Global
ADVENTURES
A DIVINE JOURNEY

KRIS JAECKLE

DIVINE ADVENTURES

Global Adventures
A Divine Journey
© 2022 by Kris Jaeckle

All Scripture quotations, unless otherwise indicated, are taken from the Holy Bible, New International Version®, NIV®. Copyright ©1973, 1978, 1984, 2011 by Biblica, Inc.™ Used by permission of Zondervan. All rights reserved worldwide. www.zondervan.com, The "NIV," and "New International Version" are trademarks registered in the United States Patent and Trademark Office by Biblica, Inc.™

This is a work of creative non-fiction. All of the events in this memoir are true to the best of the author's memory. Some names and identifying features have been changed to protect the identity of certain parties. The author in no way represents any association, company, corporation, or brand.

Printed in the United States of America.
ISBN-13: 978-1-7372768-5-2
Library of Congress Control Number: 2021914538

Divine Adventures Books
Granbury, Texas

Acknowledgements

God, who loves me so much and is the Force behind everything that happens in my life.

Greg, the ex-fiancé all over this book (and the reason for these amazing adventures), who reappeared in my life after thirty years and gave tremendous help in getting it published.

My parents and family, who have always been there for me.

Ray Hickock, who started the Young Presidents' Organization and in doing so changed the world.

Karen, my best friend from college days, who inspired me to write by writing her own books.

Nan, who inspired and guided me in writing everything in this book.

Alison, the amazing Parsons School of Design graduate who designed the perfect book cover and lent her experienced publishing advice throughout the project.

Sandra, who loaned me her beautiful mountain retreat to use while recording the book.

Sonja, who always gives wise advice.

Lynne, Kimberly, and Erika—who were encouraging roomies throughout everything.

Beth, Beth, Edna, Teri, and Brooks—Atlanta friends who helped me survive my romantic breakup.

Julie, who rolled her wheelchair across Manhattan and poured her heart into editing my chapters.

Rebecca and Kate, who went through the same kinds of experiences—in the same team position—as I did.

Dick, who allowed the use of his serene back patio while I wrote and loaned Wingman to be my faithful companion while I did so.

Kristin, who allowed me to give her pilates lessons in exchange for her writing coaching.

The Lively family, who gave creative suggestions.

Trish and Ken, members who experienced much of this with me and to whom I could always reach out to about what to say and write.

Bob, who gave me my first books on memoir-writing and got me started on my journey.

Jamie, who after adding to my humanitarian experiences, loaned me his Summit house while I wrote the book.

To everyone who encouraged me to keep the project going when I thought it would never happen.

Table of Contents

PROLOGUE

A Voice in the Night

"Kris, you're not going to South Africa for Christmas."
The darkness of the room disoriented me until I remembered that it was the middle of the night. The words had been clear, but there was no one around me. I traveled a lot, so it wasn't unusual for me to wake up in the middle of the night. What was unusual was that I heard an audible voice.

I lay there, breathing, waiting to hear more—but nothing came. Finally, I responded. "I'm not?"

"No," the Voice said. "You're going to quit your job."

"I'm going to quit my job...oh."

The Voice was calm, reassuring, and seemed to come from above—as if someone was *floating* over me. I had been praying for guidance; was this the answer? When this same kind of thing happened eight years earlier, there had also been a voice involved...

but it was an affirmation of love during a period of rejection in my life. That experience had been life-changing.

Trying to figure out what this could mean, I thought back to my boss sharing with me earlier in the day that my next assignment would be in Victoria Falls, Zimbabwe, and it would require me to be away from home—again—over Christmas. I hadn't really had time to process the assignment, except for noticing its timing.

This "supernatural" direction was also puzzling, given that I loved all the travel that came with my job. The last eight years of working for the Young Presidents Organization (known as YPO for short) had given me amazing opportunities and bettered me in all kinds of ways. And another trip to Africa would be great, given my last incredible YPO assignment to South Africa during the fall of Apartheid—which had allowed me to interact with Nelson Mandela.

The project I was currently working on—that would culminate this summer in Pontresina, Switzerland—had several months to go. Sandra, the YPO global president's wife to whom I had been assigned on the project, had quickly and easily become one of my favorite people. The way we had bonded from the beginning made me feel I had a mission to fulfill with her. Why would I be asked to leave that assignment?

On the other hand, I had just submitted applications for a graduate degree in international relations, so maybe this was a kind of divine "advanced notice" that I had been accepted to one of those?

While crafting my applications, several things had become apparent to me. The last eight years' travels to Europe, Africa, Mexico, New Zealand, Taiwan, India, Washington DC, New York City, Canada, and Bermuda had allowed me to meet and work with all kinds of CEOs, world leaders, and educators. Consequently, I had built relationships with, adapted to, and worked within these varied cultures. I had also learned to organize complex and top-notch programs for some of the most demanding people in the world—while become extremely confident and learning to take strong initiatives (many times "out-of-the-box" initiatives).

So, why wouldn't a top-notch graduate school accept me? This voice seemed to be telling me that they were!

But when I thought again about Sandra and Switzerland, I wondered about the seeming change in direction for what was to me, anyway, a Divine connection. I loved working with her and wanted to be sure I finished her project. Our initial meeting had allowed me to share an extraordinary experience I had with Mother Teresa in India. At the end of the story, she had wept, telling me about her sister-in-law's death—despite everyone's fervent prayers for her healing—and its negative impact on her belief in God. She had been quiet for another moment, and then said my story helped her think that maybe there still *was* a God.

That meeting had created a special bond between us, which was strengthened as we traveled to Switzerland in preparation for the global board meeting she and her husband were hosting there. No, I couldn't leave until I finished out their meeting, and that was still a few months away. As I thought about the voice, I realized it hadn't given me a precise point in time; it had just told me to quit my job. Also, were I to stay through the Switzerland project, I would be done just in time to start graduate school in the fall. So that timing made sense, and I began to feel excited.

On Monday, the first thing I did was call Sandra about the message from the voice, and she was kind in her reply.

"Well, I understand, Kris. Life throws interesting things each of our ways, and I don't doubt the authenticity of what you heard. I'm just glad you're going to stay through the board meeting—and you may even end up where I live when you get to graduate school."

I appreciated her understanding and confidence.

My next stop was at my boss's desk. "I just want to let you know that I'm leaving YPO at the end of this board meeting," I told him.

He looked at me, seemingly unaffected. I then emailed my other boss, who didn't even reply. No one seemed to be protesting my resignation, but I stayed positive by focusing on what I suspected was going to be my upcoming adventure at a top-end grad school.

A few days later, I arrived home to find an envelope from The Fletcher School, one of the schools where I had applied. I felt such anticipation—and here was the acceptance letter! I tore it open and read the short message on the letterhead. My first response was shock, and then tears filled my eyes as I read to the end of the page. They didn't feel I would be the best match for their school. Columbia University's similar response followed a few days later. Immediately, feelings of rejection began welling within me. My first response to everything negative in life was rejection, and here again was evidence of my being a "reject." Graduate school had rejected me—and YPO hadn't argued against my leaving.

I was tempted to get mad at the voice that had awakened me, but in all fairness the only direction given was that I wasn't going to Africa. *I* had assumed the graduate school acceptance part. Panic began to quickly take over as I realized that I had no "next step." I had already turned in my resignation, so YPO was no longer an option.

I again pondered the direction the Voice had given me. Why had it made me so confident in giving my resignation? Every time I had tried to leave YPO in the past, the offer of another amazing venue or interesting person to whom I would be assigned had sucked me back in. This Voice had been so powerful and unusual that I had obeyed it without thinking. But I had apparently been wrong about *why* it had spoken to me and what it meant.

Feelings of rejection and anxiety faded with those reassuring thoughts, and a sense of peace came over me. I continued to work on the board meeting with the strongest drive of excellence I had ever put into a project. And during that time, the feeling of inner peace remained—almost as if I were in a holding pattern—though it wasn't clear what the hold was for. The Kris Jaeckle just a few years ago would have panicked and run to someone asking for help, talking about how unfair life was and asking what the Voice had really meant (although that couldn't happen here, given its clear, straightforward instruction). None of that was happening, however, and I attributed this newfound confidence to my recent bungee jump experience in New Zealand where I had learned to hold steady in front of a big, scary, unknown destination.

A few days later, the phone in my office rang from a number in Tulsa, Oklahoma. I had attended college in Tulsa for a time but couldn't think of anyone I currently knew there.

"Kris, it's Scott Yard. How are you?"

My brain ran through names that I knew. Oh yes…*Scott Yard*. He was a quiet, reserved member with whom I had worked on a few projects. Our first experience together, however, had been one to remember.

It was in Napa Valley, California, at a YPO area conference. I had not been involved in any aspects of planning the event, but a few of us were brought in from the Dallas office as temporary helpers (we called them *crew* at YPO events). One of the things to which I had been assigned was to help with an afternoon golf tournament. Scott was tournament chairman; a perfect assignment for him. He had won the Junior PGA Golf Tournament when he was sixteen, and his golf expertise had earned him a scholarship at the University of Texas where he became captain of the golf team. He still golfed as a hobby, but in the past few years had bought an Italian pastry company and, in this new role, decided to join YPO.

I was put in charge of setting up signs, checking people in, organizing teams, and going over details for the tournament. But about an hour before it started, he began following me around—double-checking everything I was doing and expressing fears about the tournament not going well. I had finally turned to him and said, "Scott, chill!"; me, at thirty-two years old, addressing this austere and intimidating CEO in such a manner. I knew at that moment that I had probably lost my job, as he could have me fired for my disrespect. But amazingly, he calmed down and the golf tournament went forward without a hitch. After that, we crossed paths on projects in Bermuda and New Zealand, though I hadn't seen him since New Zealand.

His voice pulled me back into the present. "Kris, is there any way you are looking for a job?"

His question took me by surprise.

He continued, "I am getting ready to sell my company to take a year's sabbatical and run the YPO Tulsa chapter. I've been praying about the person I would want to work with me, and I can't get your name off my mind. So, I'll ask again: Is there any way you're looking for a job?"

Now shocked, I replied, "Scott, did you hear that I quit my job?"

"No," he said, "I had no idea. Besides, with our 8,000 members around the world, how would I have heard that you had quit your job?"

I cautiously replied, "Well, yes—I am looking for a job. I gave my resignation notice a few weeks ago in anticipation of grad school but it doesn't look like that is going to happen for the fall. So, it's interesting that you would call. But I am going to re-apply to grad school, so if I come to work with you, it might not be for more than six months."

"That's fine, Kris," he replied.

Suddenly, the inner peace I had been feeling grew even stronger. And as surprising as his proposal was, it had the same feel as my recent "Voice" experience telling me I would quit my job. That direction seemed divine, and now both experiences—wherever they were going—seemed to intersect perfectly. It wasn't what I

6

expected would happen, but I loved adventures—and this could open a whole new one.

I told him I would need to think about it for a few days. During that time, I pondered everything I would give up by leaving my job—but also realized that accepting his offer would be a "half-step" to the side of sorts. I wouldn't completely leave YPO—but rather work for the organization on a different level.

A few days later I called him back, accepting his offer, and he told me he looked forward to working together. Hanging up and contemplating what I had just done, I began to think back over all that had happened these last eight years with YPO—and how it had all started with the breakup of my engagement to my fiancé in Atlanta and the momentous decision I had made following it.

Chapter 1

To Have Loved and Lost

Prickling bushes momentarily distracted me as I peered in through the windows of the big, beautiful house Greg had bought for us. He was sitting at *our* dinner table with a slender, attractive woman and smiling at her adoringly. This was backwards. Why was I outside looking in? *I* was supposed to be the one sitting with him. Thinking back to what he had told me a week or two ago, I felt a sinking fear in the pit of my stomach. Was he really in love with *her* just six weeks after the breakup of our three-year relationship? He had consistently said he loved me—wholeheartedly—with the promise that his love would only grow stronger. Was there anything true anymore?

Greg and I had met while he was flying for my father at Grand Forks Air Force Base in North Dakota– which also happened to be where I was living in a beautiful, old sorority house while attending the university there. Handsome and distinguished, he was ten years my senior—and his company was much more appealing than that of the standard "fraternity boys" around me. But that had always been my pattern: enjoying the company of people older, more responsible, and wiser than me.

We had quickly fallen in love, then he moved back to Atlanta to start flight training at Delta Airlines. After a short period apart, I was sitting in our sorority phone room when I heard him ask, "Will you marry me, Kris?"

I had been carrying his picture everywhere, and I pulled it out to look at it again. He had been so loving to me in the few months I had known him. My recent visit to meet his family and experience Atlanta had brought the gift of a lovely pearl necklace. Here was the perfect opportunity to marry a man who was strong, well-educated, would make a nice salary, and be a great father—all the things which were true of my father.

As I pondered his proposal, I rubbed the pearls between my fingers and thought about my lifelong goal of marrying, entertaining, and raising great children (hopefully boys!). My desire to be a "housewife" was the only area in which we had a slight disagreement. Greg wanted me to be a career woman and felt I could be—given how smart I was. He assured me that he was proud of me, but also reminded me that his previous girlfriend had been an Air Force pilot. He suggested I become a lawyer or doctor and was happy to finance whatever I chose. I, on the other hand, felt strongly that my life's desires would keep me more than occupied.

Deciding we could eventually resolve this "small" issue, I accepted his proposal. Our love grew over the next few months, and I carried his picture everywhere with me. Waiting a year to join him seemed way too long, so I finagled my class credits to allow for a semester-early graduation. Not only would it get me to Greg faster, but it would also allow me to experience the town with which I had been obsessed since reading my favorite book: *Gone with the Wind*.

As always seems to happen with any kind of fast-track goal, a hiccup appeared: the need for three more classes to allow for graduation. The Business School dean (who, it turned out, had previously headed up an Atlanta university) stepped in, and promised he would award my degree if I would take the three classes from his former school and have their credits sent back to him. Agreeing to—and grateful for—his request, I was soon headed to Greg and the town nicknamed "the Queen of the South."

Settling into my first-ever apartment, I got a job with a very demanding lawyer—working long hours and saving what free time I had for Greg. He, on the other hand, was still training to fly his first Delta airplane and had no time available, so he encouraged me to focus on my new job and jump into taking my remaining college courses. I had never been by myself before, and the overwhelming loneliness began to fill my mind with doubts about our relationship. Then I remembered that being busy seemingly resolved issues (and he was setting a great example along those lines), so in addition to school and the job, I started visiting churches. My parents had always taken me to church growing up, so finding a church to settle into seemed like a good start.

Discovering one with a warm, intellectual congregation and active singles group, I began spending more and more of my free time there. The men I met enjoyed discussing philosophy, God, and the history of theology—and the women in the group added cultural events and entertaining to it all.

Beth, one of my favorite new girlfriends, loved talking cooking and Southern culture (*Gone with the Wind* again). Her father was a professor in southern Georgia, and one of his hobbies was making beautiful furniture for her. Whenever I stopped by her house to see the latest addition, we always had some typical girl talk. She'd tell me about her work life, and I'd tell her about Greg.

In the meantime, Greg's schedule began to slow a bit and he suggested we start looking at houses. This took me aback, as I had unknowingly begun to build my life around my new friends and emotionally let go of him. Yet, I reasoned that it wouldn't hurt to help him look and we ended up choosing a beautiful house on the north side of the city near the church I was attending. He began attending the church too and, although he didn't have time for the singles group, he encouraged me to continue with my involvement there.

One evening, when he was finally out of training and home from a trip, he decided to join me at a Minuet party organized by some of the men in our group. They had hired a dance instructor and requested invitees to dress formally, so Greg put on his Air Force "mess dress" and I joined him in something beautiful and blue. As we walked in, everyone looked at me in surprise. They apparently hadn't thought he was still a part of my life because of all the time I spent with them—and watching their reactions, I realized I needed to be honest with Greg at the end of the evening. I was, but his reaction was an apology for his lack of availability, his sincere desire to work on the relationship, and a strong confirmation of his love for me—followed by a reminder that he had bought the beautiful house for our future and us. Feeling torn both toward him and the other men in my life, I agreed to keep the relationship—but on a more casual basis.

Another special Beth showed up that night in my life—a lovely *Southern belle*—this time from Jackson, Mississippi. We both needed a roommate and considering that the men who threw the party were of interest to both of us, we decided to live together and rented an apartment in the complex where several of them lived. Greg would stop by every so often to check on me and be sure that I was finishing my degree—and I would stop by the new house to chat with him without committing to anything. I was enjoying being single, and never had there been such an abundance of friends and social activities in my life.

Over the next year, I continued to waver in my interest and relationship with Greg, even as he was consistently in my life—

supporting and always telling me he loved me, continuing to prepare the house, and talking about our future. And although he called the house "ours," I was careful to keep rooming with Beth.

As my activity in the church continued to grow, I pondered participating in one of their international humanitarian trips. When they announced one to Papua New Guinea, my ears perked up. I knew a little about this island—northwest of the Australian coast—because of an Aussie pilot named Robert. He had also flown for my father in Grand Forks and been a part of my social life while I attended university.

Robert was always full of comical Australian expressions like "frost my socks!" and "put the wind up my jumper!" He had grown up in the town of Ukarumpa on the island and was always full of *yarns* (an Australian word for stories) about how interesting life there had been. From his many *yarns*, I learned amazing facts about this place he had called home. It was remote, the second largest island in the world, very primitive, and the most linguistically diverse place on the planet (more than 850 languages are spoken there). In 1937, American pilot Amelia Earhart was last seen in its port city, Lae, before she vanished into thin air. During World War II the Japanese had invaded the island, but the Australian forces liberated it. General Douglas MacArthur used it as a base in bringing the war in the Pacific to an end. Charles Lindbergh, the famed Spirit of St. Louis pilot, had flown P38s for the deadliest WWII American fighter squadron operating out of the island.

The humanitarian trip appealed to me because of Robert, but also because it involved building a new air strip and teaching children at one of the country's scarce public schools. So, I committed to go and talked my boss into giving me unpaid time off as a gift for finishing my college degree—even though my fellow staff thought I was crazy for wanting to do this. Little did any of us know what this would open for the rest of my life; I just thought it would be a fun international trip with a good cause backing it. Greg, proud that I had finished my degree, made it clear he didn't want me to go—

13

though he never said why he was against it. He simply broke off our relationship when I refused to waver from my plans—which brought me a surprising sense of relief.

Flying that distance around the world was fascinating—but also tiring—as my body lost all track of where it was and when it should sleep. After a five-hour flight to Los Angeles, we boarded a fourteen-hour Qantas flight to Sydney. Our three-hour early morning layover there left me dead on my feet with lack of sleep before we finally boarded our four-hour flight to Port Moresby, the capital of Papua New Guinea. After landing we were given a surprise treat of papaya, one of the native fruits of the country, and I loved it.

As our team descended the plane's steps to a dirt path leading us inside the airport, we felt like a winning team of actors walking to the Oscars stage. A large group of short, native people attired in little-to-no-clothing watched us intently from behind the fence. After picking up our bags, we were invited to join the mission team leader for a walk around the area before our flight up into the mountains, which would be followed by a four-hour truck ride to our final destination. He suggested staying close together during the walk because of the area's reputation for crime.

While game to do some exploring with the group but needing a quick "pit stop," I made my way to the bathroom, only to discover that the toilet was a simple hole in the ground with a dirty seat on top—and with no toilet paper anywhere to be seen—all of which was a preview of many unexpected things to come. Making my way back to the group, I found that our short walk around town produced even more culture shock: roads were uneven and full of potholes; broken-down cars raced around oblivious to any traffic laws; trash everywhere; and seemingly despondent people staring at us every direction we turned. Overwhelmed by it all, I was relieved to get back to the airport and onto the next airplane.

Our next descent was into Lae, the second-largest city in Papua New Guinea. We deplaned to an even larger crowd of curious natives, and were directed toward our drivers, who loaded up our bags and motioned us into their trucks—which were along the lines of army cargo trucks. At this point, it had been thirty-two hours since we left Atlanta, and the infrequent catnaps hadn't made up for the sleep I needed. I felt I had never been this tired in my whole life!

The sun was just setting, and the resulting darkness—as well as the vibration of the engine—quickly put me to sleep. Sometime later, the engine "revved" a few times and went quiet. I had gotten used to all the potholes on this "only highway of the entire country," but our security briefing in Port Moresby had included a warning that robberies along the highway were also a part of life. So, when it suddenly grew quiet I snapped awake, fearful we were being *held up*. But the driver quickly assured us with a laugh, "No robbers…just almost slipped down the side of a 5,000-foot-high mountain pass. Did I say there were landslides all along the Highland Highway too?"

My heart still racing, I looked out the window. Knowing we were nearing Robert's hometown of Ukarumpa, I tried to stay awake to see it, but the engine's vibration lulled me back to sleep.

We finally reached the mission around 11pm, and lanterns appeared as we were led through the pitch-black night to our huts. We had all been required to bring flashlights, and we turned them on just long enough to see the layout of the room and choose a bed. In no time, we unrolled our sleeping bags and fell fast asleep.

Morning came too early, and I awoke to a fellow mission team member dressed and stretching. "Shall we go look for breakfast?" she asked. Rubbing my eyes and then unzipping the sleeping bag, I got up and threw on some clothes. We made our way out of the hut to the dining area, noticing the usual interested natives looking us over—but this time without the separation of a fence.

Breakfast started what was to be an unforgettable experience of working with these sweet, indigenous people and experiencing life on an entirely different plane. We stayed on a mission compound with no electricity after dark and equipped with only cold showers. I got my first taste of Indian food, as the gentleman in charge of the compound loved to cook his native cuisine for guests. We sat inside screened-in porches while the children ran around us, throwing golden-orb spiders the size of human hands on the screens. While that part of being around the children was repulsive (the spiders had been known to eat birds), the rest of the time was incredibly rewarding. We got to see what they ate (sweet potatoes were their staple) and how grateful they were for everything given to them. They loved that we brought over used t-shirts as gifts. They were used to wearing little grass skirts or tattered clothes (or even nothing), so these t-shirts were luxury items for them.

The children were part of a special group chosen to attend the country's six public schools, and they were immensely grateful for their access to education. Many of them came from several days' "walk" away to live on the compound and attend school. We spent our time with them, teaching and playing games on the playground.

When we asked if they wanted to play "red light-green light," we were met with blank stares. "Teacher, why a red light?" one child responded. It dawned on us that none of them knew what a red or green light was because they had never been around traffic, roads that required signals, or even ridden in cars. We had to explain that "red light" meant "stop," and "green light" meant "go."

Experiences like this made me realize how much I took for granted in my life, and even with all I had, how much I complained. Also, beginning to realize my enjoyment of children, I wondered about getting certified to teach—realizing that such a certification could be used practically anywhere—maybe even outside the United States and among poverty-stricken people.

As I considered all of this, my mind circled back to Greg and our relationship. This time apart had given me objectivity and clarity to the point of deciding to pursue elementary education and consider missions—possibly in a third-world country. Should I

16

marry, I wanted a man who shared a passion for similar things, but I felt Greg was more interested in his Delta career.

When I returned to Atlanta, he was waiting to meet me at the airport. Throwing his arms around me, he told me that he wanted us to be together. Not expecting this—and knowing what I had just decided—I simply said, "Greg, I have decided to become a missionary." Once again, he agreed to be patient, and eventually I fell back into our old pattern of relationship. I liked his big house and was used to his stability and company while I was out pursuing the things I wanted to do. So, for the third year running, we were back together.

Eager to pursue my newfound goal of studying education, I found a teaching program at a nearby college and started classes. Greg continued to hover, always telling me he loved me. He tried to share a few times about what was happening with his spiritual growth, but I never took time to listen, as my heart was too jaded to hear what he had to say. There had been so many times in the past that I had tried having spiritual conversations with him—tried to connect with him on this topic—but unfortunately found myself taking those talks to other outlets because he wasn't interested. Maybe without realizing it, I had put up a wall when it came to this topic.

Around that time, I attended a concert led by one of my favorite singers, Twila Paris. One of her songs, "Send Me," seemed spot-on with where I felt my life was to go, and I sang it often:

Here am I, Lord, send me

Here am I, Lord, send me

Father in heaven, show Your mercy

Send me.

At the end of my first semester of classes, my parents invited Greg and me to join them in Florida for their twenty-fifth wedding anniversary. He was excited, but I didn't really want him to go. He

17

also seemed a bit nervous as we made our plans, and I wasn't sure why. We flew down, and after settling in, he asked me to take a walk on the beach.

"Kris, will you marry me?" he asked on that walk.

I hadn't been expecting that, but now I knew why he was nervous and once again I felt torn. It had been a while since we had discussed marriage, and I still did not feel I was truly in love with him. But we were in a romantic place—with my parents—so how could I say no? I tried throwing a few excuses out, but he had an answer for each one. Finally, I agreed to marry him. He kissed me and seemed so happy.

We flew back to Atlanta and began to look for an engagement ring. After introducing Greg to a jeweler-friend from church whose office was a floor above mine at work, we started learning about diamonds. We settled on a nicely sized, emerald-cut diamond, and the jeweler began work on the setting. Things had never gone this far before, and he seemed to grow happier, whereas my secret feelings were foreboding; however, I continued to move forward, hoping everything would work out this time.

The next step was to find a wedding dress, and I ran across a beautiful, elaborate one at a fraction of the full price. My father was happy about my usual ability to find a bargain, but Mom argued that buying the dress was a mistake—telling him, "I am not sure Kris is going to stay engaged." Given my usual conflict pattern with her, family arguments broke out with my father defending me and paying for the dress; but all of this led me to an even stronger sense of foreboding.

Our plans progressed for a few more weeks, and we set a wedding date of December 10. As time passed, a trapped feeling also emerged. Wondering about this ongoing anxiety, I realized I might have commitment issues. When in my life had I ever had to commit? *Military brat* life is about change, and I had moved at least fifteen times before attending college. Even after that, I had gone to three different universities across the country.

As I stayed active with my singles group at church, a new man appeared on my radar screen named Lee. He was well-educated and worked as a consultant for an international management firm. He was also very nice, seemed to be spiritually inclined, and desirous of spending time on the mission field. Since he didn't know I was engaged (I wasn't yet wearing the ring), he began calling me in the evenings. The more we talked, the more I wondered if he was the kind of man I was seeking. But how could he have appeared now that I was engaged to Greg? What was I to do? I couldn't break the engagement again—especially with the ring and dress purchased (and the date set)—or could I?

Other friends took me out for dinner and expressed concern that for someone about to get married, I did not appear happy. I listened to what they had to say and finally concluded I needed to break the engagement. Figuring it would be easier if done quickly, I decided I would just "lay it on him."

Greg arrived home from a trip that next day, and when I walked into the house he could tell something was odd. He tried talking about his trip, and then asked what was up. "Well, Greg, I have been thinking about this whole marriage idea again and have realized that I am not in love with you and should break this off."

"What?" he replied, dumbfounded.

"I don't want you, Greg," I repeated calmly, with no compassion or care in my voice.

"Are you sure, Kris?"

"Absolutely."

"Okay, please leave," he said, adding, "I hope you know what you are doing."

A few days later, I found all the belongings I had left at Greg's house piled on the front porch of my apartment. This was something odd for him to do and sent a feeling of finality through me; however, it didn't disturb me too much—as I was confident that I had done the right thing. I shared it with my mother, and the counselor within her immediately expressed concern that the breakup of a three-year relationship might cause "issues." I told her I doubted that.

A week after that conversation, the phone calls from Lee stopped, a behavior that seemed strange as well. He was the reason for me breaking the engagement, and this was not what I had expected from him. Another week passed with no call from either Lee or Greg. While I didn't have a commitment from Lee, Greg's silence began to make me nervous. Our three-year relationship had consisted of his non-stop love and support; it had always been *me* backing off! He never returned things and then let me alone. But those actions were now giving me time to think through my feelings, and his continued distance allowed my heart to get the clarification it needed.

Slowly, over the course of three weeks, I began to realize that I really did love Greg and wanted to marry him. In fact, I decided I was committed enough to suggest we go to the justice of the peace and get married immediately. I knew he probably would be shocked—but excited—to hear what I had to say. After all, he had been waiting so long, and had sent me stacks of love notes throughout our relationship. The problem I faced was how to tell him. Should I call? I didn't know his flight schedule, so I decided to just stop by "our" house to see if he was there. As I pulled into the driveway, however, I noticed a strange car in the garage.

Walking around the side of the house and up the stairs to the front door, I saw that the lights in the house were on—so he was home. I gathered my courage and rang the doorbell. While I waited for him, I actually *heard* both my heartbeat and my breath. I was nervous, as I knew that I had a lot of inconsistency and indecision to apologize for.

The door opened to him standing in his Delta uniform—looking so handsome. My eyes filled with tears, and an overwhelming feeling of love filled my heart. This was the way I had felt back at the sorority house three years ago when I first met him—and it confirmed how much I wanted him. Now I felt even more confident about telling him I would marry him *on the spot*.

He, on the other hand, was clearly shocked to see me and said, "Kris, why are you here?"

"May I come in?" I asked humbly.

"Why?"

"I just wanted to talk to you."

He stepped onto the porch. "Let's talk out here," he said.

That, too, was a strange response, but I accepted it and moved forward with what I had to say. He listened patiently. I got to the part about going to the justice of the peace and then was quiet. He just looked at me. Finally, he replied. "I am surprised and need time to think about it all. Let me get back to you." Then he turned around, walked into the house, and closed the door.

I stood there stunned. This wasn't the reaction I expected. He was supposed to throw his arms around me and say, "Wow…finally. I have waited so long for this. Let me get my jacket and we will head right now to the justice of the peace."

Then again, I decided, maybe he did need time to think, so I drove back to my apartment to give him the time he requested.

From that time on, I kept to myself as much as I could. My free time was spent listening to worship music and meditating on what I wanted to be my future with Greg. It was hard to repress the memories of how much I had hurt him with my marriage promises and breakups. It made me wonder if he could believe *this* promise to marry him.

The beautiful words of a Eugene Greco song I sang to myself during this time seemed to reflect exactly what I was feeling:

Teach me Your ways, O Lord my God

And I will walk in Your Truth

Give me a totally undivided heart

That I may fear Your Name

Purify my heart—cleanse me, Lord, I pray

Remove from me all that is standing in the way of Your Love

During this difficult period in my life, a woman named Teri entered our close circle of women at church and spent a lot of time encouraging me. My other girlfriends were tiring of my obsessive "Greg talk," but she was patient and kind. I was mystified at how she could be so caring without really knowing me. But I felt her love and support as I continued to think about how I had acted toward Greg and worked hard to stay positive.

About a week later, while standing over the work copier, a strange, powerful presence suddenly came over me. Then, a Voice spoke:

> *Kris, as much as you think Teri loves you—without even really knowing you—that's how much I love you! And as much as you think Greg loved you and you didn't deserve it – that's how much I love you! I am God, and I love you!*

A searing heat filled my entire body, settling in my stomach. Tears came to my eyes, and in amazement I began whispering to myself: "You love me, God, You love me? You love me, God, You love me?"

A sob rose in my throat at the shock of what had just happened to me. What was going on? What was this feeling? Overwhelmed,

I searched for a private place to retreat. I couldn't do it in my office. Then the building's stairwell came to mind. Hurrying down the hallway, I found the stairwell door, pushed it open, and after checking that it was empty, I crumpled against the wall as the door slammed behind me.

I sat there and wept, continuing to feel this amazing presence pour into and all around me. It didn't feel sad or negative…just peaceful and kind and overwhelmingly loving. I surmised that it was "love" I was sensing…and it struck me that, in many senses, love and God were the same thing. Then, I remembered the words of my worship song requesting an experience of God's love and wondered if this was an answer to that request. Another line in that song requested God to purify my heart, which struck me as interesting given the teaching of Jesus in the Beatitudes that "…the pure in heart would see God."

My breathing calmed, and the crying subsided. My thoughts shifted again to figuring out what had just happened and its origin. Wasn't God's love a given? I had been taught that at every church I had ever attended. How simple could the knowledge of that be? Why would it cause such a breakdown for me, of all people, who thought I had the knowledge of God completely mastered? I had heard it and thought I believed it—all my life. What brought this on?

As if in answer to my question, a picture popped into my mind from just a few weeks earlier: I was in a group of people waiting for prayer at the end of a church meeting. The speaker was moving down the line, touching people and praying for them as they shared their request. He got to me and paused for a moment, not bothering to ask my request. I felt his hands press a bit harder as he said, "Sweet lady, you do not know how much your Heavenly Father loves you. Father God, show this lady how much You love her." Then, he moved on. I was upset with him because I had wanted prayer for something else. And it was obvious that God loved everyone, including me.

Yet here I sat in the stairwell, having an incredible experience of God's love seemingly initiated by these two situations. Was it true, or had I maybe eaten something strange that morning? Perhaps I was having an emotional breakdown? I believed strongly in God and miraculous experiences, so that wasn't the issue; I had just never had an experience of this sort and my very rational brain wasn't sure what to do with it.

Finally regaining control (and the ability to breathe again), I walked back into my office. A minute later, the phone rang; picking it up, I heard Greg's voice.

"Kris?" he asked, sounding nervous, "Do you have time to get together? I've done some thinking and would like to talk."

"Greg?" I said hesitantly, trying once again to regain control. I hadn't expected this.

"Can you come over tonight?" he continued.

"Um, sure." I replied, and we agreed on 6 pm.

My hesitation quickly turned into excitement. How perfect was this? I had been praying so hard that Greg would come back to me and now—just as had happened the two previous times—he was accepting me back. The love I had felt in the divine experience that just happened almost seemed to confirm it in my mind. Our meeting was a few hours away, but I wanted it to be here now. What was Greg going to say? Would he now accept my apology and immediate marriage proposal?

The workday finally ended, and I headed to my faithful white small car—only to find it would not start. Was my battery dead again? Grateful that I had parked on a hill, I set it in second gear, let the car begin to roll forward, and popped the clutch. The engine chortled to life, and I sped off to his house.

He met me at the front door. I reached for a hug, and feeling the response of his arms around me, teared up. He then turned me down the porch steps and accompanied me out to the street.

So, it would be a walk? I ignored the slight, grateful at least for his company. My love for him rose in my heart again, but I determined to hold onto my feelings and just *listen* to what he had to say.

Greg started by reminding me that he loved me, and then said he needed to talk frankly and would appreciate my hearing him out. He then explained that "three breakups were enough," and he had decided to move on. Much of his decision had been reinforced by the intense soul-searching and praying he had done after my last refusal. He confided that he had found encouragement and direction from a passage in Proverbs 3:5-6 that spoke about trusting God:

> *Trust in the Lord with all your heart and lean not on your own understanding; in all your ways submit to Him, and He will make your paths straight.*

His decision to "let go of his own understanding" and let God direct his path had brought forth something amazing: Only a week after our breakup he had met someone at a satellite location of our church, and she seemed to be exactly what he was looking for. In fact, he thought he was in love and consequently wanted to continue to pursue her—and this was another reason he needed to end things between us. He also told me that based on our relationship and my issues over these past years, he wasn't sure that I would *ever* be able to commit to someone or even marry. His comment seemed in line with my thoughts about "commitment issues," but I didn't want to hear it.

We finished our walk back at the front of his house, and our conversation ended. I didn't know what to say or do; I was desperately searching for something to cling to for emotional stability. Then, the strong presence from earlier that day came to mind, along with its Divine message of, "I love you, Kris." Greg walked me to my car and wished me luck. I drove off in a state of shock, not believing what I just heard. How could this be happening? Surely he would change his mind and come back to me, as he couldn't really want to marry someone else. And anyway, who was she?

Now—two weeks later—here I was peering through the prickling bushes, all those memories racing through my mind as I watched Greg and his new girlfriend have dinner. I finally walked back to my car, trying to calm the fear and pain I was feeling. I again assured myself that he would come back to me if I just gave it some time.

The next two months were spent waiting and hoping. Emotionally speaking, I was up and down. Beth, my roommate, was going through a similar breakup in her life, and we tried to encourage each other. Teri stopped by to encourage us both in her usual sweet way. Other good friends would tell me to let go of Greg, reminding me that I hadn't been happy with him when we were dating, so why did I want him back? But all I could think of were the many reasons I wanted him. Searching for information about him from friends, I found nothing. Then, one day at the office, I looked out the window and saw what seemed to be his car in the front parking lot. I waited for him to come through our front door to talk to me, but nothing happened.

That Sunday at church, I ran into the jeweler from my office building who had sold us our engagement ring. He seemed surprised to see me, then mentioned that he had just sold Greg another diamond. My heart stopped beating for a moment as I realized that was probably why I had seen his car. I asked him the date Greg had proposed marriage to his new fiancée, and he replied that it was December 10. I felt another shock: December 10 was supposed to have been our wedding day—and he had used it as the day to propose marriage to someone else? It couldn't be true. But it was true; I heard via other sources that Greg and Susan were indeed engaged. Darkness fell over my being, and my world collapsed.

Over the next few months, it was all I could do to survive. My roommate and I kept each other going. Neither of us had ever experienced being this low in life. The God I had experienced for my whole life disappeared. That was strange, too, considering my recent God/Love experience in the stairwell. It had been so real, supernatural, and life-changing, but now it was gone. Absolutely. I couldn't eat, couldn't sleep, couldn't stop obsessing over how I had wrecked my life by taking Greg for granted. Oddly, whenever I saw any kind of trash it would send me into a tailspin, and I started to wonder if the trash wasn't a physical representation of my "trashing" Greg and the life I could have had with him.

My desire to live began to wane, and it was all I could do to go to work. Or maybe going to work was the only thing that kept me alive? I spent Christmas with my family in Florida, and for the first time, I let my brothers love on me. Everyone saw what terrible emotional shape I was in and how gaunt I had become. I talked with my father and asked if he had ever doubted there was a God—because his example of that belief was probably the most powerful in my life. "No, Kris, I have never doubted that there was a God," he said, "but I know that a lot of people do. It just hasn't been an issue for me."

I thought about his answer and then wondered if he had ever had a serious romantic breakup. He and my mother had never divorced, so that wasn't an issue. And he had never mentioned anyone romantically significant before marrying Mom. He had been obsessed with the Air Force and flying from the time he was a little boy. As he grew older, that passion had remained his life's goal and he hadn't planned to marry; he just happened to stumble across Mom a few years into his career and she had been "added in" to the plan. She had then followed him everywhere and was always by his side.

When Christmas ended, I returned to Atlanta. As I continued to think about everything, I concluded that this "no-God" experience happened because I had taken someone's love (which represented God's love) for granted, then lost it. I remembered the Scripture in the New Testament that said, "Whoever does not love does not know God, because God is love" (1 John 4:8).

It made perfect sense: God came from love, and my love (love I had taken for granted with Greg) was now gone. Thank God I still had my father's love, though I was yearning for *some* kind of God-feeling to come back to me. Thinking through all of this, I decided that I would never again allow myself to trust someone when they told me they loved me; I now knew that love could go away and I could suffer this pain again. The safest way to keep this from happening was to *never* fall in love again or marry, so I vowed I would not.

My parents invited me to visit them at their home in Louisiana, and I took them up on their offer. I remember arriving at their house, still not able to sleep. I was realizing how EVERYTHING in my life was full of Greg: what I thought, what I cooked, what I talked about. One day while I was there, I called a friend back in Atlanta who told me that she had run into Greg and that he looked like he was doing great. After that conversation, what little recovery I had made was totally gone, and I was lost again in a mire of despair.

Out of the blue, Mom suggested that we drive over to Dallas to visit her mother and I agreed. Grammy was fun and jovial, and Mom thought that being around her would cheer me up. It could help Grammy, too, as both her husband and eldest daughter had recently died within a few months of each other. It would also be another change of scenery and could maybe help me move on.

When we got to Dallas, Mom excitedly showed me a newspaper job listing for a position within an educational organization—one that involved international travel. She suggested I apply, but my only thought was the fact that I had nothing to wear and was only in town for a short time. Besides, all I cared about was Greg and what had happened. Unbeknownst to me, she made up a resume and sent it to the recruiter. Meanwhile, I focused on my grandmother. We used a lot of the time to talk about what had happened with Greg over the last three years—as well as what could happen in my future. It didn't seem to cheer me up, however.

On my second day in Dallas, Mom received a call from someone and abruptly handed the phone to me. The woman at the other end of the line asked if I was the person who had applied for the position at the educational organization (called "Young Presidents Organization" or "YPO"). I looked at Mom, and realizing what she had done, gave her the *evil eye*. Then, I focused back on the call, and though I had no interest in the position, admitted that I *was* the person who had applied.

"We're setting up interview times with the team project manager, Linda," the person said. "Are you interested in talking to her on Thursday morning?"

"I'm leaving town tomorrow, so I won't be available then." I responded, feeling relieved since, again, I had no interest.

"Well, Linda really wants to meet with you. If she were available tomorrow morning, could you rearrange your schedule a bit?" I looked at Mom, who was rapidly nodding her head. Obviously, she was listening to the conversation.

"I don't really have a suit in which to interview, and I'll be in a hurry."

"That's okay. It will just give the both of you an opportunity to feel each other out—and you can learn more about the job," she said.

Finally agreeing to the interview, I hung up the phone. Mom began to dance around the room. "This sounds so fun…and it could be a fresh start for you. You need to get out of Atlanta—plus, you'll only be three hours away from us."

I still had no interest in the job and was only interviewing to pacify her. The next morning, I put on an old knit dress, borrowed some shoes from Grammy, and headed to YPO headquarters.

While waiting for my interview, I read the organization's history posted on the wall: It was founded in the 1950s by a young CEO in Rochester, New York, who had taken over Hickok Leather, his father's 300-employee belt and jewelry company. He didn't have much experience in running a company but felt there must be others in his "shoes," so he gathered a small group of them together in the Waldorf Astoria Hotel in New York City. The result of that first meeting was an invitation-only association with the theme of "Better Presidents through Education and Idea Exchange." Also, the joining requirements were listed: the potential member had to be a CEO or president by age forty-two; have at least fifty full-time employees; and the *company* had to make at least US $7 million per year. Then, all members were forcibly "retired" at age fifty—though the number "fifty" was never mentioned—only the word "forty-niner" from retirement point forward.

My reading was interrupted by a call to Linda's office. Once I was seated, she told me the position for which I was interviewing was in the "Universities" division, and I seemed to have everything they were looking for in terms of skills. She also explained that "universities" were educational experiences designed exclusively for members and their families that featured top-notch speakers from around the world. The job would involve supporting her and wearing "many hats" as she headed up a five-to-seven-person team that reported to members of the organization acting as the university "chairmen." These people had their own companies to run, so they laid out ideas and it was the staff's responsibility to make it all happen.

Linda then shared an article from *Inc Magazine* about the YPO universities:

> *Universities draw on luminaries from the worlds of art, education, business, and government, "resources" who not only speak to gatherings but may also chat informally with members. For example, our members might wind up sitting by a pool, talking with James Michener over a cup of coffee. Speakers at YPO events have included ex-presidents, Henry Kissinger, Gloria Steinem, Moshe Dayan, astronaut Alan Bean, Playboy's Christie Hefner, social activist Jesse Jackson, former FCC chairman Newton Minow, and Coca-Cola*

director Donald Keough. After he was ousted as Richard Nixon's chief of staff in 1973, H. R. Haldeman spoke on crisis management.[1]

The article went on to say,

> *Universities are generally held in exotic locales. You might have dinner at the bottom of a volcano in Hawaii or a formal ball at a palace in Paris. The social events have given YPOers something of a rich-playboy reputation, but despite the pleasant distractions, learning better business management remains the principal concern. One member, recalling his first university, talked about the amazing choice of speakers followed by the same number of choices of afternoon activities in the area. We arrived on a Sunday and got so absorbed in everything that, by Thursday, my wife was saying, "Do you realize that we're in Athens?"*

Watching for my reaction, Linda then explained that if I joined her team, our upcoming project was the Vienna University. The venue out of which we would be operating was the Hofburg Palace—which had been used to rule much of Europe from the thirteenth century until World War I.

"Working here is a life-changing experience," Linda insisted, "and this particular division allows you to get to know world-changing leaders—as well as travel the world in an amazing way. Are you interested?"

It was hard for me to respond positively, as I didn't want to move and I didn't really like Dallas. All I could think to say was, "If you offered me the job, when would I need to be here?"

"Within two weeks."

I couldn't make that happen, even if they did offer me a position, so I thanked her for her time, and she escorted me out. When I returned home, Mom asked me how it went. I didn't have much to say, but she was excited.

---

[1] https://www.inc.com/magazine/19820901/4558.html

"Do you realize that if they offer you a job, you have a place to stay? Grammy says you are welcome to use her extra bedroom until you find a place to live."

I didn't respond, as I just didn't care. The next day, I returned to Atlanta and my job. Working there was boring, but I had the job mastered. Toward the end of the first day back at work, however, my boss abruptly told me I would need to start looking for a job, as his workload was slowing down. That was unexpected—he had never said anything like it in the three years I had worked for him. Maybe it was good that I had interviewed for YPO, though I didn't care much about either job. Plus, I had heard through the grapevine that Greg would be getting married in two weekends—which made it even harder.

Three days later, Linda from YPO called. "Kris, YPO would like to offer you a job. Can you be here in ten days?"

I almost dropped the phone. This was a good thing, given what I had been told about losing my current job—but how could I make it happen in ten days or less?

"Can you give me a day to think about it?"

"Sure, but we need you here ASAP. We are only three months away from the start of Vienna."

I assured her I would have an answer the next day. They weren't offering moving expenses, so that would be an obstacle to overcome. When I called my mother and gave her the news, she and Dad offered to come to Atlanta to help me move.

But when I told my boss about it all, he said, "That is very interesting, Kris, but I am not sure you have the kind of experience they need."

His response got me riled, and now I wanted to take the job just to prove him wrong. Although it would be difficult to leave all the friends I loved in Atlanta, they encouraged me to take it. I finally decided to say yes and between my friends and my parents, I was packed and moved to Dallas the weekend Greg and Susan got married. I should have been excited at my new life on the horizon, but that weekend I was the saddest I had ever been, realizing that everything happening to me was closing the door to Greg forever.

I reported for duty at YPO the following Monday. I didn't even think about how the song "Send Me" might be playing into all of this. Nor did I know how much my seemingly hopeless, purposeless life was about to embark on a series of Divine adventures I could never have imagined.

Chapter 2

Waltzing in the Palace

Mozart could have been here—walking with me—toward the Stephansdom (St. Stephen's Cathedral) in Vienna. We would have turned off the Zeditksgasse, veered onto a tiny street, then said our goodbyes outside his apartment at 5 Domgasse. He could have glanced out his window at the cathedral's magnificent spire whenever he wanted. Maybe it was an inspiration for the masses he wrote? Or maybe it was just me juxtaposing my thoughts of Greg to something else. Every breathing moment of my life still seemed to be obsessed with him—though my busyness over the last few months at least gave me something else to occupy my time. But my heart ached when it thought of him; plus, I was using this job to prove that I *could* be the professional, accomplished woman he had always wanted me to be.

Kate, standing next to me, interrupted my thoughts. "This is the only one of Mozart's apartments in Vienna that still exists today. All four of its floors house museums about different aspects of him."

When we had left the Hilton on our walk to work, she had agreed to show me Stephansplatz. She knew Vienna much better than me and could provide some background while we walked. "This year is the 200th anniversary of his death, and the city is in celebration," Kate explained. "My father says that YPO didn't know this when they chose Vienna for one of the 1991 universities. That seems odd, though, given how famous the anniversary is and how much Dad knows about Vienna. His grandfather left here after World War I and settled into the New York area. Our family has traveled between the two places since then."

Kate's father, Jim, was the fourth generation CEO of the family cosmetics company founded in Vienna that made many famous fragrances. He was arranging the speakers for this university, and when I interacted with him during the planning process, he mentioned that he had a daughter, Kate, who was just finishing college in Denver and would love to be part of the university's crew.

We had happily arranged for it and now she was here.

"Kris, do you like your job? Is the staff nice? What is it like to work with the CEOs?"

I knew Kate had some experience with these YPO universities because she had attended one with her family the previous summer in Switzerland. But she had been a participant at that one, whereas here she was working.

As I thought about how to respond, memories from the last three months raced through my mind. Leaving Atlanta to take this job had brought on the usual sense of excitement and hope that a new "duty station" always did, but the reason for doing so still dominated my every breathing moment: the tragic breakup with Greg after our three-year relationship, his almost immediate connection to another woman, and their subsequent marriage. And his total cutoff and marriage left no hope of a future with him. For all I knew, his new wife was already pregnant. The dead silence about him out there led to an even stronger yearning in my heart for it all to come back. I felt like I was being sucked down into a big whirlpool with nothing to grasp for help.

Upon arrival to Dallas, I had gotten settled in with my grandmother, and then found a place to live through an Atlanta friend. My new roommate had gotten me a job at the famous "Cooper Aerobics Center," and invited me to a very active church full of singles. So, my social life was growing, but the job at YPO had been a series of "ups and downs." The YPO members, when they were around, were interesting and I enjoyed every minute I spent with them. Many were like the senior military officers around whom I had grown up: They led people and made things happen— yet didn't operate under the auspices of the military and seemed to have more direct responsibility for money.

The day-to-day job, however, was with the YPO staff who hadn't been very friendly. Behind my back, they called me "Corky"— after Corky Sherwood, the perky, Southern, former Miss America character from the TV show *Murphy Brown*. The harder I tried to be sweet and thoughtful to this mostly female staff, the more they seemed to make fun of me. And because I spent more time around them, that aspect of the job was the trade-off. It wasn't an intellectually taxing job, but it took a lot of organizing and the hours had grown longer the closer we came to the start of the university.

Focusing back on Kate, I responded that since I had not yet worked on-site at a university, I would have to wait to give her my opinion until it was over.

As we continued toward our destination, my senses drank in everything around me. If my three months of busyness hadn't gotten me out of my "Greg" depression, hopefully the elegance of Vienna would: street cars rattled by; formal but warm people nodded as they said, *"Grüß Gott!"* ("Good Day!") to each other; buttery, sweet smells from tiny pastry shops overtook my nose; and historic buildings delighted my heart.

37

We turned a corner and a large square opened in front of us. I stopped in my tracks. In front of me stood the cathedral. So, this was the Stephansdom that Mozart had looked at every day from his apartment. I had to strain my neck to see the top of the 445-foot-tall south tower with its gothic architecture resembling lace. Information we had sent out to attendees in advance had taught me that the ornately patterned roof, covered with hundreds of thousands of glazed tiles organized into diamonds and zig-zags, was complemented by eagles and coats of arms. I instantly understood why its beauty and history made it one of the most recognizable symbols of Vienna. Consecrated in the year 1147, it had been built on a fourth-century Roman burial ground and served as head of the Archdiocese of Vienna for centuries.

Standing there gazing at this magnificent structure, a sense of gratitude filled my being. I suddenly began to feel I *had* made the right decision in taking the job; what else would have brought me to work in Vienna? The city was definitely my taste: antique, intimate, beautiful; and I was experiencing it at an amazing level. We would be working in the former winter palace of the Hapsburg family; we had the top speakers in the world; our exclusive social events would be held in the most famous venues; and our attendees were top-notch leaders from around the globe.

I was also conscious that Vienna had a dark side during World War II. Our closing keynote speaker, Victor Frankl, the celebrated author who had survived the Nazi death camps, was a living reminder of those dark days. He would be taking a small group of members with him to Mauthausen the day before his keynote to let them get a feel for what he experienced. I was greatly anticipating hearing all he had to say.

Kate reminded me that we needed to move on, and as we started walking again I studied the architecture of the buildings. Made of stone with fancy carvings, they housed stores and hotels. I also noticed little "hooks" on their outside walls. Kate didn't know why they were there, so we looked for someone to ask. Up ahead, a portly gentleman in lederhosen stepped outside his cigar shop for a quick smoke, and we decided to approach him.

"*Grüß Gott, frauleins.*"

"Can we ask you a question?" Kate said. "Why are there little hooks outside the doors on the stores?"

"For leashes, *natürlich*. One cannot bring a dog into the store."

Many people walked their dogs in Vienna, so it made sense. But this was a novel concept. Hooks on the buildings for leashes? Even more interesting was the man's accent. I loved how it had a southern German sound yet was distinct.

The sign behind him read, "*Montag–Freitag, 10.00–17.00.*" Those hours seemed short for a workday, but I had read enough about the city to realize this was Viennese tradition. Only recently had stores even started opening on Saturdays, and right now that was only once a month from nine until noon. The feeling of leisure here was so unlike that in the United States, and I wondered if our 24/7 mentality had anything to do with our frenzied pace of life.

During the last part of our walk, the conversation shifted to my difficulty in getting up that morning. "While I know part of it was the time change, I can't help but think it was also related to last night's party," I said.

"But it didn't run very late," said Kate.

"True. I think it's more about the brandy," I replied sheepishly, "I haven't had much experience with drinking."

Pausing, I expected her to make fun of me for my lack of experience with alcohol, but she didn't say anything. I could tell she was thinking about last night too. We had traveled to Grinzing, a town northwest of the city bordering on the Vienna Woods for a private dinner organized for university committee members and our staff. Grinzing was a wine tavern village dating to the Middle

Ages, and one of its restaurants boasted the largest Wiener schnitzel in the area.

We had just gotten settled at our tables when what seemed a fun-loving group of Eastern Europeans walked in. Dr. Walter Landmann, who was university chairman, introduced them as being from a special program. Circling the room, they called out salutations and—after greeting us all with kisses on our hands and cheeks—encouraged us to try shots of apricot brandy, a native Romanian drink they had brought with them. One man took a seat next to me and introduced himself as being from Budapest.

"Budapest?" I questioned myself. Then I remembered Dr. Landmann had designed this special program to encourage entrepreneurship in the newly freed, former "Iron Curtain" countries.

"You have a business?" I asked.

"Yes," he said as he poured the brandy into a tulip-shaped shot glass. "It is not so much official…"

He handed me the brandy. "We were underneath…how do you say *underneath?*"

"Underground, you mean?"

"Yes!" he exclaimed, watching me intently. I raised the glass to my lips, throwing back my head. The drink went down quickly, burning my throat, and I picked up the faintest taste of apricot. After two shots, my lack of experience with alcohol left me feeling unsteady.

He moved his attention and brandy to someone else, and I tried to focus back on what was going on around me. YPO committee members were laughing and talking with these entrepreneurs about their cities and traditions—and all that was going to happen during the university. I heard "Sehr gut" (*very good*) and "Kitünő" (*excellent*) and watched heads nod as they interacted. Listening to the talk about their traditions and history helped me understand even more about the former Austro-Hungarian Empire: It had been second in size only to Russia until the end of World War I when it had lost the war and been dissolved into a handful of smaller countries. Yet, these people didn't act like it had dissolved at all—they seemed fiercely proud.

Dinner went on and I talked to some other committee couples, including Calvin and his wife, Lynna. They were from England and were the "hospitality chairmen" for this university. In addition to owning a scaffolding business, they were updating an estate in the English countryside. His accent and fun personality seemed to draw attention to him.

Next I met Will and Alice, members from Seattle who were the "transportation chairmen." Will's company had introduced YPO to a communication system similar to what was now "email." This implementation had saved YPO thousands of dollars by allowing the university chairmen and the coordinators to communicate via computer rather than extensively traveling during the planning stages of the university.

Will and his wife had brought their daughters, Cathy and Alicia, to help as crew—just like Kate. Their family seemed very warm, open, and inclusive as they pulled me into their circle during this trip. I also learned they were Mormon and wondered if this closeness between them was a reflection of their religion.

Our discussion about the previous evening was interrupted by Kate pointing out another beautiful building: St. Peter's Church. "They're not sure if this church or Stephansdom is older," she mused. "The foundations date back to the 1100s, but what you're looking at is the baroque version with a domed ceiling built in the 1700s."

I liked it too, but it didn't quite feel like Stephansdom. All these buildings—they were all so spectacular—how could I not become desensitized to it all? Then, glancing at my watch, I saw that it was 8:45 am and realized my workday started in fifteen minutes. I began to feel nervous as I thought about the day's responsibilities: unpacking the 300-box shipment as well as meeting and organizing the rest of our Viennese helpers, who—in addition to Kate and Will's daughters—would make up the local crew for the university.

"How much further is the Hofburg? I can't see it," I asked.

"The map shows us turning to the left here onto the Hapsburgergasse," Kate replied. "Then it should be straight ahead."

A minute or two later, we could see a statue in front of an impressive gate topped with detailed ironwork. It was the famous, grandiose *Michaelertor* gate, and it led into the palace. Although we had toured part of the Hofburg the previous night, I again felt goose bumps. This was where I would be working for the next two weeks: in a palace. The Hapsburg Dynasty had resided in this building filled with museums, chapels, and libraries, but it now served as home to Austria's head of state.

On our tour, we had walked through rooms that were venues for some of Vienna's most famed events: balls. These ornate rooms accented by gold walls, ceilings, and mirrors reminded me of the scene in *The Sound of Music* where Maria steps into Captain von Trapp's ballroom just before meeting him. Awed by its beauty, she dances with an imaginary partner. Thinking about this, I began to envision how our members would make their own memories here during the closing ball. We had also visited the chapel where the renowned Vienna Boys Choir sang Mass every Sunday. Then, the next stop on our tour had been the home of the world-famous Lipizzaner stallions, the elegant white horses used for the Spanish Riding School—the four century-old dressage academy. Their private show on the palace grounds would kick off Wednesday night's social event.

A glance at my watch again brought me back to the present, and we hurried up to the office area where our local crew waited. Some of their parents were YPO members, while others were descendants of the former Hapsburg Empire ruling class. Dr. Landmann had chosen these young people because they knew the city well, had traveled extensively, and had good people skills. I liked them and felt a kinship almost immediately because they were so professional. Maybe it was because the culture I grew up in—the military officer culture—was more formal and European-based.

I explained to them that after helping unpack all the conference materials and organize registration packets, they would assist during the class breaks to direct people to bathrooms, meals, or any place in the city they wished to explore. "In the evenings, we will also assist with the social events by directing people onto transportation buses and showing them their dinner seating assignments," I said, adding, "although we don't usually attend the social events, I have heard we might be invited to Friday night's ball at the Hofburg."

Fortunately, the preparation days went smoothly. I got to know Kate, Cathy, and Alicia better—as we usually walked from the hotel to the palace together. Those days also connected me even more to the local crew. They had started to accessorize their "crew uniforms" with Italian scarves, classic jewelry, and high heels, which inspired me to begin tucking a fresh flower behind my ear every morning. I also followed their example of letting the men open my doors and be chivalrous. Their inclusion and friendship were proving an emotional lifesaver, given that the Dallas staff's teasing continued here.

The closer we came to the opening with its increasing arrival of members, the more I felt a puzzling but intoxicating energy around me. I finally realized that it was the feeling of *power*. It felt like each CEO carried their own "field" of power with them, and when 400 of them gathered from around the world, this field of power was concentrated and heavy.

It was also interesting to watch the pecking order among YPO members. They were obviously "kings" of their own "kingdoms" at home but being here presented a whole new realm to conquer. I sensed they were "jousting" for new positions within this global fraternity when I heard comments such as, "How did Glenn get to be international president for next year? Whose executive committee did he head up?" or "How do you think this university will be rated? Do you really think Stefan was a good chairman?"

The university flowed smoothly that week, and then on the final day, the Dallas staff started buzzing. "Did you hear? They've invited us and the crew to tonight's ball here at the Hofburg. Are you going?"

I was excited, to say the least. The crew asked me to join them shopping for ball gowns. "We'll help find you a beautiful dress, and tonight we'll show you how to waltz. We'll even go to a champagne bar afterward."

My eyes misted again as I thought about how kind Kate, Cathy, Alicia, and the rest of the crew had been to me over the last two weeks. I gladly accepted their shopping invitation, but then my eyes caught the clock. It was time for Viktor Frankl to start his talk. I heard that yesterday's Mauthausen visit had been sobering, and members were on "pins and needles" for what he had to say today. Anna, one of the local crew, accepted an offer to join me in listening to Frankl's speech. "He's my great-grandfather and really wonderful. If you want, I can introduce him to you afterward."

We walked in just as Jim, as part of his introduction, was explaining that Frankl's 1946 global bestseller, *Man's Search for Meaning,* was the basis for today's talk. He reminded everyone that the *New York Times* had voted it one of the "ten most influential books in the United States."

Frankl, an Austrian neurologist and psychiatrist, who everyone now knew had survived the Holocaust death camps, spoke English with a heavy Austrian accent. He began by giving his educational background and mentioned his first academic paper had been published by Freud when he was only a teenager. Although he had kept copious notes on everything he studied and practiced on patients in his early career—even drafting a book about it—

44

the Nazis had destroyed it all when they forced him, his wife, and several family members into a prison-camp for Jews.

Frankl then related how he and his family were eventually transferred to the notorious Auschwitz prison camp, where upon entry he walked past Josef Mengele, the camp's famed "doctor of death," and narrowly escaped the gas chambers. During this time, his parents and brother had perished and his pregnant wife was sent to Bergen-Belsen—where she died. Through all the immense suffering he encountered, he realized that he could still decide his attitude rather than just "giving in," and he felt gratitude was one of the most powerful attitudes that could be chosen—second only to love.

Frankl also spoke about what he had observed about his fellow prisoners of war. Many of them, feeling they had nothing left to live for, ended their lives by throwing themselves into the camp's electrified fences. Their families had been killed, their businesses destroyed, and they were being tortured and starved. He then told of his amazement at how his background in counseling people to stay alive had prepared him for this experience. He remembered how, when he had been on staff at various hospitals and schools before the war, suicide rates actually *dropped*.

Realizing he could use this horrific time to study even more about what really gives people hope and meaning in life, he began to rewrite his book inside his mind. During this dark period, he also reached another of his "hallmark" conclusions: Even in the most painful and dehumanizing situations, life has potential meaning—and, therefore, suffering was meaningful. "What is to give light must have burning," he had written.

Frankl closed his speech by talking about success and by reading a quote from the forward of a recent update to his book:

> Again, and again, I admonish my students both in America and Europe: Don't aim at success—the more you aim at it and make it a target, the more you are going to miss

it. For success, like happiness, cannot be pursued; it must ensue, and it only does so as the unintended side-effect of one's personal dedication to a cause greater than oneself or as the by-product of one's surrender to a person other than oneself. Happiness must happen, and the same holds for success: you have to let it happen by not caring about it. I want you to listen to what your conscience commands you to do and go on to carry it out to the best of your knowledge. Then you will live to see that in the long run— in the long run, I say—success will follow you precisely because you had *forgotten* to think of it.[2]

Frankl was greeted with a standing ovation, and people crowded around him. Once the room had emptied he walked over to us, and after hugging Anna, she introduced him. Before even shaking his hand, I felt amazing electricity pass through me. The man had almost a "saintly" aura about him, and the profound feeling of hope he emitted engulfed me.

After that day's activities were over, I was so tired I couldn't imagine doing anything but going back to the hotel and lying down. But the crew suggested that if I joined them for an espresso— something new for me—I would soon be ready to look for a ball gown.

Realizing I might never have this opportunity again, I reluctantly agreed. Leaving the Hofburg, we hopped on one of the city's Ringstrasse trams. Still feeling tired, I wondered how I would survive the afternoon. But the scenery quickly distracted and re-energized me with each stop we made. The history of the Ringstrasse, one of the most spectacular boulevards in the world, was so interesting: it had been a circle of walls that the Hapsburgs used to protect their city and beautiful buildings from invaders. It wasn't until young Emperor Franz Josef made his famous "Es ist Mein Wille" proclamation in 1857 that the walls came down, and

---

[2] *Man's Search for Meaning* by Viktor Frankl

he ordered the Ringstrasse designed to showcase the grandeur and glory of the Habsburg Empire's centuries-old capital.

Once we reached the "Rauthausplatz/Burgtheater" stop, it was only a minute's walk to Cafe Landtmann, one of Vienna's five-top coffeehouses. Some of its celebrated patrons included Freud, Marlene Dietrich, Gustav Mahler, and Paul McCartney.

As Alexis ordered for me, I thought about my lifelong dislike of this stimulant. The aroma had always been heavenly, but its bitter taste kept me at a distance. Maybe it would be different this time? I watched people sip coffee and take bites of luscious-looking desserts. Sweets were my favorite, and the pastries here—and around the rest of the city—were enticing.

The server brought us three cups of steaming liquid, followed by three glasses of water. "This is a *mélange*—foamed milk with espresso," Alexis explained. "If you like, add some sugar to it, then drink it in a few sips. Follow with the water. It should wake you up."

Watching the elegant way she sipped, I tried to follow suit. But even steamed with milk, it tasted like poison to me. I dumped in sugar, then finished it while trying to maintain a smile. Thinking back on the history of coffee, I remembered how this drink had initially been mistaken for camel feed—and maybe that wasn't so far from the truth.

All Vienna, however, was mad for coffee. During the Turkish siege of the city in 1683, a Polish/Ukrainian tradesman named Jerzy Franchiseck Kulchickee—who had been captured earlier in his life by the Turks but eventually made his way back into Vienna—helped save the city and become a hero. Kulczycki had then used the coffee beans left behind by the Turks to open the first coffee house in Vienna, and even concocted the idea of adding milk to the liquid.

When I asked Alexis if this story was true, she said yes and pointed to the picture of a Turkish-looking man on the wall—adding that a celebration in his honor was held annually and that every coffee house in Vienna had his picture on their premises. As I studied his face, I could feel myself waking up and getting excited. "I feel much better," I announced. "Let's go look for dresses."

On the way, the crew stopped to show me the University of Vienna and Sigmund Freud Park, which was a part of the city I hadn't yet explored. My companions told me that during the summer, the park was the top place to sunbathe because the city brought in lounge chairs and served free "Vienna mountain spring water." But it was the building behind the park with a white, lacy façade that produced a reaction similar to the one I had felt when I first laid eyes on Stephansdom.

"That is the Votivkirche, arguably the most famous neo-Gothic church in the world," Alexis pointed out, noting that the brother of Franz Josef had it built to thank God after a failed assassination attempt on the young emperor's life.

From there, we finally made our way to Kleiderverleigh, a huge bridal store. "You find a beautiful *kleid*—gown—that is in your size, and you rent it," Alexis said. "They can help you to fit it, but we must find one *schnell* as the ball starts in four hours."

I looked at a long rack full of dresses in my size, then started searching through them. First, I pulled out a flowing, full-length red chiffon dress and held it against myself. Then a fitted, full-length baby-blue silk dress caught my attention. Hmmmm.... all the gowns were full-length. This was like a fairy-tale dress shop full of stunning gowns, and they were all so gorgeous. How would I ever make up my mind? The crew helped me search, and then one exclaimed, "Perfect for Kris," handing me a black sequined gown with collar and waist trimmed in gold. It was simple but very elegant and sophisticated.

When I tried it on, the fit was perfect and I thought about the fact that I had never dressed this way before. To my surprise, the fee included delivery to the hotel, pickup, and cleaning. So, we all departed, agreeing to meet at the ball at 7 pm.

While dressing in my hotel room, I was grateful for the cup of espresso. Without it, I wouldn't have had the energy to go to the ball, as I had never been so exhausted. Gayla, one of the Dallas staffers, was professionally dressed and waiting for me in the lobby—as everyone else had already gone to the event. When she saw my gown, she asked if I had brought it with me. I avoided her question, as I wasn't going to volunteer information about the afternoon's excursion. While the staff had spent time together around town during the week, they had excluded me; I wasn't about to share my special time with the crew this afternoon—or about how I had rented a gown.

Arriving at the palace, we could hear a Strauss waltz emanating from the ballroom. The light from the chandeliers was romantic, and all the tables were aglow in candles. I chose to bypass the Dallas staff and sit with the crew. Alexis sat across from me, attired in a stunning, sequined red ballgown—her hair cascading down her back. She nodded her approval at me and then whispered something to the young man next to her. I was glad to be at this table; they knew the culture and would include me in everything as much as they could.

The evening began with a performance by dancers in dazzling white gowns and long-tailed tuxedos performing a waltz. Next came the Vienna Choir Boys with their sweet and heavenly voices, and as they sang "Edelweiss" I was transported to another realm. These two opening events made the perfect preview to what promised to be a magical evening.

After a traditional dinner of Weiner schnitzel and apfelstrudel, the orchestra started up again and the waltzing began. I had never learned how to waltz— staff hadn't been a part of the waltzing lessons offered each afternoon—so I decided to sit and watch. My Viennese friends who had participated in the city's ball season for years immediately headed out to the dance floor. As Alexis passed, she whispered, "We will tell the men to ask you to dance too!"

I studied everyone closely, trying to catch their rhythm, moving my feet underneath the table to simulate what I thought were the steps. I had recently taken up "two-stepping" in Dallas on weekends, and the waltz seemed to mirror its "one-two-three" feel (or did "two-stepping" mirror the waltz's "one-two-three" feel?). Suddenly, one of the men on the crew walked by and offered his hand for a dance. I smiled nervously and hesitated, but he took me by the hand and pulled me up. "Hold onto my shoulder and hand," he insisted. "I will lead, and you will follow me. I have led many women before, and I can do it with you. You will dance."

Nodding at his instructions, I attempted to let him lead, but I got mixed up on the steps and became frustrated and embarrassed. Slowing down, he began once again with his first step and gently drew me along. I took a deep breath and relaxed. Suddenly, I was following him. He smiled, and I smiled back. Before I knew it, the two of us were circling the floor in perfect rhythm to *Weiner Blut, Weiner Blut, da-da-da, da-da-da, da-da-da*. The dance ended and he started to lead me back to the table, but I begged, "Geoffrey, please…one more dance? I am just beginning to understand how it works."

Looking back at me, he accommodated. But at the end of the second waltz, it was clear he preferred a more practiced partner and we returned to the table. My Viennese friends encouraged several other men to offer their hand, so I enjoyed a few more dances. Suddenly, my mind drifted back to Atlanta with Greg at the Minuet party. He had been so handsome, and I had so taken him for granted. Yes, I was in Vienna in a magical event, but I still felt the sadness.

I felt the espresso wane, and between that and my usual sad "Greg" feelings regaining their strength, decided to head back to my room. I thanked everyone for the evening. "This has been so wonderful, as if I'm in the middle of a dream. Here I am in a lovely gown, waltzing in a royal palace to a live Viennese orchestra, with delicious desserts at the table—but I am so tired that I must go back to my hotel."

Alexis protested "But Kris, we are now going to a champagne bar. You must come. That is what one always does after a ball." Everyone else was nodding their heads in agreement. "Come with us for just one drink—a glass of pink champagne—then you can go back to the hotel."

Kate, Cathy, and Alicia said they would go, but I thought about all the work ahead of me tomorrow. I had to pack everything in the morning and wasn't sure how long it would take. It took one more minute to ponder the options: home to bed—or a nightcap of pink champagne in a Viennese bar surrounded by a charming European crowd who had been gracious and kind to me. My decision was made; I was going.

Entering the champagne bar, the elegance of the place with its soft lights and clinking of glasses overwhelmed me. One of the men told the waiter to bring "Rosa Champagner" as we took our seats on velvet couches and chairs in front of tables lit by candles. When the waiter arrived with long-stemmed flutes filled with the pink, sparkling liquid, I tried to act like I knew what I was doing—raising my glass as a toast was made.

"To our wonderful city…with the best of champagne."

Everyone took small sips, nodded their approval, then set the glasses down on the table in front of them. Conversation amongst our group would normally have been carried on in German, but given that we Americans were among them, the crew members were gracious enough to converse in English.

After two glasses, I began to feel tipsy. A few minutes later, my head started to nod and several of the crew smiled at me. Kate volunteered to get me home, and everyone said their *gute nacht*. Back at the hotel, it took all my energy just to insert the key into the door, remove the gown, and collapse onto the bed—where I instantly fell fast asleep.

The next morning, I awoke with a start. The clock read "10:04." Packing had started over an hour ago. I tried to jump out of bed, but an incredible throbbing in my head stopped me. A headache? In the morning? This was a new experience. Then thoughts of last night's champagne drinking came back to me. Could this be my first hangover? I had imbibed more than I ever had in my life, which would explain this feeling. It could be added to my rapidly growing list of *firsts* on this trip to Vienna: Austria, shots of brandy, espresso, a formal ball with waltzes, and working in a palace once occupied with royalty. But the time hit me again, and I realized that breakfast would end in twenty minutes. I had a big job to do today, and the other staff were probably already hard at work. Standing up much more carefully, I took two aspirins as I dressed.

After a quick breakfast of *birchermuesli*, an Austrian cereal that was yet another "first" experienced in Vienna, I made tracks for the Hofburg. Heading up to the area we had been using as offices, I saw that no one was there, and—judging by all the taped and labeled boxes—realized they had come much earlier to do their packing.

When I finally completed my task, I wandered back into the ballroom where last night's gala had been held. To my surprise, it was exactly as it had been left the night before. Strolling around the room, I took in the sweet scent of the flowers, and tears welled in my eyes. After all the pressure of the past few weeks, I felt a sense of relief and a little more objectivity–as well as an overwhelming mixture of feelings. The strongest emotion—stronger than the sadness last night of losing Greg (at least at this moment)—was one of wistfulness. It was hard to believe it was all over!

Closing my eyes, I could still hear the notes of the various waltzes as I had whirled around the floor in my elegant ball gown partnered by handsome Viennese men dressed in tails. The evening had been like something out of a fairy tale, and as I reflected I wondered how this could ever have happened to me. Vienna had been so romantic that I wondered if my vow to never again let myself fall in love after my breakup with Greg had been premature. Glancing around the room full of wonderful memories, I felt just a trace of hope arise—in both myself and a potential new life. I had been occupied with many things over the past few months in Dallas: line dancing, new friends, and planning for this university. But, here in this story-tale setting, for the first time since Greg's rejection and subsequent marriage, I had felt traces of the sadness cloud over me begin to lift—even if just a little bit.

Chapter 3

The Beautiful Northwest

The rays of the western sun felt warm, and a light wind whipped through my hair as I rotated the jet ski handlebars to rev its engine—which produced an adrenaline rush. Following Cathy's lead as she took a full circle around Mercer Island for fifteen miles, I got a bird's eye view of its intriguing houses—many with private docks—while keeping a half-mile from the shore. The blue waters of Lake Washington danced and sparkled as we jetted around, my wetsuit keeping me at just the right temperature. Turning my head away from the shore, I could see sailboats with their raised masts and powerboats bobbing about. And to think my Vienna experience had led to this unexpected adventure!

My visit to Will and Alice's home was the result of a strong connection I had formed with them at the Vienna University. Will had noticed my emotional and spiritual struggle during that trip and had been kind enough to share some of his similar internal conflicts over the years. I had also enjoyed getting to know their daughters, Cathy and Alicia, as they served on the crew. Alice was exceptionally sweet and thought I might enjoy seeing the Pacific Northwest, so when they extended an invitation to visit them at their home on Mercer Island, I was convinced to say yes.

Once my plane landed in Seattle, Cathy was there to pick me up. As she drove me onto Mercer Island and down the eastern edge of the shore, I fell in love with everything I saw. I had noticed a foot-shaped island with bridges off either side as the plane approached Seattle Tacoma airport, and I asked her if this was that island. She responded that it was—and also the most populated island lake in the whole United States. Situated just east of Seattle in freshwater Lake Washington, Mercer Island was first the home of the friendly Snoqualmie tribe who gathered berries and fished there. Cathy explained that in the mid-1800s, the tribe had rowed one of Seattle's founding Mercer brothers over to the island for the first government survey in 1860, which gave it the Mercer name.

She went on to tell me more about the history, starting with its notoriety and accessibility being established in 1889 when Wisconsin speculator C.C. Calkins bought large amounts of its acreage on credit. He hoped to make it a resort and began by establishing a community named "East Seattle" on its northwest shore. He then built a lavish hotel and nearby steamboat landing ("Calkins Landing") that greatly increased traffic to the island. However, eventually he ran into problems with creditors and after supposedly losing everything in a card game, the hotel shut down and then mysteriously burned in 1908—and with it, the resort community idea.

East Seattle was still there. And since the first bridge to Mercer Island was built in 1940, the population had grown steadily to the point of it now being one of the most exclusive and private places to live in Seattle. The technology boom was taking place here at this point, and Cathy mentioned that several YPOers and technology moguls were settling around the area.

As she pulled onto their property, I noticed the private dock with a large cabin cruiser and several small machines sitting beside it. She explained that they were jet skis, personal watercrafts that made circling the island fun and easy. While she was telling me about the jet skis—and encouraging me to take a ride on them as my first adventure here—we entered the house, and Alice greeted me with a hug.

On the way to my room, Cathy pulled me into the den. "Look out there," she said, pointing toward an enormous glass window covering the wall from floor to ceiling. I caught my breath, as in the distance over the Bay loomed a majestic, snow-capped mountain. "It's Mt. Rainier," she said, smiling. "We wake up to it every day. Isn't it amazing?"

Fifteen minutes later, I had changed into my swimsuit and we headed toward the dock. To me, the jet ski looked like a "water motorcycle," and I wasn't sure how to get on it. But she demonstrated the correct way, stressing that the jet ski only worked when the rider stayed *balanced* and *centered* and kept the throttle active by rotating the handle, which controlled propulsion and steering ability.

We took off slowly at first so I could get the hang of it, but as we began the fifteen-mile loop around the island, my unsteadiness rapidly turned to confidence and even a little cockiness. I was instantly humbled, however, when during my first try at crossing Cathy's wake, I twisted sideways, accidentally let go of the throttle, and the jet ski and I separated. Circling back around to where I was struggling in the water, she explained how to turn the jet ski upward and step on it from the rear—then reminded me to always keep the throttle activated, and we were off and running again. When we finished the full loop, she complimented me for being a quick study and encouraged me to join her for another go-round. She didn't appear certain I was adventurous enough to do this, but I immediately responded, "Absolutely...let's go for it!"

Our second time around gave me even more confidence—especially with staying afloat—and I was able to notice more of what we were passing. There were other jet skis and boats, and I felt like a dolphin swimming and skipping waves, especially when I kicked the engine up to full speed at sixty miles an hour. This time around, though, I kept my eyes open for Calkins Landing, and pinpointed it just south of where the I-90 bridge, the Murrow—which connected Seattle to the island—was in the process of being repaired after sinking two years earlier. Continuing around, I could see more beautiful houses with docks on big lots full of huge trees. Then, when we were almost back home, Cathy pointed out the Beach Club. After pulling back into their dock, she told me I had passed my "check ride" and was welcome to take the jet ski out whenever I liked—which I thought very generous.

Later that evening at dinner, I met their oldest son Bruce who had just returned from his standard two-year mission trip. These trips were apparently a rite of passage in the Mormon/LDS faith for eighteen-year-old boys, who were strongly encouraged by the scriptural admonition to "go therefore and teach the nations." But Bruce and I didn't quite seem to connect the way I had with his sisters; maybe we were just at different times and places in our lives.

Over the next few days, the family invited me to participate in church activities with them and I discovered their religious culture was much like the Baptist one I was currently experiencing in Dallas: both believed in proselytization to lead others to their faith; both strongly encouraged social interactions with others of their same faith; and both held Sunday morning and evening services and studied their faith's religious books (*Bibles* for Christians; the *Book of Mormon* for LDS). While Christians believed that Jesus Christ had only appeared once on earth in the first century, Mormons believed God and Jesus Christ had both appeared again in 1820 to

Joseph Smith—followed by a visit from an angel named Moroni who shared with Joseph where to find ancient "golden plates" containing writings from God to former inhabitants of America. It was from these plates that he had built the Book of Mormon.

I thought back to the Voice I had experienced in the stairwell and the Love that had overwhelmed me. Viewing all these similarities helped me see how close-minded people could get within their own religions. They went through all their "motions," their classes, their studies, their meetings; but where was the Love I had experienced in the stairwell?

All these questions swirling through my mind were unsettling. There had to be something more. The jet ski rides and breathtaking views had been wonderful, but because of my troubled soul the talks with Will were my favorite part of my visit. Following on our spiritual conversations in Vienna (he had experienced a "God" crisis of sorts too, although his involved his Mormon faith, whereas mine was about my Protestant faith), we dove further into comparing all kinds of cultures, beliefs, and how exposure to them could open one's mind. He talked about how his first mission trip started his intellectual and spiritual expansion, and that his YPO experiences and travels had enhanced it even more.

His comments led me to reflect on my humanitarian trip to Papua New Guinea and how it had deepened my spiritual walk, but I also realized that it was my romantic crisis that had initiated my more profound thoughts about God and the world.

The talks with Will at their home lifted my spirits, and my sense of sorrow since the Greg breakup seemed to lighten even more. It was a blessing to be with this family, and I wished they were going to attend the upcoming YPO "family university" in British Columbia—just a few hours north of where they lived and where I would be serving as crew—so that I would be able to see them again.

YPO family universities were a somewhat new addition to the organization's global offerings and were scheduled during the summer when families had enough of a break in their hectic schedules to be able to come together for a week. The previous year's event had been held in St. Moritz, Switzerland, but the upcoming one in British Columbia would be split between Whistler and Vancouver. I had volunteered to be crew because I had never been there and had heard that Whistler—a ski resort in the Rockies with the second longest vertical drop in North America—would provide beauty and wonderful outdoor activities. Vancouver—a bustling, scenic, and ethnically diverse West Coast seaport—didn't appeal to me as strongly, but I figured it would play its part in my getting to experience Whistler.

When the time came to head to British Columbia for the family university, everyone started in Whistler. Originally named London Mountain because of its heavy fogs and rain (but re-named at some point for the call of the hairy marmot prominent in the area), the YPO families spread out in various accommodations throughout the resort. Those of us on the staff, however, were assigned more casual quarters with bunk beds which made for some short tempers. It was quite different from what I had experienced in Vienna where we all had our own spaces within top-end hotels; no matter how irritated we became during our stressful workdays we always had the option of retreating to our own room. These rustic cabins in the mountains, however, provided no solitude and we also had the added annoyances of mosquitos, bugs, and my least favorite: spiders. But here the scenery was pristine perhaps due to the valley having only opened to development in the last seventy-five years.

After the first three days of exploration, education, and outdoor activities in Whistler, all 1000 attendees were transported via private train to the more luxurious Pan Pacific hotel in Vancouver for the second half of the university. This direct two-hour ride ran along the tracks of the famous "Sea to Sky Corridor," named for the stunning views it offered along the way.

Prior to taking the fabulous ride, the members had been told that the Corridor had first opened around 1915 via an inaugural train that connected Squamish, established as the terminus of the new railway and named on behalf of the indigenous people of the area, all the way to the north of Whistler. The new line both opened a faster means for more people to reach the fertile Whistler/Pemberton area and establish farms as well as a faster method to transport their livestock, shortening the Vancouver cattle drive by three days. It wasn't until 1956 that railway operations were established from Squamish south to Vancouver (steamboats originally brought people from there to Squamish), and then a highway was constructed in 1962. But tourists still preferred the train line.

After we loaded members and their families onto the train for their journey south, we finished shutting everything down and then started our drive on the Sea to Sky Highway. On the way to Squamish, we passed the Black Tusk—an old volcano—to the east, followed by the snow-capped, jagged peaks of the Tantalus Mountains to the west. Squamish had been originally established as a logging town, and on our short stop there, we learned how logs had been pulled from the Squamish River and placed on the railroad for delivery to Vancouver.

From there, the Sea to Sky Highway opened onto the Howe Sound, with a deep blue expanse on one side of the road and cliffs and mountains rising off the other. About a mile south we stopped again, this time at Shannon Falls, the third highest waterfall in British Columbia, where we took the fifteen-minute trek up the road to view the spectacular 1100-foot drop onto the boulder-strewn watercourse near where we stood. Someone in our group explained that these falls had been created long ago by a receding glacier and were classified as "horsetail" waterfalls because the descending water begins in a small stream and then widens to create a lot of mist, maintaining contact with the granite bedrock behind it for most of its path.

It was easy to be overwhelmed with all this scenic sensory input, and I could understand why the Sea to Sky Highway had been voted as one of the "top five best rides worldwide." The landscape along the highway also laid the groundwork for Vancouver, which was surrounded with snow-capped mountains, dense forests, and beautiful beaches along the Pacific coastline.

As we entered North Vancouver, we decided to make one more stop at a famous suspension bridge, The Capilano, named after a river honoring a Squamish chief (which, in their language, meant "beautiful river"). In 1889, a 460-foot hemp-rope and cedar-plank bridge had been suspended 230 feet above the river, and over the years, it had been reinforced and replaced by newer materials. Now, in addition to being Vancouver's most recognized visitor attraction, it was also used in films and TV shows. Set in a lush forest, the swaying bridge provided an adrenaline rush; as we crossed it, we saw some kayaks below and what one person thought was an eagle watching spawning salmon.

Once we reached Vancouver Harbor and settled into the Pan Pacific Hotel, we all breathed sighs of relief when we were assigned our own rooms—and headed straight to them to enjoy a hot shower. Classes were held in the attached Convention Centre, and nearby was the world-famous Stanley Park featuring forests, lakes, bridges, lighthouses, gardens, totem poles, and a famous aquarium.

Since I knew that the upcoming Taipei University chairman, Sidney, was attending the Whistler/Vancouver University, I went out of my way to give him top-notch customer service. The first time I had met him was in Vienna; he had been there for a few days to market Taipei University and get a feel for how universities were run. I also discovered that, like some other Taiwanese citizens, he owned a house in Vancouver...so he was on-site taking notes about everything. During a few quiet minutes on a break between classes,

I mustered up enough confidence to ask him to tell me more about his native country and he graciously obliged.

Chapter 4

Tai Chi in Taipei

Sidney began by explaining that his country was discovered by the Portuguese, who named it "Formosa," which means "beautiful island." However, much of it had not been kept beautiful, and since then its name had been changed back to Taiwan—meaning "sandy island" in Dutch.

He also explained that just after World War II and Mao Tse Tung's Communist Revolution in Mainland China, a Chinese leader named Chiang Kai Shek led a group of over two million followers in a short-term escape to Taiwan. He established the "Republic of China" there, which continued to be recognized as the legal government of China by the United Nations. Chiang designed his stay to be short-term, believing he would return to his home country within ten years. Sidney said when that didn't happen, Taiwan became the permanent residence for Chiang and his fellow citizens—including his father—who had given up all of his wealth and the family's Shanghai hotel. "Were it not for our friend, America, who considered *us* the Chinese government, it would have been even worse." he insisted.

He continued sharing that, despite all his losses, his father remained a kind and generous person and ended up in leadership in his new country—all of which set an outstanding example for him while growing up in Taiwan. Sidney served his required military time after secondary school but wasn't sure what to do for a career without a college degree (rather a standard thing for YPOers, I was learning).

He looked for a job with American Express, but their requirement of both a college degree and an ability to speak English thwarted that idea until a friend of his was able to offer him an entry-level job with them. This was in 1971 when Taiwan had just been replaced by Mainland China on the UN Security Council—which was causing a great deal of economic chaos for Taiwan and angst for ex-patriates who feared losing touch with their home countries. Sidney felt badly for these people, many of them English-speaking, and would check their mail several times a day as well as forward it to them after they left, oftentimes at his own expense. This also motivated him to learn the English language, something he had been avoiding. Word of his outstanding service reached American Express, and in the ensuing five years, he was promoted to head their Taiwanese operations. From this position, he was able to turn the company's profits and keep it operating on the island. He observed that much of that achievement was due to his love for customer service and helping people—which ultimately led him into the hospitality industry—similar to his father.

"I have always wanted to change the world," he confided with sincerity, emphasizing that one of the ways he was trying to better his native Taiwan was by increasing tourism. "That is why I accepted my Prime Minister's invitation to open the Ritz Carlton in Taipei. We wanted to give top-notch luxury and customer service," he told me. The number of employees he took on to run the hotel had provided him the opportunity to join YPO, experience other cultures, and invite others from around the world back to his much-loved island.

When I asked why we weren't using his hotel as the venue, he replied that it wasn't large enough to accommodate YPO—but that the newly opened Grand Hyatt Taipei had more than 800 rooms and could easily do so. The rest of the chats we had about both his personal story and experiences in Taiwan increased my excitement about working on his university—even though Taipei wasn't exactly one of the destinations on my bucket list. I soon realized that his positive energy drew me to him, and his goal of changing his corner of the world was one we had in common.

These personal encounters with YPO members always fascinated me. It was interesting to hear the stories of where they were from—and the choices they made to be standing in their current shoes. I imagine my willingness to converse probably made things worse when observed by the Dallas staff, but I thought little of it at the time. I wasn't trying to outshine or outdo anybody around me; nor was I trying to rub shoulders so I could name names. I was just being my usual curious self—as well as trying to get past my life-shattering break-up with Greg. Every conversation, every trip to a new place, and every immersion into a culture allowed those pieces to reform me.

Six months later and 8,000 miles around the world, I landed on the tiny island of Taiwan. My first order of business seemed a mission impossible: double-check tiny names on watches. How on earth was I going to do that?

One of Sidney's ideas had been to give personalized watches to every guest as they checked in for the university. Although watches weren't unusual gifts at these YPO functions, he had enough connections with the Chinese jewelry industry to acquire quality ones. Then he had the event's logo—as well as each attendee's first initial and last name—imprinted on them. Counting attendees and spouses, that came to 900 watches—and they were all being produced here in Taiwan!

The good news was that the watches were ready. The problem for me was their grammatical accuracy. Our databases *had* to keep correct member name spellings, so I knew that the right information had been supplied. But given that it was a Chinese manufacturer— and given the basic concept of statistics—there were going to be errors. So, this double-checking procedure would take some serious time, energy, and patience.

We had scheduled our arrival into Taipei a few days earlier than usual—as well as hired extra crew—in order to accomplish this detailed task. And it was me who got to supervise it all in addition to my usual job of unloading event materials, setting up the offices, and organizing the crew. Attendee nametags were a different deal because we always customized them in Dallas so that they were ready for attendees; we also brought our nametag engraving machine with us everywhere we went in case corrections were needed. But names on watches? Just thinking about it gave me a giant headache.

Our first day there we spent adjusting to jet lag and doing initial set-ups. I was already getting stressed, so I decided to get out and about to have a look at the city before everything got too crazy. At breakfast, I asked one of my Dallas co-workers, Missy, if she would like to join me on a walk.

"I don't know," she hesitated. "I don't really care for the gray haze that seems to be hanging everywhere." She then reminded me that the poor air quality was the result of their failure to establish environmental guidelines decades before, as they hadn't expected to be on the island long enough for the country became industrialized.

"True, there's a lot of pollution," I countered, "but it would be interesting to walk over and watch the group of people across the street who are performing that interesting form of movement."

"Oh, you mean *tai chi?*" Missy asked.

I nodded my head. I had first noticed these groups involved in tai chi on the ride in from the airport as we approached the Chiang-Kai Shek Memorial. The sun had begun to set, and as we drove by, at least a hundred older women were outside performing movements slowly and fluidly in sync with each other. I had never seen such a thing. And while setting up the office the day before, I had gazed out the window at one of the parks across the street and seen all kinds of people doing it there too.

It made sense that Missy would know about tai chi. She was the team's copywriter and had researched everything Taiwanese in detail before putting anything on paper for the attendees.

"OK," she agreed, "I'll walk across the street and watch it with you. Morning is a better time to see it."

We finished eating and walked over to watch. There did seem to be a little less haze…and a lot more people practicing. Missy explained that while the meaning of tai chi was "supreme boxing," it was often called "meditation in motion" due to its focus and breathing—and was known to bring a sense of calm wherever it was practiced. While some believed tai chi started in the twelfth century, actual proof of existence could only be traced back to the mid-nineteenth century.

We walked around the park watching the people move slowly and in rhythm, and then Missy returned to the hotel. But I stayed, wanting a few more minutes to observe. It had been interesting to watch these people perform tai chi, and in light of all my stress about the watches—as well as my love for exercise—I wondered if I could just try to follow along for a few minutes. Smiling at a few people, I quietly positioned myself in place at the back and took a breath.

Stepping the left foot at an angle, I followed them as they rocked forward—pushing my arms out and open—then rocked back while pulling them back in. I did this about ten times with the left foot, then switched to taking the right foot out at an angle and repeating everything to that side ten times. Someone noticed me and spoke English, saying the move was called "Calming the Waters." The next move, "Pushing the Waters," involved leaning to the left with elbows slightly bent and palms of both hands pushing to the left for ten times—and then leaning to the right with palms of both hands pushing to the right for ten times. Next came "Over the Drum" on each side—which again meant a left diagonal step with arms long out front—palms facing each other—and a slight push out and up with a slight pull back in. Amazingly, I could already feel myself breathing more deeply and becoming calmer…so I stayed another five minutes. Then, sensing the pollution rising, I headed back inside more confident that I could handle the watch-checking job.

I saw Sidney shortly thereafter, and he still had his gentle and kind air, although he was much busier trying to handle all the soon-to-arrive leader-guests—and those 900 watches. Whenever I saw him after that in the hallway, he would smile and twinkle his eyes at me. The Grand Hyatt was a beautiful venue, but after our staff's arrival dinner at Sidney's boutique Ritz Carlton Hotel, I preferred it to where we were staying because it reflected more of his spirit.

This university worked similarly to the one in Vienna the previous year: Speakers on all topics had flown in from around the world for the array of morning educational classes, while all manner of excursions and activities outside the hotel were on tap in the afternoon. And as always, there would be top-notch evening social events in significant places.

Things seemed to be moving forward without a hitch, and one of the speakers whose name had caught my eye was Stephen Covey, the author of a global bestseller, *The Seven Habits of Highly Effective People*—which I had heard about, but not yet read. While delivering gifts to guest rooms the first evening, I had entered his room only to see a *Book of Mormon* lying open on his bed, its pages dog-eared and heavily underlined. I hadn't realized that he was a Mormon, but after my recent stay in Mercer Island and discussions about spiritual issues with Will, I made a point of finding out when Covey would be speaking so that I could stand in the back of the room and listen to him.

Covey's talk was titled "Emotional Bank Accounts," based on a concept in his book. In his view, every time something good was added to a relationship, it was a "deposit" to the emotional side of a relationship—whereas fights or negative discussions caused issues in relationships, so they were called "withdrawals." One of the wisest things that could be done in a relationship, therefore, was to make many "deposits" so that when a withdrawal had to be made (a confrontation or fight or something along those lines), there was more than enough to cover it and the relationship would stay healthy. His concept intrigued me, and I pondered its significance in both my past as well as future relationships. Going forward, I could definitely work on making deposits. Looking backward, I wondered how the balance had been in my relationship with Greg. Wasn't I always complaining about him to my friends? Maybe this was why our "withdrawals" felt more like overdrafts laced with hidden fees. Communication would definitely need to play a part in my future relationships, but I first needed to balance my *own* account to see where I stood. I still needed to figure out who *I* was and what *I* wanted.

A few days before the black-tie closing event, those of us on staff were told to submit our names if we wanted to attend, as there weren't enough seats for the entire group. Those chosen would check members in, then find an empty seat for dinner toward the back of the ballroom. Before leaving Dallas, I had read that the closing venue would be at the historic Grand Hotel built in 1952 by Chiang Kai Shek and later praised by *Fortune* as one of the top ten hotels in the world. The fourteen-story, palace-like building— one of Taipei's most famous landmarks—boasted gilded tiles and vermilion columns, so I had been inspired to bring an elegant sleeveless, full-length red taffeta dress with matching full-length gloves—just in case.

71

Staff members from a team who had recently returned from the closing event in Monaco assured us that probably no event could ever top that one: an evening in the Sportsman's Club with its glass walls retracting into the floor as fireworks went off in the harbor. Taipei wasn't on a bay as was Monaco, but the Chinese had invented fireworks, so who knew? Maybe it would still be worth going. So, I submitted my name and kept my fingers crossed. I wanted to *be* in red to match the beautiful red hotel. A few hours prior to the event, my boss let me know I had been chosen to attend, and I was excited. Another staff member made it clear to everyone, though, that she was upset for not being chosen and announced that she had brought a beautiful dress too—but it didn't matter. Feeling sorry for her—and seeing no one else offer their seat, I told her she could have mine. But she was so put out that—in front of everyone—she dramatically put her hand to her forehead and insisted, "No, no, Kris—you go; I'll just stay here and find something to do," then walked away.

I decided to take her at her word and ran to my room to change. I already loved my Taipei watch (Sidney had surprised the staff by also having the watches personalized for us), so after I zipped up my full-length, tight-fitting mermaid gown and slipped on the long red gloves, I fastened it over my right wrist.

As I settled into the registration desk with my fellow workers from the Dallas staff, one of them—who was wiser and had been with YPO far longer than I—leaned in and said, "Kris, you look very lovely, but you might want to remember in the future that this is *their* party and your job is to look *professional.* Don't out-dress them. Plus, you are being paid by them...not the other way around."

I understood her logic—which I felt she had communicated in a kind way—and wondered what the YPO members would say when they saw me. But as they checked in, they only offered compliments...and a few asked where I had gotten the dress. *They* didn't seem too concerned about what I was wearing.

When it came time for dinner, a senior staff person signaled for me to take the seat beside him, so I headed in his direction. I had enjoyed getting to know him during the university, finding his expatriate background in Hong Kong quite interesting. He had joined the YPO staff a few years earlier and worked his way up to heading the Asia/Australia/Pacific's region, which contained the second largest percentage of the organization's global population. We had a great conversation about Hong Kong and its upcoming return to China, but he maintained that when it happened many people would leave to live in countries without Communist influence. While our talk was stimulating, my second glass of wine made me drowsy and I remembered that—just like in Vienna—I had a shipment to pack up tomorrow, so I excused myself and headed back to the hotel.

On the ride back, I thought about the champagne bar in Vienna after the closing ball—and how kind Alexis had been to me during that university. My thoughts then shifted to how nice it had been to have her in Dallas last summer after her father had arranged a YPO internship for her before sending her on to graduate school in Paris. It had been fun to watch how she worked and how much she reminded me of myself. She would get assignments, rapidly learn the system, complete them in record time and then twiddle her thumbs—confirming my observation that YPO jobs weren't overly-intellectual.

Alexis and I had also spent a lot of time together personally, and my family had even taken her with us to San Antonio. She had enjoyed the city's Alamo and Riverwalk—and loved my family—and the day after we returned from that trip, an overnight package addressed to my parents arrived from Vienna. To their surprise, they opened the wooden box to find a Sacher Torte, Vienna's most famous dessert. The circular cake iced in melted chocolate had a picture of the Hotel Sacher imprinted inside the cover—and had been sent personally by her father. We were all delighted, to say the least.

The next morning, after packing the shipment to go back to Dallas, I needed to be at the airport to fly out. Sidney had stopped by the hotel to check on everything, and thoughtfully suggested that I ride with a Taiwanese chapter member. He said she was soon heading to the airport and had room to spare in her private sedan.

On the way to the airport this woman was gracious and kind, and as her driver took us through the streets of Taipei she pointed out various landmarks and expounded on the history of the island. She spoke of her appreciation of the United States's consideration of her country as the "real China" despite pressure from the United Nations and, more recently, its continued support of the right of her country to self-govern despite Soviet threats after the Sino-Soviet split.

As she shifted the conversation to economic and military aid, she expressed even more appreciation for the billions of dollars the United States had contributed—especially between 1950 and 1965. She also acted like it was a privilege to have me—an American—in her car. I wondered if she knew I was just a YPO employee; or had Sidney maybe told her something else? No matter, I was grateful for seeing Taipei through her eyes because it made me aware of how much we took our independence and freedoms for granted.

On the long plane ride home, I realized that the Taiwanese had inspired me with their love for their native country. They were very committed to the success of this tiny island in the middle of the South China Sea despite all the odds against it.

My thoughts soon turned to what Will had said about the YPO helping him grow intellectually and spiritually. Now, it seemed to be having that same effect on me. I had not planned on working for YPO a year ago when I was in the depths of despair. I had not even *wanted* to go to work for them. Then, I had heard Viktor Frankl and been inspired—and was finding that Sidney had inspired me too, with his twinkling eyes, his top-notch customer service, and his kindness. I hoped I was like him in all those ways.

As I continued reflecting on all the people I had been privileged to meet during the past year, I thought about one of my favorite Scriptures, Jeremiah 29:11, "'For I know the plans I have for you,' declares the Lord, 'plans to prosper you and not to harm you, plans to give you hope and a future.'"

I had thought during the encounter in the stairwell the plan was for Greg and me to get back together. However, taking one unknown step after another had catapulted me further than I had ever imagined myself to go. Maybe all of this—my impromptu job interview and well-timed layoff—had little to do with chance and was indeed God's Divine plan for my life. Maybe I just had to follow His lead.

Chapter 5

Meeting a Prince

"D id Henry VIII really build this castle for Anne Boleyn on the grounds of an old leper hospital?" I asked Ron, my new boss, as we walked into St. James's Palace, the venue for the evening's social event at the YPO London University.

"He did," Ron replied—explaining that the infamous couple had their initials "HA" carved into the Gatehouse in her honor. "It is the most senior palace in all of England—and not open to the public—so we are getting a truly exclusive venue for tonight's event. And I just found out who our royal host will be."

It was hard to believe I was in another royal palace. Just an hour ago, I had been loading members onto transport buses from the Grosvernor House Hotel's Park Lane entrance with its sign topped by five flags. The wives all had on lovely outfits, and I had wished that I was attending the evening's event too. But as I had already learned in both Vienna and Taipei, staff weren't invited to social events unless it was to check members in—or if a few seats needed to be filled at the closing party. That was how I had the good fortune to waltz the night away in Vienna and wear my favorite red ball gown in Taipei.

I had also been thinking about this evening's gift deliveries to YPO members' rooms at the Dorchester—the more exclusive of the two locations in which the members were staying. I had never been in such a fancy hotel, and felt I had to tiptoe around everywhere. On the first night of gift deliveries, I had noticed that each room's ceiling had a small arrow pointing the same way. I initially assumed this was to direct guests to the hotel exit, but I later found out that it was called a *Qibla,* an Arabic symbol showing the direction toward Mecca. Apparently, the Sultan of Brunei—who had acquired and updated the hotel over a decade ago—had one put into each room as a show of his Muslim devotion.

Ron had interrupted those thoughts by asking if I wanted to check guests into tonight's event with him. I was caught off guard. "Don't you think that might cause even more problems with the staff?" I asked him. "They seem to be especially upset with me at this event, with their usual accusations that I get too close to the members—even though they don't seem to *want* to do things with members. Plus, who will coordinate gift deliveries to the rooms?"

"Kris, the hotel staff can coordinate the deliveries. That is one of the things they do for a living. And don't worry about the other staff; just meet me back down here in fifteen minutes, and we'll go together."

Smiling at him, I had nodded and then headed up the elevator to my room, wondering what I should wear. My elegant, deep green satin and velvet cocktail dress, or beautiful red pantsuit with red stones and gold embroidery? Concluding that my attire should be more professional (I remembered the advice given to me in Taipei), I chose the red pantsuit.

I hurriedly dressed, then looked at my hair and wondered what could be done to make it look more sophisticated. But a glance at my Taipei watch made it clear that if I wanted this chance, I had to get downstairs *now*.

So, I met him as requested; he had a hackney cab waiting and ushered me into the back seat with Don Camp, our event photographer—who smiled and told me I looked nice. Don and I had met during the registration party, where he had set up shop in front of a professional look-a-like Queen to snap pictures. He seemed to know *just* what to say to people and how to position them as he worked his magic. After that, throughout the event, he was everywhere. Mustachioed, glamorous, and smooth, Don was one of those Hollywood paparazzi types who always seemed to know how to catch the right moment for everyone. He was constantly running—camera bag slung over his shoulder—and snapping photos at every turn. He also went out of his way to take pictures of the staff, as he knew that would be another token in his favor regarding being asked along to the next university. After each day's photographs, he posted all of them for members to buy. But for me, he would always snap special ones and slyly hand them over with twinkling eyes.

On the short journey to St. James's Palace, Ron listened as Don and I speculated about the host. Andrew and Fergie's recent separation made them an impossibility; Princess Anne had already been a keynote speaker; and we knew it couldn't be Queen Elizabeth. For the last few days, members had been saying they hoped it would be Prince Charles and Lady Di. And given that their official portrait still hung everywhere—with Londoners seeming nonchalant about their rumored potential separation—it seemed that this was a possibility.

"It's Prince Edward," Ron finally announced from the front seat.

Prince Edward? I didn't know much about him. Don didn't either, even though his Hollywood home base usually had him on top of the latest celebrity gossip. Ron then told us that the prince had studied history at Cambridge, opened the recent

Commonwealth Games in New Zealand, worked at Lloyd Weber's theater company in London where he had met someone rumored to be his girlfriend, and was in the process of forming his own TV production company.

His girlfriend? That caught my attention. "He has a girlfriend, Ron?"

"I thought you'd be interested," Ron replied with a laugh. "No one is really sure if that is true, so he is considered to be single."

Hmmmm…what girl wasn't interested in meeting a single prince? Was he handsome? Part of the military? What kind of girlfriend was he seeking? My mind considered all these questions. But Ron didn't know much else; he was more focused on Prince Edward getting through all the crowds and shaking everyone's hands. And he re-reminded Don to take *everyone's* picture.

As the cab dropped us at the entrance to St. James's Palace, I studied the red brick construction and remembered what I had learned in last evening's newsletter: The brick had been costly when Henry VIII used it to construct this Tudor palace. Then it had served as the main family residence until Queen Victoria decided in the early 1800s that she wanted to live in the more formal palace, Buckingham. Although St. James's Palace still hosted the official Royal Court, it also remained the residence for some of the lesser Royal Family. And the celebrated Chapel Royal, with ceilings painted by Hans Holbein, was used to host official events and charity receptions.

The rooms designated for the YPO social event that evening were already full of members, and Don went off to take photos. An official-looking woman—the Prince's assistant—was pointing and directing, so Ron immediately went over to her. She apparently had sent some staff around the room to remind YPO members that when they met the Prince, women were expected to do a small curtsy—and the men a bow from their neck. I watched her example and practiced—just in case I got to meet him.

Suddenly, Prince Edward entered the room, and I watched him from a distance. Everyone was doing fine with their formal greetings, and he seemed to be a natural at handshaking. He had 750 hands on his agenda that night, so he rapidly moved through the crowd—not stopping for much conversation.

The closer he got to me, the more I noticed that his impression was very normal. If I met him on the street, I might not have known he was part of the royal family. That reminded me of what I was learning at these YPO events about wealth and status: People who possessed it didn't need to prove that to others. The ones new to it, however, were often set on proving their status.

One of the small groups of members that included a committee member and his girlfriend motioned me toward them. The Prince came by and stopped to talk to the girlfriend, reminding her that they had met at a party a few months ago. She seemed flattered, but given how lovely and sweet she was, it would make sense that he would remember her.

Without warning, he turned to me. I curtsied, expecting him to move on, but he stopped to talk. I heard a "click," and saw Don out of the corner of my eye. "What is your name?" the Prince asked.

"Kris," I said, gripping my champagne glass. Why would he want to talk to me? I noticed members turning to notice the attention he was giving me—and then heard another "click."

"Welcome. Are you enjoying my palace?" he asked, pointing to himself.

"It's beautiful," I responded somewhat breathlessly. He smiled and moved on while I stood there, wondering if he had really stopped to chat with me?

A few minutes later, when the Prince had finished all his greetings, his assistant walked toward me and casually said, "His Royal Highness may be having cocktails later in case you want to join him."

I did a double take; was she speaking to me? *Inviting me to have cocktails with the Prince?* Don must have heard it too—as he was snapping pictures—because he whispered into my ear and asked if I was going to accept. It *was* a bit of a Cinderella moment. But before I could say anything, Ron walked up and tapped my shoulder, telling me we needed to get back to work. I didn't think he had heard the invitation, but I also knew I couldn't tell him *no* about getting back—especially since I was still on duty and he had gone "above and beyond" in asking just me to come along. I sighed and headed out the door with him.

Once we were dropped at the hotel and I finished the few things I had to do, I thought back again to what Don and I had both seemed to hear. It would have been another fabulous first—really the opportunity of a lifetime—to join Prince Edward for cocktails. And I guess I *could* have found out where the cocktails were if I had pushed for it. Ron would probably have let me off for the evening, and who from the staff would have known what happened—given that none of them were even around when we had returned? So much had happened in that instant at the palace that it had been overwhelming. Now that I thought it through, I was a bit sad I hadn't snatched the opportunity, but the evening had still been amazing—and I was grateful to be a part of it.

When I had first arrived at the Grosvenor House in London where the events for the university would take place, I felt its age and history. Calvin, the hospitality chairman I had enjoyed meeting in Vienna—and who, this time, was the education chairman (in charge of the fifty or so speakers brought in from around the world)—was there to greet all of us at breakfast. While he had been in Taipei for a few days to market this event—and had come through Dallas once or twice during the planning process—he was *definitely* in his element here: London, one of the capital cities of the world.

After breakfast, I started unpacking the shipment, and Matt, Jason, and Amy, three crew members, came by to introduce themselves. I thought back to how they had gotten involved: Matt was the brother of Gretchen, someone who had quickly become a good friend after we met in Dallas a few months prior.

While sharing during one of our morning walks that I would soon be traveling to London as part of a work assignment for my job with an organization called "YPO", she stopped and looked at me in surprise. It turned out that her mother, Trish, was dating an engineer, Ken, who belonged to YPO—and they had just been at the Taipei University. Not only that, but they were soon headed to the London one. And since I had also shared some stories about the Vienna crew, she brought up her brother, Matt. Attending Texas Christian University and currently in London as an exchange student, she wondered if he —along with some of his American friends—might be able to help at the YPO University?

That idea struck a chord with me; We did need crew for the London University just like we had in Taipei and Vienna, so after checking with my boss the arrangements were made for them to serve as crew. Plus, it would give Matt a chance to be around his mother.

So, as I met the three "TCU"ers that first day, I was very impressed. Matt was tall, dark, and handsome with a definite "Texas" feel. His friend, Jason, was from his fraternity and was just as handsome—though from a blond perspective. Jason, who was smart, mature, and sophisticated, seemed to emanate a bit more of a "leader" feeling. And from all the questions he asked about the event, I could tell he was trying to grasp everything to which he would be exposed. The way he thought and asked questions made me want to spend more time around him, but I figured a *lot* of people probably wanted to spend more time around him. Matt's other friend, Amy, was a sweet redhead. She was also very smart and an obvious hard worker.

In addition, my two main hotel contacts were already proving to be valuable. Whenever I needed the smallest thing, they were "on it." One was Angus, our British Conference Services Manager, and the other was Marco, the Italian Catering Manager. Angus was even-tempered, quiet, thoughtful, and very efficient. His consistent "straight face" made it difficult to read his thoughts or feelings, but I soon found out that this was a part of the male British personality. It was also somewhat second nature to me—given my extended exposure to military men.

Marco, with his passion, emotion, and expressiveness, was an entirely different story—and something I hadn't before encountered. Clearly married, he still kissed, flirted with, and called "beautiful" anything—and everything—female he could find. I didn't know how to flirt, so when I didn't respond he seemed confused and gave up. Everyone else on the hotel staff just seemed to take that aspect of him with a "grain of salt." What I didn't know was that he was behaving in a standard Italian male way.

Thinking about the possibility of YPO staff behavior turning stressful (as had happened in both Vienna and Taipei), I realized that meeting these special people could prove to be helpful and made a note to treat them in a very thoughtful way. And Ron, who was even-tempered and kind, would help as well—although he was just learning the ropes as he worked on the event with our department supervisor, Becky. He had come aboard YPO after Linda—who had hired me for the Vienna University—left for another job (and her departure had almost made *me* leave for another job!).

On the YPO member side, there was an American expatriate, Bob Payton, who had come to London in the late 1970s and become somewhat of an icon in the city as he helped transform the centuries-old culture of London to more modern times. His first project had been to introduce deep-dish pizza—and American casual dining. Following that, he introduced more restaurants and then bought an English estate that he refurbished and turned into a country house hotel. Ron sang Bob's praises—especially after a planning trip where they did a "pep talk" to the Grosvenor

House senior staff and explained expectations of a large group of demanding American guests.

Simon was the overall event chairman. Quiet and intense, Simon had started the concept of frozen food sales in England. He began with a freezer in his garage, and within a few short years had begun to revolutionize the grocery business. Consequently, the English tradition of shopping for fresh food daily in local markets was changing to the American way of buying larger quantities of food once or twice a week—and saving money in the process. Packaged vegetables and meats—among many other things—were now available for purchase; frozen, and in larger quantities.

As I thought about it, the whole YPO member committee for the London University were "new money" in England—and it was their money that allowed them entry into just about everything. Most also had estates in the country—purchased from the English aristocratic class who either now couldn't afford them or just wanted to sell them for some reason or another.

Just in front of Grosvenor House sat the famous Hyde Park with acres of green space and a lake that offered Londoners the opportunity of walking, running, biking—or even swimming. The English were famous for building in-city parks, and this was my first experience with one of their masterpieces. I had enjoyed the Stadtpark in Vienna, but it was much smaller and newer than this one.

Hyde Park's history went back to 1536 when King Henry VIII seized the Manor of Hyde from the Catholic church and established it as his royal hunting ground. A century later, "common folk" were given access to this royal hunting ground by King Charles. When King William and Queen Mary ruled England, they established a home near the park, Kensington Palace, and created a broad avenue called "King's Row" that ran through the park to their other home at St. James's Palace. When the road soon became known to house highwaymen and robbers, however, they lined it with 300 oil lamps for safety—the first use of street lighting in all of England.

During the reign of King George II, his wife had 300 acres in Hyde Park fashioned into a garden and dammed the river to create Serpentine Lake. I also discovered that in the early 1820s King George IV ordered a "makeover" for the park. And, during that reconstruction the two arches serving as its entrance gates were constructed as memorials to British victories in the Napoleonic wars: The Wellington Arch and the Marble Arch.

One day while setting up for the university, I was talking to Jason—whom I indeed loved being around—as he was always thinking and philosophizing. We shared similar political and spiritual beliefs, and as we took a break over a cup of tea, he asked if I had been to Speakers' Corner.

"Speakers' Corner? What's that?" I replied.

Jason explained that this famous place in Hyde Park had an interesting history related to free speech and demonstrating. Situated in what was originally known as Tyburn—a small hamlet where people were executed for being criminals, traitors, or even martyrs—it had become famous as a place for making speeches as early as 1108 when those being hanged were given a right to say something before their death.

"These speeches became a big form of entertainment for the masses, but they could also turn rowdy and dangerous—as public holidays for the working class would be created for specific hangings," Jason said.

"By the time the gallows were dismantled in the 1700s, more than 50,000 people had been executed there. And over the next century," Jason continued to relate, "the Tyburn hanging area became a place where public marches began and ended. But in 1866, after the police attacked a crowd that had been banned from meeting there and then set up railings to prevent further demonstrations, there were three days of rioting. The next year, 150,000 people defied another ban, so an Act of Parliament finally established it as a place to demonstrate and act freely."

"Since then, Speakers' Corner—also referred to as the 'Forum of the Common Man'—has become known around the world as a symbol of free speech," Jason said.

I have always been fascinated by history, so I asked him to tell me more. "Lenin, Marx, and Orwell have all used it." Jason went on, noting, "There is one older gentleman, Baron Soper, with whom I love to watch and debate—and who has been coming to Speakers' Corner on Sundays since 1942. Soper was the nickname given him because he liked to preach on a soapbox."

In Jason's view, this Methodist minister was quick-thinking but controversial, so he drew large crowds. "We share totally different political beliefs and ideas on Christianity—despite his being a Methodist minister—though we both have a strong love for God as the basis of our lives. He espouses socialism and pacifism—but I love to hear how he thinks because it sharpens my ability to debate what I believe. He got his start as a socialist in the Labour Party because he was so affected by poverty as a young man."

After learning all this, I wanted to go to Speakers' Corner and see Lord Soper. Jason had me sold on experiencing this man—plus, it would be fun to see Jason in action. When we left the hotel after finishing our setup, we headed to the Marble Arch tube stop and as we approached a circular black iron fence, we saw a handsome, white-haired man attired in a black cassock and clerical collar who was speaking from a stand with "West London Pulpit of the Methodist Church" posted on the front. His speech was passionate, refined, clear, and he was leaning forward with crossed wrists.

"It's him: Lord Soper," Jason said, guiding me closer into the crowd. The topic of debate—for the moment—seemed to be the existence of God, and when someone asked him if God was *really* dead, he responded, "Funny, you rascal, I hadn't heard He was unwell!"

When the arguments with others slowed for a moment, Jason tried to engage him in a debate on Thatcherism. He listened to Jason's question, then spoke to the crowd:

"My young friend here asks why I am such a critic of our former prime minister, Mrs. Thatcher. Young man, capitalism is an unfair economic system based on stealing. Are you a Christian? Would you not agree that Christians were told to love and share? I do not think of Mrs. Thatcher's economic philosophy as being any form of loving and sharing! It is more like shoplifting."

I was taken aback by his criticism of Thatcherism, given what she had done for the British economy and her pro-American stances. However, Jason was ready with his reply when two other debaters jumped in more forcefully with their comments. Soper repeated the other debaters' questions, then went into his answer—his voice raising in decibels.

Jason leaned over to me. "This is how it goes, Kris. You can see how passionate he is about his beliefs. When his staff gets him set up out here, he starts on a topic and then wants to debate. It's always interesting to come over here and watch. I've actually learned a lot about British politics by sitting in on this event."

The next evening, there was to be a preview for the Mexico City University, our team's next event. In the same way Sidney had come to Vienna to market Taipei and Calvin had come to Taipei to market the London University, two of the Mexico City event's chair couples, the De Leons and the Cibolos, had chosen to put on a tequila tasting at this university. Jose Cibolo had red clay *caballitos* (shot cups) made—with "Universidad de Mexico" painted on them—and brought them along with several top-shelf tequilas to entice people to register.

I had asked Matt and Jason if they wanted to help staff the event, and they readily agreed, telling me they had never done a shot of tequila—and hoped the bottle wouldn't have a worm. I also saw Trish (Matt's mother) during the day, and she said that she and Ken would come—if for no other reason than to see Matt. So, I knew there would at least be a few people there.

As we set up that night with Jose, he told us about the history of this drink associated with Mexican ranchers, cowboys, and bandits. He then explained that it came from the cactus-like blue agave plant, which grew well in the volcanic soil around Tequila, Mexico. Native Mexicans had been using the plant to make *pulque*, a fermented drink, long before the Spanish explorers came to their country, but when those *conquistadors* ran out of brandy in the 1620s, they tried distilling the native pulque and created the first tequila—which had evolved ever since.

Jose stopped talking as he noticed Ken and Trish walking up—donning his sombrero and a smile. As he explained the Mexico City marketing materials to them, Matt, Jason, and I joked about trying tequila shots. Jose heard us laughing and turned to offer us a cup. Ken and Trish chimed in with an encouragement, and when Don walked up with his camera, we were all set.

Jose reminded us that Mexicans often drank their tequila *neat*, but since it was our first try he recommended the *tequila cruda* method. That involved salt and lime, as the salt killed the burning sensation in the throat and the lime mellowed the flavor. After handing us each a *caballito*, he poured the tequila and waited. We licked our left index finger area, using our right fingers to sprinkle salt over it. Then, picking up the cup in our right hand and a lime wedge in the left, we licked the salt. Looking at each other with courage, we inhaled and downed the full shot, following it with a squeeze of lime. I felt the burn and appreciated the lime, but the look on Matt and Jason's face was one of strong distaste—and Don caught it perfectly. He was always in the right place at the right time!

Gerardo and Dorothea De Leon showed up soon after the tasting started, and everyone spent time tasting, laughing, and joking. More members stopped by on their way to the evening's event at the House of Parliament, and they signed up as they tried a shot or two of the tequila. By the end of the event even more people had signed up, including Ken and Trish, and it all seemed a success.

After it was over, Matt and Jason headed back to school and I mused the tequila shot while walking to our office—realizing it was yet another fun *first* for me. I was greeted by an empty room when I got back; apparently the Dallas staff had left for dinner out somewhere in the city. Feeling a bit lonely as I sat at my desk, I heard a noise and looked up to see Marco and Angus in the hallway, looking at me a bit shyly.

My smile encouraged them to walk into the room, and Marco said, "Why are you so sad, Kris? Why don't you come with us, as we have a surprise for you!"

While unsure as to what they might have, I agreed and followed them down the hall to a small meeting room. When they opened the door, I saw a table set for a formal candlelight dinner—the kind prepared for their top-tier patrons' room service. Motioning me to sit, they began to serve me a delicious meal.

"We are so appreciative of how kind you have been to us and do not like it when you are sad," Marco said when he had finished serving, and sitting down next to me, he put his arm around me with his typically Italian affection. "Is this not a happy trip for you?"

Angus didn't say anything as he stood there with his inquisitive eyes, looking strong and supportive. The difference in their behavior was so marked: Italian affection versus English reserve.

I wanted to respond, but decided it was too complicated to explain the tension with the Dallas staff. Besides, it would make it seem like I was complaining. Instead I smiled, telling them I appreciated my beautiful romantic dinner.

Suddenly, Angus spoke up, "Kris, we know the university is almost over. Do you want to stay for a few more days? We have asked our manager, and the hotel thinks it can offer you a complimentary suite."

I was surprised at such an unexpected—and wonderful—gift, especially given my desire for a place to stay for a few extra days. YPO had paid for my room through shipment pickup day, and I had already asked Matt if there was any way to stay at his college. But Angus's offer was a much better option, and a *suite* would allow me to house my parents, who had expressed the wish to come over to London for a few days while I was there.

"That would be *so* awesome!" I replied. "Would I still get to see you?" I asked, looking directly at Angus.

"I will be around, Kris," he replied, but committed to nothing else.

I secretly hoped that meant he would have time for dinner or a show because I was feeling attracted to him. Of course, Greg was still the prominent male on my mind, but it was nice to feel that someone else might eventually take that place since he was permanently gone. Even if nothing happened with Angus, though, the gift of the free suite left me on cloud nine.

After the university ended, I moved into the complimentary suite—which was icing on the cake to everything else the Grosvenor House had done for me. It allowed me to give my parents a top-notch, initial "over the Atlantic" experience, and the hotel's history as a World War II Officer's Club was the perfect complement to Dad's background as a retired Air Force pilot and colonel.

When they arrived, we went to see the musical *Les Miserables*, then made plans to catch *Joseph and the Amazing Technicolor Dreamcoat* on another night.

We spent the next few days visiting military history monuments around the city. This included the Tower of London's White Chapel—built by William the Conqueror and containing a millennium's history of military weapons, soldiers, and combat skill—as well as Westminster Abbey. My father was especially intrigued by the Abbey's coronation chapel built by Benedictine monks in 966 and its WWI Tomb of the Unknown Soldier.

One day while walking through Green Park, we met a retired Royal Air Force (RAF) gentleman who told us about the exclusive RAF Club nearby. He explained that England—with its enthusiasm for airplanes and pilots—provided it for commissioned pilots, and suggested we stop in to see what was going on there. It sounded like another ideal place for my father, so we walked in that direction.

The building housing the club was stately inside and out. We learned it had been established at the end of WWI by the president of the British Air Board, who gave instructions to the chairman of the Royal Flying Corps Club to "ensure a permanent Club House worthy of the airmen and their 'brilliant and superlative heroic work.'" After gaining entrance by proving Dad's military officer pilot status, we discovered a book fair on one of its floors and were surprised to find a book about dad's favorite plane that he had flown: the Supersonic B-58. So, we bought it on the spot.

We also peeked into the elegant main ballroom after seeing a notice about a lecture being held there by Britain's most renowned test pilot and long-term Club member, Eric Brown. His accomplishments, starting in WWII, included holding the world record for the most aircraft carrier take-offs and landings; flying the most types of aircrafts in history—including captured WWII German, Japanese, and Italian types; and transitioning the military flight industry into jet and rocket technology.

What struck me even more was this man's seeming "luck," including escaping from the Nazis, living through the downing of an aircraft carrier, and surviving eleven aircraft crashes. Club members who knew him told us that despite all these incredible escapades and accomplishments, he was understated but incredibly positive, and I wondered if that positivity was a big part of what had kept him healthy and alive. It also occurred to me that he would have made a fabulous keynote speaker for the London University. He reminded me of Viktor Frankl, our main Vienna University keynote who had survived Auschwitz, as I knew that Frankl's positive energy had kept others—as well as himself—alive. The RAF Club staff also shared that Brown was involved with getting the Smithsonian *National Air and Space Museum* set up, so I hoped that sometime, between London and Washington DC, I might be able to meet him.

My parents and I spent our last day at the Westminster Cathedral, a beautiful neo-Byzantine building, studying lists of inscribed soldier names who died in various wars. For Dad, seeing in person the military history he had spent many years studying was an amazing experience, and I was grateful that our special visit together had all worked out.

On the other hand, it was hard to think about leaving London after my wonderful three weeks, but to my delight, Angus asked me to join him in one of the hotel restaurants on my last evening in London. Once again, pondering the romantic attraction I felt toward him, I wondered if I was getting anything back besides warmth and kindness. Had he felt the same sparks flying but just not expressed them? Would he even have asked the hotel for my free suite if he hadn't wanted me around a bit more?

We enjoyed a nice dinner, and afterward, asking if I liked to stargaze, he led me to a quiet, dark area on the hotel roof. As we stood there, he didn't speak much—whereas I chatted away due to my nervousness—but then I grew silent too. Moving closer, he brushed himself against me, and I drew in my breath, wondering about a kiss. But nothing came—just the sound of his wonderful accent as he pointed out a few stars, then told me he would miss me and hoped I had a safe trip home. Then, he walked me back to my suite.

Once settled into bed, I thought about what had just happened. While there was no magical kiss, I *had* felt Greg step a little bit to the side and the first inklings of desire for someone else step forward. A larger crack seemed to be forming in that "I will never let myself love again" wall. Maybe my heart was gradually opening, and as I drifted off to sleep, I sensed that this newfound feeling portended romance in the future.

Chapter 6

Latin Lovers

It all started with a kiss on the neck—in an executive conference room in Dallas, no less. Not that this kiss was planted on *my* neck. But I could almost feel the soft touch of his lips as if I had been the object of this highly romantic yet very public gesture.

All of us sitting around the table gasped, uncertain how to react. The man who had startled us with his unexpected act of sensuality was Gerardo, the chairman of our next university in Mexico City. None of us knew much about him except that he had run the Mexican Stock Exchange, and his wife Dorothea was the granddaughter of a former president of Mexico. They were flying through Dallas not long after we had completed the London University, so a quick introductory meeting in the YPO conference room had been hastily organized.

Ron had put together a quick agenda, and the first item was potential keynote speakers. We had heard that the education chairman for the university, Jose—the YPO member who had run the tequila preview party in London—was trying to get Nando Parrado, one of the survivors of a Uruguayan rugby team's plane crash high in the Andes, to be a keynote speaker. The recently-released movie *Alive* depicting the unbelievable seventy-two-day survival story, including grisly details of cannibalism among the survivors, had just been released. So, it made sense that this topic would be the first thing brought up.

Thinking back to when we had entered the room, I noticed that Gerardo was already at one end of the table and Dorothea at the other. We took seats along each side and waited for him to speak. He rose, glanced at Dorothea, and paused, then picked up the agenda and laid it back down, looking at us with a shy smile. Setting the agenda aside, he began to walk alongside the conference table. "Our university," he said softly to us, "will be the highest-rated in YPO history."

He didn't sound the least bit cocky. Given his position as former head of the Mexican Stock Exchange, as well as his wife's social status, arrogance could be expected. But he seemed quite the opposite: quiet, kind, and understated. He continued with his point, noting that the last time the YPO had come to Mexico, the members who attended had given that university their highest rating ever. "I want the people who come this time to love our university, love our education, love our social events, love their friends, and love our country," he stressed with sincerity.

As he reached the opposite side of the conference table, he placed his hand on Dorothea's shoulder, gently pressing her head to the side with his other, and leaning down, placed his lips against her neck for just a moment. Her eyes closed during this kiss and when he let go, she slowly straightened her neck, gazing up at him with adoring eyes.

We all sat there speechless, watching as he casually walked down the other side of the table and sat down. No one knew what to say. All I could think was how much he had seemed to like the word "love." Ron finally broke the uncomfortable silence by trying to re-focus on the agenda, but none of us could pay attention. We were still thinking about that *kiss*. None of us had ever seen anything like it, even at a YPO party—let alone a YPO planning meeting in the conference room. Was Gerardo one-of-a-kind, or just your typical "Latin lover"? No matter, my mind was already made up that I wanted to do my best to make his university top-rated because, in my view, he was a special man.

Certainly, Mexico City was going to be an interesting follow-up to London in that they were both historic capital cities. From what I knew, Mexico City's European-based origin dated to the sixteenth century, whereas London had been founded by the Romans at the start of Anno Domini. Mexico City had also been inhabited by the Aztec Indians from as early as the thirteenth century, and by the time the Spanish arrived, had a population of almost 200,000 people.

Hernan Cortes, the Hapsburg-financed explorer who conquered the Aztecs, had introduced Spanish culture into its indigenous culture. One of those Spanish lifestyle habits was taking siestas. Another was very late dinners. Ron had learned from his visits to Mexico City that the city was still operating under these auspices and, given that most of our attendees were used to 24/7 operating hours and dinners starting around 5 pm, thought these facts should be mentioned in the pre-university newsletters to prepare our guests.

A few weeks later, Jose stopped by our office to discuss the education program with Ron. He also brought his son, Jose Jr., who was so exceptionally handsome that I couldn't keep my eyes off of him. Jose stopped first at my desk to thank me again for my help during his tequila preview party in London, and then introduced his son. I noticed Jose Jr.'s shirt had a University of Texas logo, so I asked why he had chosen to go to college in Austin, given that one of his father's sources of pride was being a graduate of Notre Dame. As he explained his choice, I tried to focus on what he was saying, but he was so good-looking it was hard to keep from staring at him.

After finishing his answer, he looked at me intensely, but said nothing else. I suddenly felt a strong wave of attraction, and my tongue—now stuck to the roof of my mouth—didn't seem to work. The uneasy silence continued for a moment, then he seemed to lose interest and turned to join his father, who was now sitting at Ron's desk.

My lack of confidence in my own attractiveness washed over me, and I wondered if that was why I hadn't been able to respond to him. Or was it maybe that the intimidation I felt around his father also emanated from him? It was interesting to compare his father to Gerardo, as Gerardo was more approachable despite having held a far more prominent national position for the country.

My thoughts were pulled toward Ron's desk as I heard Jose talk about his continued lack of success in connecting with Nando Parrado. Jose was sure there would be some profound thoughts on leadership and teamwork learned from his horrendous experience, but apparently Parrado hadn't done much public speaking about the event and wanted to leave it in his past. So, Jose had a new idea: fly to Montevideo and approach him in person; would the university budget allow for this? Remembering that YPO speakers were never paid—but rather had their flight and hotel expenses covered and then could attend the entire event for free (whereas members paid "tuition" of at least $8000 to attend)—Ron told him the budget could probably cover this expense. But would it be worth it if Parrado continued to say no?

Listening to their discussion, I wondered why Jose was so confident about Parrado—especially since he didn't have much speaking experience. I also knew that part of Parrado's story involved people eating each other to stay alive, and to be honest I didn't want to hear about it. Would YPO members have the same reaction? Or was the "shock effect" of cannibalism what made the story stand out? I preferred positive stories and thinking back to Vienna felt Viktor Frankl had been amazingly positive despite his horrific WWII prison camp experience.

As they continued their discussion with Ron, I pretended to work as my thoughts drifted to Jose Jr. My desk sat across from Ron, and I looked up once to discover Jose Jr. looking over at me. I felt a rush of heat through my body, and I looked away in embarrassment. It couldn't be that he was purposely looking at me, could it? Handsome men were never interested in me.

At the same time, it made me think of a recent incident. While country-western dancing in Dallas one night, a nice man who was my partner had remarked, "You are way too smart for me," and didn't ask me to dance again. His comment had upset me. Was *smart* threatening? What was I supposed to do…not talk? Giggle? My brain was always going, analyzing, trying to figure things out, connecting; that was just my persona. Considering what had attracted Greg to me, I realized that I was very confident at the end of my college days. I guessed it was somewhat based on my intelligence and hard work, as I had put myself through college with a job. But another attraction might have been my father commanding the Air Force base where Greg and I met, as it gave me a bit of notoriety I probably wouldn't have otherwise had.

With all these thoughts running through my head, I kept on working at my desk and an hour or so later, father and son stood up to leave. Turning to me, Jose said a gracious Mexican goodbye, while Jose Jr. continued in his silence—though he shot me another quick look, arching one eyebrow. I wasn't sure what that look meant and was disconcerted, although it seemed to confirm his arrogance.

Once they were gone, I asked Ron why Jose Jr. had come with his father and learned that Jose Jr. and his sister Mary would be part of the crew. A small smile escaped my lips as I realized I would see him again. Ron caught my smile and reminded me to stay low-key as I had been advised after the London University. There had been a bit of a to-do over whatever perceived behavior I had exhibited there, so much so that the staff had included a sarcastic line or two in their post-university poem about my "taking such good care of the hotel staff." The implication was that I hadn't taken care of the Dallas staff, which astounded me because whenever I *tried* to help the other staff, they had blown me off. Or maybe they had found out about my going with Ron to St. James's Palace? In any event, my boss had asked me to please stay out of the limelight and not mention invitations to do things with YPO members.

This pettiness made me want to leave YPO, but if I did I wouldn't get to meet such interesting people or go to such fascinating places. By now, I had started feeling bored with my job, as there wasn't much to it but typing, organizing, and packing. Ron seemed to sense this too and promised he would search for new things to challenge me.

As the time grew closer to Mexico City, I started casually dating a fellow church member who was tall, blond, and sophisticated: Ed. Very nice and extremely sociable, he recruited doctors and nurses for emergency rooms. One night as we chatted about his company, Ed mentioned that their founder/CEO, Dr. Lawrence Wright, was going to Mexico City. The fact that he was going about the time I was going made me wonder if he was a YPO member, so I asked Ed to find out. When he found out Dr. Wright was indeed attending the YPO university, I told him I would track him down during the university and connect with him—which seemed to please Ed.

Our relationship was still in the budding stage, and so far, we had gotten along well except for a few hiccups in communication. He simply didn't talk as much as I was used to men talking. My father and both of my brothers were articulate and outgoing, so I thought that was a male trait in general. But now I questioned my assumption, as Ed's lack of communication at times made me wonder if he was really even interested. It could have been my imagination, but sometimes I felt he showed more affection to his dog than me. As I got ready to leave for Mexico City, however, I put my concerns about our relationship aside.

The day before we left for the university, Calvin and a few other English YPO members stopped at the office. They had bought Harley Davidsons and were riding across the United States before having their motorcycles shipped back to the UK. It was hard not to laugh as they showed off their black leather riding jackets because they looked so out of character for YPO members. However, it was a fun moment in the midst of all the last-minute prepping.

On arrival in Mexico City, I experienced the same shock I had felt at seeing other third-world countries. Our ride from the airport showed poverty was visible in every direction, and trash littered the ground everywhere. Mexico City had just been labeled the most polluted city in the world by the United Nations, but as I looked around to make a comparison with the hazy skies that had surrounded me in Taipei, it didn't seem so evident. I remembered that we had been warned to drink only bottled water and not eat food sold on the streets. Given what I was seeing, I was fairly certain I wouldn't even be tempted to do so.

When we checked into our hotel, the Camino Real Polanco, I noticed Chapultepec Park across the street. Hailed as one of the largest urban parks in the Western hemisphere—and visited as much as Paris's Bois de Boulogne or New York City's Central Park—its forest of bald cypress trees, called *ahuehuete* in Spanish, were more than a century old and known to re-oxygenate the Valley of Mexico. Mexico City also housed the second largest number of museums in the world (I had just been in the city with the *greatest* number of museums: London). I made a mental note to try to visit the park, and since several of our evening social events would be in the museums, I hoped I would be included in one or two of them as well so I could get a flavor of the city's main attractions.

This area of town, the Polanco neighborhood of the Miguel Hidalgo borough, was known to be the "Beverly Hills" section of

Mexico City because of its shopping, mansions, and restaurants—and was one of the top real estate markets in all Latin America. The hotel's architect—when he had designed it for the opening of the 1968 Olympics—had referred to his project as a hotel-museum: combining Mexican modernist style with reminisces of pre-Hispanic pyramids. It almost had the feel of an airport, given its overall size and abundance of long corridors leading to its large guest rooms as well as conference areas; it was also full of bright colors and top-notch pieces by famous artists and sculptors. The last YPO Mexico City university had been held here—the one Gerardo had said produced the highest YPO event rating ever—and I wondered if the hotel had played any part in that rating, given that it had hosted visits from many kings and presidents.

While we were getting our offices organized, Don Camp stopped in to ask us where he could set up his picture tables. I was glad he was here, as I always found him fun and interesting. I especially liked how he found ways to make people feel special, including me.

Jose Jr. and his sister Mary arrived with their father to learn what their role would be. They had both agreed to help with the educational aspect of the university and were excited because Nando Parrado had finally agreed to speak after their father had visited him in Montevideo. Jose Jr. and I exchanged glances a few times while they were in the office, but once again he didn't say anything directly to me; another man who didn't communicate! Well, it probably didn't matter as I had Ed back in Dallas and needed to stay away from any romantic involvements here. On the other hand, how could I be sure what he would be up to while I was gone? Maybe a little fun on the side (if the opportunity arose) could be interesting. Then again, Jose Jr. probably had lots of women hanging around him. And my brain flashed back to how consistent, faithful, and trustworthy Greg was until he had finally decided to move on because of my inconsistent behavior. It had now been three years since we had gone our separate ways, yet so many of my thoughts were still on him. On the other hand, Jose Jr. was a distraction—and I enjoyed distractions—so I focused on him.

Setups pressed forward, and while he wasn't around much, he did show up at the opening party and sat next to me. Don Camp finished his work at the registration party and made this his next stop—doing his usual chatting and snapping pictures. He stopped and took our picture, and after that, Jose Jr. began to talk and flirt a bit over his first glass of wine. I didn't know much about flirting back, so I paid equal attention to everyone at the table rather than focusing on him.

Remembering that Jose Jr. would be working education, though, I decided to volunteer to work there as well, and one day, had enough time to serve as a room coordinator for two of the university faculty: Dr. John Paling and Dr. Gerald Bell. I felt fortunate to be assigned to both after I heard them speak. John Paling was an Oxford graduate with a great sense of humor who used animals to teach about leadership. His speech, given in his wonderful British accent, was titled, "Up to Your Armpits in Alligators: How to Sort Out What Risks Are Worth Worrying About." He had me laughing the whole time, including when he made the comment about his wife "being an American—well, really a Texan—which was 'almost American.'"

Dr. Bell had a more serious personality. A top leadership professor from the University of North Carolina, he had written a book called *The Achievers*, focusing on traits that make a leader. Although listening to him was like trying to drink out of a fire hydrant, the point he made that struck me most was, "There is no such thing as a multi-tasker."

I had always felt that my ability to multi-task made me more effective, but he insisted that focusing on more than one task made someone less efficient at *all* tasks. I approached him afterward to talk about multi-tasking, and he was gracious enough to give me his time—and a copy of his book.

Nando Parrado's keynote talk was coming up soon, and I debated whether to attend. Although I did not want to hear the repulsive part of his story, I decided there must have been a reason that Jose had worked so hard to get him. Hoping I had—so far—done what my boss had requested about staying low-key during the university, I asked for permission to go and promised I would stay inconspicuous. Ron agreed, saying he would join me, and the two of us entered together and walked to an area behind the stage as Jose was finishing his introduction. Parrado appeared very nervous to me, and I hoped his speech would go well. If it did, he might launch a speaking career; it would also be a feather in Jose's cap for all the effort he had put forth in convincing him to appear.

After thanking Jose, Parrado stood there and shuffled his notes. Everyone waited for him to speak, but he said nothing. People started shifting in their seats. Finally, he set his notes aside and looked out at the audience. "I should not be here," he announced. "I should be dead on a glacier in the Andes."

That got everyone's attention—including mine. Maybe it *would* be worth listening, although, in my mind, the jury was still out. He began to relay his story from the beginning, talking about being on the way to an exhibition game with his Catholic school's rugby team and all their supporters—including his mother and sister—on a Uruguayan Air Force plane that crashed while flying over the Andes, forcing the passengers to survive for seventy-two days in extreme circumstances. Of the forty-five people on the aircraft, eighteen died in the initial impact or within the first week. Given the extreme cold of the 12,000-foot altitude where their plane lodged, the survivors managed to find safety in the broken fuselage, though eventually another eleven died due to injuries and the elements. He then shared how he felt throughout those sixty days—as well as during the following ten-day trek for help with a fellow rugby player, Roberto Canessa (all without any mountaineering gear) —and then the final two more days leading rescuers back to the survivors.

As I listened to his story, I homed in on what seemed his bitterness toward God because the crash had killed his sister and mother—and because the experience had happened to *him and his rugby team* and not to other people. It seemed to me that his survival would produce gratitude, but he spoke only about all the negative things he visualized while up there—like what it would feel like to freeze to death and how the life he had wanted would never happen now (no wife, no children, no career) because he *knew* he wasn't going to survive.

When he reached the part about what they ate to stay alive— what it looked like and how they prepared it—I felt he was too graphic and started to walk out. But then I heard him say that after he decided to assume the role of leader for the group, he experienced an overwhelming feeling of confidence that they would survive— followed by a "jolt" of joy so powerful that it almost lifted him off the ground. He had no idea where the jolt came from but shared it with the others to encourage them. That admission turned me back around to keep listening…at least there was *something* positive he was saying.

Parrado next focused in on making a vow to his father that he would struggle—even through pain—on a trek through the Andes to find help to get home to him. After he chose another survivor he thought strong enough to make the trek with him, he then went back to despairing that he would die up there—and imagining how it would happen. His negative energy and visualizing were very powerful, and I had to wonder how much it influenced two strikes that came against them: first, the avalanche that buried their plane in even more snow, killing eight others and almost him, and then a blizzard that brought on winds so intense they could not even stand up. When he and his chosen partner finally departed and then reached the 15,000-foot peak they needed to cross, he thought about the beautiful perspective it gave of the surrounding Andean mountain peaks—yet also became angry as he thought about how much more he would have to endure (if he could endure) before potentially reaching help.

Suddenly, in the midst of those feelings of anger, Parrado described how a sense of his father's love washed over him and made him realize that love could not be crushed. "There is nothing more powerful than love," he said dramatically, as if he were stopping a camera to give an editorial comment. Continuing with his dramatic story, he relayed that he was suddenly rejuvenated, confident that he would keep walking until he could walk no more.

Looking at my Taipei watch, I realized he had been speaking for seventy minutes—already ten minutes over his allotted time—but no one in the audience seemed restless or bored. Far from it, they were all glued to their seats at the incredible story he was telling. Parrado continued, describing their descent from the majestic peak slowly into a valley. On the ninth day of their arduous thirty-eight-mile journey, they came across a cow—and then a herder—and then finally some rescuers. From there, his story wound down to how he guided helicopters back to their friends still at the crash site—seventy-two days after the harrowing ordeal had started.

Parrado gave all this a moment to sink in, then reminded everyone that he should not be here at the Camino Real in the Ciudad de Mexico—he should be dead. Then he was quiet, and another glance at my watch showed that it had now been ninety minutes. The room was silent as he stood there—just as it had been before he started—and then a thunderous applause erupted, followed by a standing ovation. Members rushed forward to talk to him. Before leaving the room to go back to work, I looked over at Jose Sr., who seemed relieved and proud—as it was exactly the kind of reaction he had hoped for.

That night, while lying in bed, my mind was spinning with thoughts from the speech and how I agreed and disagreed with some of his conclusions. I found myself again comparing Nando Parrado to Viktor Frankl. Frankl's speech had been much more uplifting and encouraging than Parrado's. Then again, Frankl had been speaking for forty years about his experience, whereas this was Parrado's first try. I also wondered if maybe Parrado had a different personality than Frankl? Frankl had spoken about his focus on positive things despite the difficulties of his prison camp experience and had concluded that people need a *reason to survive* amid hopelessness. So maybe he was, by nature, a *glass-is-half-full* kind of person, whereas Parrado was a bit of the opposite.

I also thought about the fact that while Frankl's belief in some sort of Universal Being was *strengthened* through his horrendous circumstances in the Nazi prison camp, it seemed that Parrado had *lost* his faith in the Catholicism under whose rules he had been raised—an experience that stripped him of his hope and trust in what he knew of God. Parrado had even spoken of the mountains as the personal adversaries against which he was competing.

A lot of Parrado's struggle reminded me of my feelings about God and life after my breakup with Greg. I had wondered if God was so loving, why hadn't He allowed us to mend our relationship? Why had He allowed me to struggle with depression and an overall distrust in love?

Given his hostility at what had transpired, it was amazing to me that Parrado had been able to survive the devastating circumstances of his mother's and sister's deaths and the seeming hopelessness of the crash situation. I knew I had days when I felt low enough to quit—and those had been over a romantic break-up, not a matter of life or death. Thinking of what might have been Parrado's crash "survival reason," I wondered if it was the "necessity of winning through pain": a conclusion he had drawn as a little boy after hearing his father share about a rowing race in Argentina he had won by pushing against competitors—despite the pain of his throbbing muscles. Maybe he saw the Andes as his "competitors" and wanted to beat them despite the pain he had to endure to do so? I also wondered if maybe the idea of suffering was an *imprint* received from his father's story—and this crash might have somehow been a result?

I wanted to think that his father's love and prayers had sent him energy. But since Parrado mentioned in his speech that his father thought he was dead (and had sold everything reminding him of his son after hearing about the plane crash), I wondered if it might instead have been the prayers of so many others who had relatives involved in the crash or were from the Catholic school.

Still unable to sleep, I reflected again on his conclusions about love and its power, realizing, though, that the kind of love of which he spoke was more related to people and family than God. I had learned through my own difficulties that a trust in divine love (1 John 4:8 says that "God is Love") was the only thing that didn't disappoint. Trusting in divine love, however, required surrender to something higher; once that happened, that love evidenced itself in all kinds of ways—however the *Divine* chose. I had discovered that it is like a life of surprises if one can trust and become more intimate with the *Divine*. Loved ones, knowledge—anything—could disappoint if it wasn't on the divine level, and I wasn't sure that Parrado understood this. Yet I also remembered how many times he referenced strength in his talk, not only referring to his father's rowing story but also to his pondering who would be "strong enough" to join him on his trek for help. Perhaps it was his trust in strength that had allowed him to persevere?

My thoughts then shifted to my father and what he had experienced in Vietnam as a B-52 pilot. He had always been so positive in the letters he wrote home to us during that time, talking about how fun it was to grill dinner and to interact with Sucks, their squadron dog. Pondering further, I realized that he had even made stories about his difficult military school sound positive and comical; one of my favorites was the story of igniting "comet bombs" against opposing squadron dorm rooms to make them messy just before scheduled squadron inspections; of course, as a child I never thought about what it was like to have to do the resulting clean-up in the few hours before the inspections. I realized my dad was probably a "glass-half-full" person too, and I had probably inherited that trait from him.

All these thoughts circled me back to my interactive experience with the force of Love just before Greg had ended our relationship. Mine was a Presence, a Voice—a Divine love experience—whereas Parrado's was a realization about the love of family. I was glad I was starting to feel more confident about my relationship with God again, or at least He was feeling *there* as opposed to the spiritual vacuum that had resulted after the breakup.

Gerardo's talk to us at the Dallas office about his "love" goal for the university also popped into my mind; had he known what Parrado was going to say, or was it his own personal philosophy of life? I had secretly enjoyed watching his romantic behavior toward Dorothea throughout the university. They would often sit cuddled together as they observed what was going on. It would be interesting to find out what caused their strong intimacy—as I figured they had been married at least twenty years and knew that marriages could fail by that point. Finally, I fell asleep—grateful that I had attended the talk.

On the final day of the university, the staff was invited to attend the closing party. I had brought along a ruffled, royal blue cocktail dress with a sparkling belt buckle just in case we were asked—and looked forward to attending while staying low key. When I arrived, Ken and Trish Byers asked me to join their table. Jose Jr., looking even more handsome than ever, was there and pointed to the seat next to his. As I took it, I slightly brushed his arm, prompting that same feeling of tension and attraction I experienced whenever I was around him. We both chatted with others around the table, and I wondered if anything tonight would happen between us.

I noticed that the member on the other side of me was Dr. Lawrence Wright. As I thought about the familiarity of his name, I remembered that it was Ed's boss; what a coincidence that he would be at my table! The timing was perfect to make a connection, so I introduced myself and mentioned Ed from back in Dallas. I also relayed his kind words about the company, then asked if he and his wife had enjoyed the university. They told me they had—especially Nando Parrado's talk—and mentioned wanting to see *Alive* when they returned to Dallas.

After we finished our conversation, I thought back to Ed and his continuing lack of communication. Did that mean things between us were over? What exactly did it mean when men didn't communicate? This had been the first time on the trip that he came up in my mind. Should my lack of thoughts toward him be a indicator that I was no longer interested in the relationship? Or maybe that our relationship was even more casual than I had realized?

I looked toward Jose Jr., who was eyeing the dance floor, then he stood up and headed toward it while also throwing me a glance. Was he asking me to dance? I didn't know much about Latin dancing, so I wasn't sure how to respond. Plus, going out there would put me in front of everyone despite my promise to lay low. On the other hand it looked like great fun, and given my love for dancing maybe I would pick it up fairly easily. I mentally struggled for a moment, then gave in to temptation and joined him with the group of committee members on the dance floor. To my surprise, a few others from the Dallas staff followed my initiative—which made me feel better.

The cha-cha-cha was easy to learn given the beat: one step forward, replace it back, then sway the hips and march the feet three times. Next came the mambo. I watched everyone for a moment, then followed them with a sidestep, return to center; other sidestep, return to center. I was having a great time moving my arms with the rhythm, and once again I got the steps down easily. Jose Jr. confidently stepped close to and then away from me, brushing me slightly, which again raised my pulse. Then we both turned to watch Gerardo and Dorothea, who, in their usual understated manner stepped onto the dance floor next to us and began to swing around, fully entwined.

As the music and dancing continued, the YPO Mexico City members cheered me on as I learned the steps, then looped their arms through mine as we hooked up in a line. Don Camp was running around shooting photos, and he stopped once in front of us to snap Jose's picture as he pointed at Don and did his signature "eyebrow raise." That arching look was the same facial expression that had so intimidated me the first day I met him—and it still did so. But I was now even more attracted to him, and as both of us began our second glass of wine we danced even more closely together.

Ed fleetingly crossed my mind, but the excitement of the moment (and probably the wine) brought my thoughts back to the present. After the musicians took a break, Jose went over to talk to his father, mother, and sister—and then shot me a look as he walked out the ballroom door. I took that as an invitation to follow, waited a minute or two, then subtly made my way toward the exit. He was waiting in the hallway, and the second I met him he grabbed my hand—drawing me toward him and asking if I wanted to go to my room. I wasn't sure how to respond, but his assertiveness was enticing as I told him my room number. He led me down one of the long "airport" hallways in the right direction, then stopped to pull me into a small alcove and began to passionately kiss me. I enjoyed every second, responding equally—or so I thought—but I felt him release his embrace slightly, as if to ask me if I wanted to "keep going."

I thought I did, but was simultaneously in deep thought about whether he was really attracted to me—or just heady with all the wine and dancing? Didn't alcohol lead to release of inhibitions? If so, he must be attracted—right? Then I suddenly wondered if it was *my* passion and inhibition that was being released by the alcohol?

I decided to go with the moment and nudged him toward my room while thinking about whose desires were stronger. It had been quite a few years since I had been with Greg in any kind of passion, and I remembered him often being the person who kept us "in check" during those times. When we got to my door and I fumbled to get my key, Jose abruptly pulled away. Confused, I turned to look and there was his sister Mary coming down the hotel hallway with another member of the crew.

I found that odd; had she seen us leave and found a way to follow? Jose was breathing heavily—as was I—as we considered how to handle this interruption in our plans. But it was clear there was no way to get away from her, so he stepped aside and said, "Buenas Noches" very politely—as if everything was under control and he had just been escorting me to my room. Terribly disappointed yet slightly relieved, I calmly said the same to him and Mary—watching him join her and walk away—and walk away—and then entered my room alone. My hands were shaking and my heart beating a mile a minute as I collapsed into in a chair. Loosening my sparkling belt, I forced myself to breathe slowly in order to calm down and think. There was no way to find him now, as we hadn't talked about his room number. Still feeling all that sensuality and passion between us, I sat there and wondered what, if anything, would happen next. Would he wait awhile and then return? Or was it another *might have been* romantic adventure—like what happened with Angus in London—except progressing a bit further? Gazing out the window at the bright lights of Mexico City, I kept hoping…at the same time realizing that only time would tell.

Chapter 7

A Paris Intermission

As seemed to be the case with other romances in my life, nothing progressed with Jose Jr. and me. Ed and I dropped our relationship back to a friendship and I once again busied myself with work during the day and any activities I could pick up in the evenings.

Thinking about it all, I felt like I had, somewhere along the way, lost who I was. Upon returning from Papua New Guinea, I had been so sure of myself in that I wanted to become a missionary and work with children. But here I was—four years later—in almost the exact opposite position. Huts in native jungle villages had been replaced with five-star or exclusive locations and simple children learning to read replaced with CEOs. It was all a bit much to process, especially since I had grown bored with day-to-day work at the Dallas office.

Thankfully, Ron came to me with additional responsibilities, and it seemed to awaken something I thought I had lost: hope. His proposal was for me to take on the children's program for our upcoming university in Maui—which would provide a much-needed challenge from the day-to-day routine to which I had become accustomed. And even better, it involved working with children from the age of five all the way up to college level.

Although I had begun working toward my elementary school teaching certificate in Atlanta before accepting this job, my hopes to complete that goal in Dallas had been washed away by the busyness of YPO. Managing the children's program was at least a step in the direction I'd originally planned for myself, and I was looking forward to Maui for that reason alone.

All of this took my thoughts to someone else who had stayed on track with her career goals: Alexis. Her Dallas visit and internship at YPO after the Vienna University showed how easily she had mastered her responsibilities and confirmed my conclusion that I had a generally easy job—though oftentimes a busy one. Soon after that Dallas visit, she had started graduate business school at the Haute Etudes Commerciales (HEC) in Jouy-en-Josas, France, and we had stayed in touch through her three-year program. I had gone to visit her during her final spring break earlier in the year, and in doing so, enjoyed my first trip to Paris—a special birthday present to myself. It had also proved to be interesting and fun and had me wondering what it would be like to do a YPO university in this incredible city.

The vacation had started with Alexis picking me up at Charles-de-Gaulle Airport in a small, Beetle-looking car with the name "Citroen 2CV" on it. She explained that it was called a "Deux Chevaux" (meaning *two horses*) after being developed by the French in the 1930s to help shift the farming transportation culture from horses to vehicles. Conceived to allow four people to transport 50kg of farming goods to market at 50km per hour, it had to be fuel efficient and also steady enough to transport eggs over unpaved and muddy roads while doing so. I remembered that the Germans had somewhat of the same goal when they designed the "Volkswagen" (meaning *people's car*), and apparently during WWII had even tried to steal some of the tools designed by the French for the manufacture of this car.

It took us an hour or so to drive from the airport to Jouy-en-Josas, where she settled me into a room in her emptied-out dorm. A few hours later we headed into Paris from a local stop of a train called the Reseau Express Regional (RER), then connected to the Paris Metro to have dinner at the Café de la Paix near the Opera House in downtown Paris. During the trip she explained that the Paris Metro was extensive, well-organized, and easy to follow—and I realized while we were at the the the Café de la Paix that it reminded me of Café Landtann, the coffee house she had introduced me to in Vienna.

Once we were in town, I found the Parisians to be rather "testy"—correcting me if I spoke incorrect French and impatient in helping me with anything. When I commented on this, Alexis shared that the French countryside's culture was a bit different—which made me wonder if I would experience that difference if I visited Versailles later in the week.

The next day she stayed in Jouy-en-Josas to focus on her graduate project. My goal for the day was to see the Louvre, the world's largest museum, and as I waited for the RER I grabbed an amazing pastry at a nearby bakery. Enjoying it on the way into Paris, I switched onto the Metro then exited at the Palais Royale stop. Gazing in awe at the former palace turned museum, I entered through its IM Pei-designed glass pyramid. Trying to head toward the *Mona Lisa*, I soon found the museum overwhelming given its size and collection of contents—as it housed a long stretch of history from the Middle Ages to the mid-nineteenth century. The more I explored, the more I realized days could be spent in the museum while just brushing the surface of its collections.

Also on my mind was this evening's venue: a restaurant suggested by Alexis. A good friend from Atlanta, Steve, would be arriving in Paris at the Gare de l'Est train station and joining us for dinner as well as a three-day stay. Steve was one of the guys from the Atlanta singles church group who had lived in the complex in which Beth and I had shared an apartment. He was also one of the key people who counseled me to break off my engagement to Greg—and I hadn't heard from him since my move to Dallas.

His Paris visit had started with our reconnection a few weeks earlier while he was passing through Dallas. He had asked for some time to "bend my ear" about a romantic situation with which he was struggling—and which he said reminded him of Greg and me. Over dinner, he had shared how he proposed to a bridesmaid at his brother's wedding only to have second thoughts, end the engagement, and break her heart. We had continued to chat throughout the night about our similar experiences and feelings, and I had casually mentioned my upcoming trip to Paris. Perking up at hearing this, he had mentioned that he would be in Europe around the same time and could possibly join me for a few days—if he could get his schedule rearranged. I had always liked Steve and thought him adventurous, and since we had never traveled together thought the idea a fun one. After he had confirmed a few days later that he would be able to join me, I had reached out to Alexis about his visit, and she had easily agreed to the idea given her busy schedule (and the available HEC dorm rooms). This had made me look even more forward to the trip—plus I thought that he and Alexis would enjoy meeting each other (he was quite the charmer).

Walking around the Louvre and thinking about Steve, I realized that in addition to his charm, he had always been intriguing to me— perhaps because he was smart and came from a family that owned a nationally recognized ad agency. Although he had clearly inherited his family's creative gene, he had gone the direction of computer consulting and ended up as one of Andersen Consulting's (now Accenture) top consultants.

Also fortunate was that he knew Paris well, and after dinner (where he *did* very much enjoy meeting Alexis), he suggested we walk to the Rue de Montmartre and try crepes—introducing me to what rapidly became a love affair with the rich Hazelnut chocolate confection called Nutella. The following day, he and I set off to explore the Musée D'Orsay and both loved it—starting with the building itself. Situated in a former Beaux-Arts railway station, the museum showcased around 2500 pieces created during the turning point of art between 1848 and 1914. The collection featured strictly French artists, such as Degas, Renoir, Van Gogh, Gauguin, Monet, Manet—the list went on and on—and as we walked the galleries, I soon realized how much I loved the beauty and gentleness of Impressionism.

One artist in the Musée d'Orsay stood out to me because of the effect Tahiti had on him: Gauguin. While his artworks themselves had not impressed me (he had started as an Impressionist under Pissarro but his trips to Tahiti morphed him toward Primitivism), the effect of being so close to nature and immersed in the Polynesian culture seemed to inspire him to paint with more vivid colors and graphic shapes. I wondered if my upcoming time at the Maui university would influence me in any of the same ways.

Enjoying my time with both Steve and Alexis in Paris, I then finished out the trip in the countryside of Versailles with its amazing palace (and gracious locals)—and before I knew it, I was back in Dallas to push forward with Maui.

Chapter 8

Maui & Justin

To: Kris Jaeckle

Children's Program Coordinator

YPO Headquarters Dallas, Texas

Canucks beat the Stars in Stanley Cup Playoffs!

Told you so.

Justin

The fax machine sat right next to my desk, and I noticed the strange note addressed to me as it spit out its contents one morning. It even had a "smiley face" at the bottom. This was a highly unusual fax coming to a business office, and I grabbed it quickly before anyone saw it. Personal faxes weren't supposed to arrive right in front of my boss's desk here at work.

Sitting down, I studied the fax more closely. Who was *Justin?* And what was the *Stanley Cup?* I vaguely knew the Dallas Stars were our city's professional hockey team. But who were the Canucks?

Suddenly, I remembered the last night of our recent planning trip at the Grand Wailea Hotel in Maui (and it was definitely a grand hotel!) in preparation for the upcoming family university. Justin and Kelly, the children of Andy and Millie to whom I had been assigned to help with the kids' program, had come with their parents to the meeting. And, we had met because my boss had unexpectedly invited me to attend this final planning trip, even though it wasn't something normally allowed for my position.

I seemed to recall that Justin was into sports. He had told me that he played ice hockey, rugby, and tennis—and maybe other sports too. He had a casual manner about him, as well as a confidence I had never seen in a nineteen-year-old—except from perhaps someone who was a pilot. But I felt pilots could carry a lot of responsibility due to the intense training they went through—and because of how their machines operated in the sky while they performed their mission—whereas Justin hadn't mentioned any flying experience. So, maybe it was the rugby playing? I remembered that Nando Parrado had been part of a rugby team when his plane crashed in the Andes. I also knew it could be a brutal, close-contact sport but I had never met an accomplished rugby player. Anyway, Justin had impressed me that night at the planning meeting with his easygoing self-assurance when he sought my attention during dinner. His fax had just demonstrated it again—but I doubted his parents knew that he had sent it to me.

Fifteen minutes later, my phone rang. "Did you get my fax, Kris?" asked the voice.

"I did," I replied, recognizing Justin's voice. "But I wasn't expecting to receive anything from you on the YPO fax machine."

"We always use our family fax machine," he quickly explained, "so I didn't think twice about it. Anyway, I told you the Canucks would beat the Stars. We are going to win the Stanley Cup this year!"

It came back to me now. The Canucks were Vancouver's professional ice hockey team. He must have explained to me that the Stanley Cup was the professional ice hockey championship and I had forgotten, but I acted as if I knew what he was talking about. After all, the University of North Dakota Fighting Sioux, my college team, were arguably the winningest ice hockey team in college sports when I graduated—and the number one event on Friday nights at school were the rough-and-tumble ice hockey games. Thinking about them, I remembered that during the annual game against our rival school, the University of Minnesota Gophers, fans threw frozen gophers onto the rink—apparently a tradition in this rivalry. How long had it been since I had left college in Grand Forks? Six years? I hadn't thought much about ice hockey since then. But if Justin played both rugby and ice hockey, he was probably a very strong guy.

For sure, Justin was bold and seemed to have a good sense of humor. His father was quiet when I was around him—except when discussing politics or philosophy—so Justin probably had a bit more of his mother's lively personality. Coming from a Russian background, his father had graduated from the University of British Columbia, gone into construction, and become very successful—but his mother seemed the overt go-getter. During our time together, she set goals, completed them, and seemed a very bottom-line type of woman. You could get lost in conversation with his father over socialized medicine or philosophy or history, but it was fun to hang out with them both and they were very supportive of their children. Kelly was a top-notch ice skater, while Justin was involved in rugby and ice hockey as well as tennis, and young Daniel (who was shy and only ten) was already busy with sports too. I thought them an exceptional family.

By the time Justin and I hung up, he had me laughing and looking forward to seeing him again. I thought about how fortunate I was to be assigned to their family. I had first encountered them at the Whistler/Vancouver Family University back in 1991, and had thought highly of them there too, seeing that nice personality mix of Andy and Millie. I didn't think I remembered the kids—especially since little Daniel would have only been around six at the time.

I worked hard on the children's program, and Millie and I drew closer with the various projects, schedules, and events we were formulating.

When it came time for the university, our arrival at the Maui airport was greeted with "Alohas" and fragrant pink and white orchid leis. I had read that leis were bestowed on all visitors to the Hawaiian Islands, the tradition being rooted in the native concept of decorating a person for emotional reasons. Hawaiians had started it when their Tahitian ancestors had used stars to navigate their way to these islands around AD 1000. They brought their lei custom along—fashioning them out of all kinds of materials, including bones, leaves, shells, nuts, and feathers—to signify rank or even signal a desire for a peace treaty. Leis eventually became the signature greeting to Hawaiian Island visitors in the early 1900s as tourism took off—and had since become globally recognized. Fresh orchid lei-making was going to be one of the YPO children's activities, and I had taken time to research the history so I could explain it to them.

As our jitney neared the Grand Wailea Hotel, Mount Haleakala towered in the background. One of the scheduled member activities at the university was a sunrise bicycle descent of this famous East Maui volcano (its last explosion had been just two centuries ago), and I hoped to get a chance to partake of this activity at some point.

Pulling into the hotel, the beauty of the grounds once again captured me. Japanese investor Takeshi Sekigushi had lavished $650 million on the hotel, and the results were readily apparent. Even check-in was a luxury experience—given the tropical, open-air atmosphere and gracious staff. Andy and Millie had also arrived; Millie and I exchanged smiles. I didn't see Justin with her, although Daniel was by her side and Andy was talking to the event chairman.

The setup went smoothly, and during that time I had a chance to have a look at the full grounds of the hotel—which included an intimate wedding chapel that led to a private beach. Exploring their children's pavilion, program, and counselors, I found the staff to be pleasant and enjoyable. One of the female counselors with long brown hair she kept in a five-strand French braid was someone I especially came to admire, as I enjoyed her touching stories about the children to whom she had been assigned. Since I had mastered the three-strand version of her hairstyle several years prior, I asked her to show me her complicated method and then used it as my go-to style for the university.

Once the university officially began, Millie did her usual expert organizing and I took a back seat—helping when requested—as well as trying to figure out if there was any way to keep ahead of her. She treated me as a partner, but she was sharp as a tack and it was again reinforced to me that she was probably a major force in her husband's success. Justin and Kelly were both good about checking on their mother and assisting with whatever they could, but I could tell their personal preference was to be in the pool or at the beach.

Whenever I saw Justin he teased me, and I gradually got to know him better. He seemed to generate a feeling of both gentleness and strength, which was a kind of energy I hadn't experienced before in a guy. The men I had known usually had one or the other, and I wondered if this combination in his personality could have come through rugby. From what he was teaching me of the sport, it required intense play—with no padding or protection—wearing out all the players in the process of a match. Once the game ended, the opposing teams enjoyed sitting together, talking, and honoring each other for the game. That seemed different from ice hockey and American football where both teams might shake hands when the game was over, but it wasn't a tradition to sit down and socialize together. As I thought about this—and the fact that Nando Perrado would be a keynote speaker here—I wondered what Justin's reaction to his talk would be given their mutual love of rugby.

No matter where we went on the island during the university, we were surrounded by fresh flowers and gorgeous, bright colors. I could always pick a lovely blossom and tuck it into my braid, which made me feel beautiful (it is easy to feel beautiful in Hawaii). Meals were eaten outside in the plentiful sunshine under the clear, blue skies. And since all of us on staff were staying nearby at a less-expensive hotel, I could run the Wailea Beach Path to my room if I wanted to take in some beauty.

This manicured route ran one and a half miles, starting at the Andaz Resort and ending at the Fairmont Hotel, and it maneuvered around top-notch condos and other hotels—with the Grand Wailea in the center. Because of its pathways leading to the shore, it allowed for snorkeling and surfing and, because of the heights of its Wailea Point portion, sometimes offered whale sightings in addition to nice views of Kahoolawe, Molokini, and Lanai. I also often peeked at the Four Seasons Hotel when walking from the Grand Wailea—since they shared the same private beach—just in case I caught a glimpse of someone interesting on property there. One day I saw Whoopi Goldberg, whom I had loved watching in *Jumping Jack Flash* and *Sister Act*.

I personally thought the Grand Wailea was more beautiful than the Four Seasons—although both properties had opened within a year of each other and had received cash investments by Sekigushi. However, only $180 million had been spent on the Four Seasons—as opposed to the $650 million spent on the Grand Wailea. The Four Seasons encompassed fifteen acres, whereas the Grand Wailea covered forty. The general opinion I gathered was that the Four Seasons had the best level of guest service, but families preferred the Grand Wailea with its dedicated children's program, various pools, and waterslides.

During our final planning meeting, Millie and I had done plenty of running around the island to double-check the venues for the kids' program, and I learned a great deal about the lush vegetation, fragrant flowers, sugar cane industry, and pineapple plantations—as well as another Maui experience we thought would be especially exciting for the children: the Atlantis submarine ride.

Millie had also come up with a new idea for family universities: a "teen book" (as opposed to a "yearbook") for kids sixteen years and older. Her concept was based on feedback from other YPO family universities requesting a way for kids to keep in touch with each other. To accommodate this, I had set up and sent out a survey to get biographical information from the kids so that our marketing department could create the book. Each teen was assigned a half-page which allowed them to tell about their schooling, interests, and contact information—then at the end were blank pages for notes from friends made during the university. Completed just in the nick of time, they had been included in the family's opening registration packet, along with schedules, notebooks, nametags, etc.

One day while attending the children's activities, I saw Daniel seated in the craft area working hard on a project. As I stood there, he walked over to me and then with a shy smile that reminded me of his father, gave me a heart-decorated, hand-made bracelet with my name on it. All I could think was that those Pottman boys could just win my heart!

As the university smoothly progressed, I grew closer to Andy and Millie's family. They were all so kind, thoughtful, and committed to doing a great job. Justin checked up on me in between his activities, and after social events began walking me to my hotel along the Beach Path. The evening after Nando Parrado spoke, his demeanor was sober and reflective, and I shared some of my thoughts about Parrado's keynote speech in Mexico City. I had had a hunch in

Mexico City that his appearance there might start a speaking career for him; a new discovery was that he had also become interested in YPO membership—so this university gave him an opportunity to see how family events worked.

In the final days of the university, Justin and I began to subtly spend what free time we had together. As we did, I felt a growing closeness and attraction—though his appeal still puzzled me given the difference in our ages. I also wasn't certain what Justin found attractive or interesting about me—even though he had reached out in obvious ways from the moment he first met me. I did feel a kinship with his mother, as both she and his sister Kelly were intelligent and ambitious. So, maybe that similar aspect of my personality didn't intimidate him.

Justin was also close to his father, with whom I had connected intellectually (except in a few political areas—but he was Canadian, and that was to be expected). One of the suggestions Andy had given me before the university was to read *Hawaii*, the famous novel by James Michener, and I had taken him up on it and fallen in love with the work. Michener had actually been invited to the Maui University to speak but turned out to be a bit better at writing. The feedback from members was that he had a lot of information to share but came across as a bit "dry." I had noticed this while reading his book and found myself sometimes skipping pages when he went into his "information overload mode" while writing about topics such as the formation of the Hawaiian Islands.

Something else Andy had shared was how much he enjoyed driving the "Road to Hana" when he was in Maui because of all the scenic stops along the way that included amazing waterfalls and a black sand beach. Andy and Millie's family had been so busy with their duties during the university that they hadn't had a chance to do many family activities and, out of the blue, invited me to stay afterward and join them for a few days of fun. Justin's face had an encouraging look at this invitation, and the next time we were alone he asked me to drive the Road to Hana with him—

as well as cycle down Haleakala together—if I chose to stay. I suspected he had urged his parents to extend the invitation, but it didn't really matter as I had already found myself wanting to experience more of Maui. So, after accepting their offer, I made reservations for a rental car so I could have more freedom—and potentially time with Justin.

During the university I had noticed all the girls hovering around Justin, and certainly understood why: He was handsome, gentle, strong, encouraging, and patient. And we were in such a romantic setting that it was hard not to feel something for him. He seemed to enjoy my company as much—if not more so—than some of the teenyboppers who had crushes on him.

Then, something came to mind that I realized might be encouraging my openness to Justin: Prozac. A new kind of antidepressant classified as a "selective serotonin reuptake inhibitor" (SSRI), Prozac was gaining popularity with doctors and therapists for its ability to deal with anxiety and curb depression. My mother, who had her master's in social work, had always kept an eye out for my emotional well-being, and recently suggested I try it. She knew how stressed I became while working the universities, and although I had been through some standard counseling for family issues at her request, I had never been on an SSRI.

A few years earlier, a cousin-doctor had tried putting me on the classic mood stabilizer Lithium after I shared about a few strong "feeling dips" during significant life experiences (and certain times of the month). Although it hadn't seemed to produce a significant change in my frame of mind, I had tried it because of my trust in him. Always checking symptoms initially by investigating body acidity, allergy possibilities, hormone issues, and other variables—he would then prescribe medication only if necessary. Another factor he had discovered running in our family was a low level of serotonin, and between the stress of universities and the serotonin issue, I wondered if I should try the Prozac to see what would happen. Being a risk-taker and deciding I could always stop if it didn't work, I had reached out to him for a prescription. Then, after mentally wrestling about it during my first week in Maui, I looked at one of the small capsules and decided to try it—remembering that my mother said it could take up to a month to be effective.

The very next morning, I woke up feeling wonderful about life and noticed that during that day, problems didn't seem to bother me quite so much. Was I finally losing some of my sensitivity? Was it just the fact that I was in a beautiful environment? As I pondered what might have changed in my routine or environment to cause this change, the only thing I could think of was the Prozac. But it was supposed to take more than a day to have an effect, wasn't it? As I continued taking it over the next few days, my feelings stayed positive and consistent. The only thing that changed seemed to be my ability to get up at 6 am, as now I could not get out of bed until at least 8 am. After speaking with my mother about this, she said the good aspects—as well as the sleep pattern change—sounded like the results other people were experiencing. She also suggested that since it seemed to be helping, it might be worth staying on it for a bit. Trusting her years of counseling experience, I followed her advice.

The university culminated with a great closing party on the beach, and everyone was sad to say goodbye. The kids seemed to appreciate the "teen book" Millie had initiated, telling each other that they would use it to stay in touch and that they looked forward to meeting up again at next year's family university. I did my usual pack-up and ship-out duties, then rented my car and joined Millie and her family at Wailea Point.

After arriving, Justin and I headed out along the Wailea Coastal Walk just as the windspeed picked up and the surf started to crash. The sky darkened and a standard afternoon rain shower emerged. There was no shelter to be found, so Justin kept me close to him with a firm grip on my hand. Within ten minutes, the wind had settled down and a double rainbow emerged. As we stood on a cliff along this portion of the Coastal Walk (no whales seen this time!), it seemed the perfect moment for a sweet kiss—which I returned. That night, I joined everyone at dinner for a discussion of the next day's activities. Since Justin and I were doing the Haleakala sunrise bike ride the next day, Millie suggested we join the family afterward for some snorkeling. Once our agenda was set, I went to bed early in anticipation of the 2 am bike ride pickup time—just five hours away.

Justin was becoming even more affectionate, and when we met in the early morning for the van pickup, he gave me another sweet kiss. During our ride in the dark up the 10,000-foot Mt. Haleakala, we couldn't see anything—which allowed us to settle in and listen to our tour guide explain the local legend about this volcanic crater-peak. Apparently, it was known as being home to the grandmother of the Hawaiian demigod *Maui* who had become famous for helping him capture and slow the sun's sky journey so the day would become longer.

Entering Haleakala National Park at 6,500 feet, we continued ascending to the 10,000-foot peak of the massive shield volcano that makes up most of the island of Maui. We finally stepped out into chilly temperatures and, while waiting for the first streaks of dawn, gazed at the millions of stars (as well as some shooting stars) we could see at this elevation. Our tour guide informed the group of the island's latitude of twenty-one degrees, which enabled us to catch both the North Star and the Southern Cross. As I stood there, I recalled stargazing back in Papua New Guinea—which had been my first introduction to the Southern Cross.

As dawn began to break, we took a seat along the rock wall to watch the spectacular sunrise in all its glory, with rays of red, orange, yellow, and blue greeting us over the clouds. I could understand why this experience had been described as a once-in-a-lifetime event—as well as why the YPO members who had done it raved about it so much.

As the skies continued to brighten, the tour guide equipped us with helmets, raincoats, and special cruising bikes featuring heavy-duty brakes. During the ride, the grades were going to be steep and there would be some sharp turns, but the tour guide assured us we would be fine. A photographer was running around, and he stopped to snap a few pictures of me sitting on Justin's handlebars as he embraced me from behind. Justin had easily lifted me up to this position, which confirmed again to me his strength as well as how easily and openly affectionate he was. He seemed clear about his feelings despite his young age.

He also proved to be the perfect companion on our twenty-seven-mile ride down—as his laid-back yet fun and confident demeanor helped ease the tension of the somewhat nerve-racking grades and sharp curves we encountered. Our descent wound us through upcountry Maui to the cowboy town named Makawao with its grazing fields where cattle had first been introduced to the islands.

The landscape rolled by, shaded by eucalyptus and jacaranda trees—past sugar cane and pineapple fields—as well as art galleries, stores, and restaurants. We also spotted orchids, macadamia and coconut trees, wild coffee trees, and many other exotic plants and flowers. Often visible in the distance as we made our way down the volcano, too, were Lanai, Kahoolawe, Molokini, and other Hawaiian Islands. Our bike ride ended around 10 am near the beach in Pi-uh, the town where our Road to Hana journey would start the next day.

As requested by the family the night before, we joined them for snorkeling at Kamaole Beach. Swimming around the lava rock and coral formations allowed us to catch glimpses of green sea turtles, yellow tang fish with black stripes, silvery needlefish, white pufferfish, and bright red pencil urchins.

At dinner with the family, Justin and I talked about our plans to drive the Road to Hana and Andy recalled his memories of its black sand beach, the Seven Sacred Pools of Ohe'o, and Charles

Lindbergh's grave. I had studied the route, which in total ran about 110 miles, and asked Andy whether it was smart for us to do the full loop—or just turn around once we reached Hana. He responded that the full loop would be interesting and allow us to view the Seven Sacred Pools—but reminded us to be careful as some parts of the road might not be paved.

I also asked Andy if he knew the history of the road that went around the island. He explained that it all had started with West Maui's King Pi'ilani back in the sixteenth century after he acquired East Maui and Hana. He built an "alaloa" or "long road," allowing connection between the two island halves. This precipitous footpath ran 138 miles over diverse terrain—with vine-ropes necessary to swing over the various gulches. It was used for the next 250 years until one-lane, gravel government roads were initiated in the 1880s to assist in transportation of goods from Hana's sugarcane plantation and mill. Eventually, the road circumnavigated the island's east shores around Hana, featuring 617 hairpin curves and fifty-nine one-lane bridges. The speed limit was, therefore, only twenty-five miles per hour. Once Kalepa Bridge was reached, the Piilani Highway or "Back Road to Hana" began and was even more serpentine and cliff-hugging than the first half of the route—which was why many people turned around and returned the way they came once they got there.

Andy had done the full circle, but he encouraged us to drive it in a clockwise route, which he felt allowed for seeing the most beautiful portions of the landscape during the morning when vegetation was still covered in morning mist. We could then stop for lunch in Hana and spend the afternoon on Haleakala's dry backside, where the waterfalls and rocky landscape were even more spectacular as the afternoon light waned.

The next morning, Justin and I put the top down on the rental car, and dressed in our bathing suits and coverups, drove a half hour to our starting place, Kahului. Just after Paia (where we had ended our biking adventure), we reached Hookipa Beach Park, a mecca for people who loved to combine surfing with sailing. Continuing, we rode past jungles thick with bamboo and ginger, pineapple fields, cattle pastures, and papaya orchards. The sometimes one-lane, sometimes two-lane, road could ascend into cliffs overlooking the pounding Pacific coastline, or turn down toward the shore—which we finally did just before Hana to catch the black sand beaches in Waianapanapa State Park. Stepping onto the dark, sparkling sand and feeling its smooth texture between our toes, we walked over to a sign informing us we could hike along the coast from there to Hana. We wrestled with the idea but decided to return to our car and continue driving.

A bit past Hana, we could hear the thunder of descending water and slowed to see the eighty-foot Wailua Falls. As enticing as it was to linger, we pushed on to catch the Seven Sacred Pools located in the 'Ohe'o Gulch which emptied into the ocean about twelve miles past Hana. Stopping the car, we studied the stunning view of black lava cliffs against the bright blue ocean, and then looking at the map, felt energetic enough to walk the two-mile Pipiwai trail to the grandest waterfall easily reached on Maui.

The trail wasn't too difficult, starting out in a tropical rainforest and threading its way through connecting pools and waterfalls. Early on we saw a gigantic banyan tree, and looking at its extended limbs and long, aerial roots, I was glad we had included a visit to the famous Lahaina one in the YPO children's program.

We continued down the path, eventually entering a bamboo forest that opened out into the 400-foot Waimoku waterfall—a sight well worth the hike. As we turned around and headed back, Justin and I talked about this amazing set of islands and all their history. Nearing the end of the trail, we decided to finish with another half-mile walk down to the pools where we could take a dip. Once there, we stripped to our bathing suits, grabbed each other's hand, and took a giant leap into the refreshingly cold water. As we swam beneath the falls, I loved feeling Justin's warm, muscular body next to mine, and he suddenly pulled me close and kissed me with a tender passion. At that moment, I thought of Gaugin and how Polynesia had seduced him with its beauty and loving culture in what seemed an earthly paradise—and I understood completely. It had happened to me as well.

Chapter 9

Into the Heart of Africa

It was the biggest spider I had ever seen—probably six inches from top leg to bottom, with golden knuckles and a yellow and black body—and it loomed larger and more terrifying as our Range Rover approached a grove of trees on the Londolozi game reserve in the heart of the Sabi Sands area near the western edge of Kruger National Park. Its web spanned a good part of the grove—a complicated, clouded mass of white silky strings. The flapping bird trapped inside kept my gaze intently fixed on it from a distance as I perched on the top seat in the back of the vehicle.

Renias, our tracker, was a sturdy black Bushman raised in the original hunter-gather traditions of a local tribe, and he sat in a foldable seat attached to the front fender. Carrying a gun and large stick, he was positioned there to discern footprints and other signs of wild animals as we drove along. He also kept an eye out for these entangling webs and then wielded his stick to tear them down without destroying the spider. Although I was an *arachnophobe*, that first morning on our safari I had learned to trust his ability to perform this task as we drove around the game preserve so that I had—as of yet—to meet any of these frightful spiders face-to-face. He always made sure the webs came down, even if it was just a few seconds before we ploughed through them.

But Renias didn't seem to have yet spotted the terrifying spider—and the bird trapped in its web—rapidly approaching us. Instead, he was busy conversing with the game ranger David, the head of our team, who was driving the vehicle. The closer the spider and bird came, the more my skin crawled. I began to lean toward the woman sitting next to me. Finally, I couldn't control it; I opened my mouth and screamed.

The web and spider came down with a *whack* as the Rover lurched to a halt. The bird flew away. Alex, a rugged white South African dressed in khaki shorts and a short-sleeved safari shirt, jumped out of the driver's seat and walked straight back to me. Taking off his safari hat with one hand and running the other through his hair in frustration, he said (in his charming native accent), "Are you *quite* all right?" His emphasis on the word "quite" confirmed his lack of pleasure.

I didn't reply. He went on, "You have seen so many kinds of animals out here today and nothing has bothered or scared you. You even walked up behind a rhinoceros when nobody else would. Why would you scream at a spider?"

My embarrassment and shame grew. Everyone else in the Rover was staring at me as if I were a lunatic or something. They might have been scared too (I thought to myself defensively), but as usual I was the only one who would express what people around me might be thinking.

"Well," I finally ventured in a small voice. "I…I wasn't sure what to do. Usually, Renias gets them down, but he didn't seem to notice that one. I just got really scared."

At the same time, I thought about what he had said about my courage when it had come to that rhinoceros. We had been out on this morning's drive—we took two drives, one at 8 am and the other around 3 pm—and out of nowhere, the colossal creature had appeared in front of us, just off the road. Alex stopped from a distance to let us see it and explain that these animals had a strong sense of smell and hearing, but poor eyesight. So poor, in fact, that they couldn't see more than a hundred feet away.

"Does anyone want to get closer?" he had inquired. "If so, you can get out and walk up a bit more. We are in a downwind, so you can get pretty close to him from behind and he won't be able to detect you, even by smell."

I was the only one to volunteer, so Alex grabbed his gun and followed me as I stepped out of the vehicle and quietly inched forward. Although rhinos didn't socialize with each other, they and other herbivores in South Africa did allow tickbirds to sit on their backs and pick off bugs…as well as warn them if anything got too close.

When we were about fifteen feet away Alex suddenly motioned me back and stepped in front of my body. He slowly gestured for me again to follow his lead, and we were able to get a bit closer. I noticed the rhino's greyish, tough-looking hide and set of ancient-looking horns oddly protruding from its head—and felt its heavy energy. A red-beaked tickbird perched on his back noticed our presence, and its immediate "hiss-rasp" call sounded shrill. With the bird's warning signal, we halted our approach. Alex motioned me to step backward and we retreated, keeping the rhino in careful sight.

Once we were back in the Rover, Alex commended me. "Nice job, Kris. That was a once-in-a-lifetime experience. Anyone can do it in a zoo, but it is different in the wild. Too bad the bird gave us away—but you got pretty close to that rhino."

I felt like patting myself on the back for my act of courage, but I just smiled.

"Did you notice its *two* tusks?" Alex remarked to everyone in the group. "This rhino would be hunted were it not living in a conservation park. Their curving tusks, made mostly of keratin, were traditionally used for ornamental dagger handles by Muslims and prized in native African folk medicine for their aphrodisiac properties. That's why this creature is nearing extinction."

His observations were met with silence by everyone in the group, and I assumed they were thinking about the potential extinction of this fascinating species, as was I. Many of these conservation parks had been set up to protect animals like the rhino, which was in danger of vanishing from the face of the earth. Londolozi had been created in the 1920s for hunting, but descendants of its founders had re-oriented it toward "wildlife tourism" in the 1960s.

Suddenly, Renias spotted something and pointed to the right. The Rover quickly took off, heading toward one of my favorite African animals: the long-necked and skyscraper-legged, yellow and brown giraffe with its short, hairy horns. I felt a sweetness about this animal's personality, even from a distance, and realized that the giraffe didn't emit the same heavy energy that had come from the rhino. That same sweet feel had seemed to come from a black-and-white striped zebra we had watched the day before. It had observed us warily from afar while swishing its tail, and Alex had explained that its razor-sharp eyes were what allowed it to keep its distance. He also shared that the zebra was the only horse in the equine family not domesticated because of its unpredictable nature and tendency to panic under stress.

Focusing back on Alex's reprimand about the spider scare made me resolve to keep myself under control. David returned to the driver's seat, informing everyone it was time to head back. Our trek on the wild side today would wind down with high tea this afternoon—with a focus on elephants promised for tomorrow. As the Rover bounced its way along the rutted path back to camp, I eagerly looked forward to the scrumptious scones they served. All the food so far had been gourmet quality, which surprised me given the somewhat primitive setting of the camp. Tea and scones back at camp was a way to avoid the intense heat of the afternoons when the animals were resting.

As I nibbled on scones and sipped my rooibos tea (rooibos was a native herb brewed by the Dutch starting in the 1700s as their alternative to the more expensive black tea), I reflected on how much power there seemed to be in this wild environment—as well as how it seemed barely under control. As I watched the animals out on the savannah, I could see the potential for violence which could erupt at any moment. At times, the native South African blacks seemed to live the same way—given both the oppression of their government as well as fractional fighting brought about because of local tribal warfare. I called it "power under control."

This was such an amazing time to be in South Africa. F.W. de Klerk, the state president, had released Nelson Mandela in 1990 after his twenty-seven years in prison, and together they had won the Nobel Peace Prize in 1993 for the peaceful termination of the apartheid regime and for laying the foundations of a new Democratic South Africa.

Our current YPO international president, Doug Smollan, was a South African. When nominated for that position two years earlier in 1991, he had the foresight to request that one of the three international universities be held in his country during his presidency. While he knew at the time that 1994 would bring the first South African open elections (and most likely the election of Mandela), he *had not* known that in 1993, Mandela and de Klerk would receive the joint Nobel Peace Prize. What he did anticipate was that his CEO-guests would experience history as it was being made.

Smollan's involvement in abolishing apartheid and personal friendship with de Klerk had also enabled him to schedule de Klerk, Bishop Desmond Tutu, and Mandela as keynote speakers during our time there—which promised to be an amazing lineup. Tutu had won the Nobel Peace Prize back in 1984 for his activism on the apartheid issue and work in human rights in South Africa.

Smollan also was aware that his friend Sol Kerzner, a South African magnate who designed global resorts, had just added an incredibly beautiful property to his famed Sun City resort: The Palace of the Lost City Hotel. Grand proportions and graceful towers framed the combination of African and Victorian architecture, and it was getting rave international reviews.

So, Smollan had decided to break the university in half. He staged the first three days in Johannesburg at the luxury Sandton Sun Hotel (located in an area labeled the "richest square mile" in Africa) to give everyone the flavor of this history-making city. Then he booked the second three days in Sun City to get the feel of Kerzner's luxury resort, which among other famous events, had recently hosted the Miss World pageant.

I had looked forward to exploring Johannesburg, but upon arrival the city had struck me as non-descript—as opposed to Vienna or London with their distinct feels. Its third-world atmosphere—similar to Mexico City—was noticeable because of the crime, trash, and poverty, but the difference between the two cities was that Mexico City possessed a distinct sense of history, given that it was more than 700 years old and home to a strong native culture that had been enriched by the even older European culture of Spain. I did not feel any kind of history present in Johannesburg.

I'd also had an unpleasant experience in Johannesburg during the first half of the university. Those of us on the crew (I was helping with the off-property activities, which YPO called "off-sites") had taken a dry run for a tour scheduled in a section of Soweto, which was a local acronym for "Southwest Townships." It was supposed to be a slum, but as we drove through it the neighborhoods didn't appear as poverty-stricken as I had expected. I had certainly seen worse in Mexico City as well as in Papua New Guinea—and New Guinea's indigenous people had appeared more primitive because they had not been exposed to much technology and were still living in huts eating mostly sweet potatoes. Yet I remembered them expressing gratitude for schools and roads and everything to which they had been given access.

As we toured Soweto and slowed to look at Mandela's house, someone had come running out and thrown raw eggs at our car. I hadn't experienced this type of anger in Mexico City or Papua New Guinea; then again, neither of those countries had gone through the oppression of apartheid. Much as I hated to admit it, all these components of Johannesburg made me long to go back to London or Vienna or the United States—or at least someplace brighter and safer. Once the Johannesburg events ended, however, Smollan had transported everyone via private bus out to Sun City where my perspective of South Africa began to change. It seemed more resort-ish in this new location and, while the hotels chosen in both cities were ideal settings for YPO events, this Palace of the Lost City complex—recently built for 830 million rand—was lavish to say the least. Walking through its magnificently decorated interior, I thought back on the history of its decorator, Teresa Carter, who was one of YPO's most prominent female members.

Carter had jump-started her hotel interior-decorating career by acquiring the contract for the Loews Anatole in Dallas. Although she didn't have the background or resources to decorate a hotel of its size (her background was in restaurant decorating), she was interested in the fact that it was slated to have seven restaurants, and her marketing proposal to Trammell Crow had promised, as a local magazine described, "some ideas for his hotel and restaurants he could not live without." When he phoned her to discuss the ideas, she was able to convince him that she could do the best job—then she more than delivered on her promise. Hotels around the world were soon knocking at her doorstep, including Kerzner hiring her for this new property in Sun City.

During her time working on The Palace, she had safaried at a local game reserve and the chief game ranger, Damon, began to pursue her. Carter was an intimidating woman who demanded excellence—but since he had tracked some of the largest and most dangerous animals in the world, he pursued with confidence. Their safari romance eventually turned into marriage and they maintained residences in both countries while he kept his safari business, traveling back and forth from Dallas. Because she had not only decorated The Palace but was also part of the committee for this University, he had come along with her and helped to organize the university behind the scenes.

We all found Damon interesting and charming, and the stories he told about his adventures as a ranger whetted our appetites for the staff safari scheduled for the end of the university. He was a great example of the "power under control" aura I found evident everywhere in the country. South African women were also confident, but in an understated way. They were beautiful, organized, fashionable, and smart—but didn't seem to have issues with men being in charge. The younger South African girls in our crew evinced this feminine attitude as well, but what seemed to stand out even more was their elegance, kindness, and an interesting fetish for high-laced hiking boots.

As the time for Nelson Mandela's speech approached, I studied up on his background—becoming intrigued by the evolution of his stance on nonviolence. He had begun with this philosophy (inspired by Ghandi, who had gotten his start on nonviolence in South Africa), but after witnessing the South African police kill sixty peaceful black protestors, had incorporated guerilla-type violence against the government. This behavior led to him being formally tried, with his 1963 trial resulting in a death sentence that was later reduced to a life sentence. His next twenty-seven years—almost three decades— had been spent in various prisons, starting with eighteen years on

Robben Island in Table Bay (which was also where Ghandi had been incarcerated 55 years earlier). This remote site off the west coast near Cape Town had long been used to isolate unwanted people (starting with lepers during the nineteenth century), and then was turned into a penal colony for political prisoners. Mandela spent his years there in a tiny cell with just a straw mat, working during the day in quarries. Eventually, he turned to nighttime studies to obtain a second law degree, and somewhere during that period began to pivot back to non-violence as the means of achieving his goal. He also tried to become friends with prison guards and worked on an autobiography focusing on forgiveness and goodness as the path toward fair government for *all* South Africans. Once released, he became head of the African National Congress (ANC).

At the time he was slated as one of our keynote speakers, Mandela had just been elected the first president of South Africa and the first non-white head of state in that nation. One of the initial steps he had taken was to try to keep some of the white members on his government staff, much to the anger of the recently liberated blacks who wanted no part of them in leadership. Excitement over his election was still running high, though, so YPO members were greatly anticipating what they would hear him say at this key moment in his country's history.

As Mandela stepped to the podium, I wondered whether he might engage in fiery rhetoric, but instead his approach was calm and centered on fairness. He spoke of the wisdom of keeping some element of experience present in the country's new leadership. Positivity emanated from him as he made it clear he wanted to establish an equitable government, forgive the apartheid past, and move forward to a hopeful future—an amazing attitude for a man who had spent the bulk of his life behind bars.

Listening to him, I sensed much kindness—and as he finished his address, the members all rushed forward to shake his hand. The energy radiating from him became even more powerful as the crowd pushed him close to me, and while I didn't get to shake his hand, the magnetic force surrounding his persona engulfed me in a profound way.

Once again, I thought back to my experience with Viktor Frankl in Vienna and realized the similarity of their thinking. Was it because they had both forgiven after suffering so greatly in prison settings? Frankl and Mandela had both said that they had used that oppressive, trapped time in their lives to become "better" rather than "bitter" and I knew that was an extreme—if not impossible—but disciplined decision to make. What had I heard someone once say? Having bitterness toward someone was like drinking poison and hoping it would affect the other person.

I then found myself contrasting Mandela's speech to Nando Parrado's talk in Mexico City about surviving his plane crash. His oppression had been the result of a cruel—though beautiful—environment rather than by humans. He perceived the Andes as his "enemies" and was determined to beat them—which, in his case, was one of his greatest motivators to stay alive. Frankl had not tried to overthrow the Nazis—that would have been a sure death sentence—but he had survived and grown stronger in a concentration camp full of their hatred. He had even used his pre-war experiences as a psychiatrist treating suicidal patients to help his fellow prisoners maintain hope, and his incarceration had ironically allowed him to strengthen and refine those principles, making them—and him—more resilient.

Likewise, in prison Mandela hadn't tried to overcome his oppressors or pit them against each other. Instead, his years in jail had seemed to lead him toward wanting to bring everyone together on an even playing field for the betterment of his people. Despite his conciliatory attitude, though, a few of our South African YPO members were leaving the country now that he had been elected. Everyone worried that there would be upheavals in how the country operated—as well as a backlash from many of its formerly oppressed citizens. Wasn't that what had happened in the United States after the Civil War? Things didn't just turn around overnight into a society with equal justice; even now, one hundred years later, there were still major social issues in America that hadn't been resolved.

No matter, I felt certain that Mandela's inspirational speech would be the highlight of the university, although we still had several days of activities to go in the elegant Palace of the Lost City Hotel. Fortunately for me, Don Camp was on hand before he had to rush off to the Middle East on another global photo shoot. He was his usual energetic self in Johannesburg for the first half of the university but had a surprise in store for me during the second half while we were in Sun City.

Over a casual cup of coffee, he and I had chatted about how difficult it was to make it in the modeling and acting world in Los Angeles. "Everyone is so artificially enhanced and perfectly beautiful in Hollywood," he commented. "But, Kris, you are so fortunate. You seem to have a lot of natural nice features—which I think is really refreshing. Would you be open to me doing a quick photo shoot of you? I hear there are all kinds of interesting places in the Lost City: wave pools, simulated villages with entry gates and towers, jungle areas. Did you bring a bathing suit you could wear?"

I was taken aback for a second. Don photographed Hawaiian Tropic girls and other top-end models for a living—and I certainly wasn't one of them—so where did this come from? But he seemed to be his usual nice self and perhaps was offering this as another way of keeping himself on YPO's radar screen for future university photography assignments. Thinking about my new black swimsuit embroidered with pearls, I agreed to the shoot—realizing that I would need to keep it low key. Later that afternoon, we met at the wave pool—Don with camera in hand, and me in my swimsuit— and we bounced around interesting Lost City locations, with me changing from one outfit to another. At the end, I thanked him for introducing me to another "life first": modeling. Then he departed to take pictures of members at that evening's event.

Once the university ended, I joined the staff for our safari in Londolozi—certain it would be another memorable adventure. The luxury camp, the name of which meant "protector of all living things," had the Sands River flowing through it. And it was where, on our very first morning out in search of game, Alex had spotted that rhino and I had ventured out with him to take a closer look. My act of bravery, however, was followed by the screaming episode over the spider—one I hoped everyone would soon forget.

The next morning, we set out with the goal of getting up close and personal with elephants. Renias was in his usual place at the front as Alex drove us toward one of their favorite watering holes. As the landscape whizzed by, we could spot all sorts of animals in the distance: giraffes, hyenas, zebras, and maybe a cheetah or two. Alex slowed as we approached the watering hole, and then weaved in and around the area as Renias reported signs of elephants to him.

According to Alex, Renias was looking for several prominent things: track prints of round, five-clawed front feet and ovular, four-clawed back feet; track lengths of about 24 inches; and *scuffs* at the front of the track with smoothness at the back—which, if not correctly observed, could cause you to follow the track backward. Finding and following those signs then led to trunk mark signs in serpentine "s" patterns along the tracks and water digging marks along a riverbed.

Suddenly, Alex issued a "shhhh" as Renias motioned him to bring the Rover to a stop. We could hear the rustling of branches, so we waited breathlessly to see what might emerge. Renias motioned to go forward with the Rover, which Alex did very slowly. Renias whispered that the watering hole he often visited with success was coming up and it seemed we might be in luck—given the snapping sounds he was hearing in the bush. Just ahead, we could see a small stream running over a drop in the road, and beyond that appeared a mother elephant and her baby.

146

Forging ahead, Alex carefully drove into the stream, getting closer to the pair. He then shut the engine off so we could watch, all the time indicating the need for quiet voices. We all agreed that elephants weren't beautiful animals because of their abnormally long noses, flapping ears, and wrinkled hide, but they were impressive—and enormous!

In the midst of our talking about what we were noticing and asking questions, Alex abruptly told us all to freeze and be quiet. We had inched in very close to these mammoth creatures, and apparently the mother had heard us, turned around, and was now heading straight for us. Suddenly, a complex feeling passed over me—like a strong sense of fear or anger. I thought about my ability to sense human emotions and wondered if I sensed animal ones too. I knew that elephants had been proven to emote; perhaps what I was sensing was her anger or fear?

Renias raised his gun as Alex tried to start the engine—which was catching, for some reason. I felt the tension increase and said a prayer for safety. The mother was now confronting us directly and raising her trunk in an aggressive trumpet. At just that moment, the engine kicked in and Alex slowly started to back the Rover away from her. The mother gradually lowered her trunk as she watched us move away, and once she felt a safe distance between us, turned around and led her calf off in the other direction.

Alex and Renias looked at each other and breathed a sigh of relief. The rest of us did the same. "That was a *really* dangerous situation." Alex observed. "We were too close, as she was very angry. I think we're done for the morning; let's head back to the camp."

That afternoon after enjoying tea and scones again, we headed out for another ride in search of wildlife. As the Range Rover navigated its way through the bush, I glanced over at Candy, my bunkmate on this trip. She had joined YPO just a few months ago after getting the educational project manager job I had wanted—which had very much upset me.

She didn't know this, however, and on her first day at work we shared an elevator up to the main floor. Normally I was a very sweet and kind person, but soon as I found out who she was and the job she was starting, I made it clear that it was supposed to have been *my* job. She must have understood how I felt because, to my surprise, she worked to become my friend and then asked if I wanted to be her bunkmate on the safari. I cautiously accepted her invitation, and during the few weeks we were in the office together realized how much alike we were.

Candy and I were both well-traveled, but in different ways. She was internationally educated and had run art galleries around Europe; she had received one of her graduate degrees from the prestigious but understated Thunderbird School of Global Management. She was smart and driven to excellence, and the more I got to know her, the more I liked her. We held deep discussions at night before falling asleep under our mosquito netting about what we were experiencing on the game rides *and* about what had just happened during the educational conference—especially Nelson Mandela and his keynote address.

South Africa society was still undergoing so much upheaval—with all kinds of good and bad things swirling around it. Someone had told us that the person who had tossed eggs at us in Soweto was Nelson Mandela's wife, Winnie Mandela. She had also been an anti-apartheid activist, and since its end had been asked several times to step down from her political positions due to accusations of murder, violence, and corruption.

She and Mandela had been married over thirty years—though much of that time had been spent separated—and while it was thought that she had played an instrumental role in his early days of radicalism, I wondered if their current marital separation was partially due to their decidedly different approaches toward changing their country. She had also been put into prison for crime, but that only seemed to make her harder and more radical, contrary to Mandela's prison time, which had softened him in some ways. We considered all this in thinking about Mandela's speech and the message he was trying to get across. On our last night of the safari as Candy and I nestled in our camp beds, I shared how my difficult breakup with Greg had brought me to YPO, and she, in turn, opened up about a recent romantic breakup she had endured. "It was scary, Kris—it really shut me down from other relationships."

Her comment caused me to think about Greg and the vow I had made to *never let myself get that badly hurt again,* reflecting on my romantic life since then and the strong drive that kept pulling me back to visit Atlanta every few months. I also thought about my desire to prove that I could be the kind of career woman Greg wanted, and my success at YPO seemed to have accomplished that. I still missed him, even though four years had now passed since I last saw him. And those feelings were waning even more due to all my church involvement, personal and professional travel, and time with my parents and friends.

Candy continued talking about her own situation, explaining that she had recently attended a weekend seminar from a global organization that had a local office in Dallas, and how it seemed to have an impact on the way the painful breakup had affected her. Before she attended the event, she had been asked to set a goal of some kind. Then she joined a large, diverse group of intellectual people who listened to each other relate stories from their lives while being questioned and guided by a moderator. "I didn't share any stories—in fact, only two or three people each day shared— but the crazy thing is that as you listen to those people, you start realizing things about yourself that you had never seen before," Candy said. "By the end of the weekend, I got a big insight into a pattern that had been true my whole life—and had affected my romantic relationships. And all I did was sit and listen. It might be something interesting for you to try."

"It sounds like a bunch of people who are victims," I replied with a frowning tone. "Does it involve God in any way?"

"Yes, I wondered about the victim mentality too, but it didn't come across that way at all," Candy answered. "And there wasn't any kind of reference to God—it dealt more with life in the here and now—but it is based on Christian principles, such as love, forgiveness, truth, and generosity." Candy then insisted she felt I was well-versed enough in my beliefs that I would be able to handle it. "From all you have shared during this trip—and even from what you have said about Nelson Mandela and what you noticed about him—you seem to be open to learning new things while pulling from the foundation in which you believe."

My respect for Candy was growing, both due to her intelligence and drive for excellence, so this opportunity sounded intriguing. She had already talked me into staying an extra night in London during our homebound layover to see the Apsley House, the home of the first Duke of Wellington. She had mentioned its magnificent architecture and amazing collection of classical art, noting that we had just enough time to see it—so I decided I would learn even more about her tastes once we visited it together.

As she finally drifted off to sleep, I reflected how much I had loved the time on safari and might even want to work in South Africa on a safari team. The whole YPO university and safari afterward had impacted my life in unexpected ways: the amazing and impactful Nelson Mandela, the power and feel of this country on the very tip of an extraordinary continent, and all the wildlife in community with each other.

Gazing up at the night sky, I realized that it was every bit as black—and the stars every bit as bright—as it had been in Papua New Guinea or Maui. As I pondered both countries, it seemed that so much of the primitive nature in Papua New Guinea related to the humans, with their tribes—in just the last generation—emerging from cannibalism. South Africa was primitive too, but more because of its animals and their interactions with each other.

It occurred to me that South Africa had experienced longer contact with civilization, starting in the thirteenth century when the Dutch had explored and mapped the country as part of their efforts to create a new Silk Road route to China via the Cape of Good Horn. As I mused about how many of these unusual species they had seen in the process of their discoveries, sounds from outside the camp caught my attention: the grunting of hippos, howling of hyenas, and fading roar of a lion followed by what I thought was a very low hum, which Alex said was the way giraffes communicate—so maybe the lion had been stalking them?

The nighttime scenery and sounds all seemed to reveal the amazing God to whom I was growing closer again—but on a much larger scale than ever before. My project assignments in Europe, Mexico, Asia, and now Africa *so* gave me a sense of being on divine adventures, but this safari seemed to have enhanced my concept of God as being an exotic Being in addition to everything else I had thought of Him. He had created such an astounding world, and I was just now getting to know it.

Chapter 10

Bellissima Firenze!

I stood riveted to the spot, gazing upward at the most glorious male body I had ever laid eyes upon. Absolutely nothing was left to the imagination—from the taut muscular chest to the perfectly chiseled manhood on display between his powerful thighs.

"What are you staring at, Kris?" my co-worker Dennis asked in a teasing tone of voice.

I blushed. I couldn't deny my secret fascination with a certain part of the anatomy exhibited in such precise detail. But every inch of Michelangelo's fourteen-foot-high, massive marble *David* held me spellbound, and I had to break my concentration on it to step closer to a curator as he explained the creative process of the most magnificent statue in the world.

He started by explaining that the original block of marble (they called it "the giant") had been imported to Florence in 1464 from the Mediterranean coast to be sculpted into a Biblical character and hoisted high on display in one of the Cathedral of Florence's niches.

Two artists rejected the block for fear that its many imperfections made it unstable, so the marble lay neglected in the cathedral courtyard for twenty-five years. But in 1501, a twenty-six-year-old Michelangelo, already one of the best-known and paid artists of that time, was asked to take on the project. He did so enthusiastically, working in secret for two years to fashion his extraordinary statue of David. Unlike most artists of the period who depicted triumphant heroes after their victory, Michelangelo produced a revolutionary take on David by imagining him just *before* his legendary battle with Goliath. His creation produced a youthful shepherd standing relaxed but confident in a classic *contrapposto* position—his weight resting on the right leg with his left leg slightly forward as he turns his head to concentrate on the upcoming test.

While listening to all of this, I realized that what captivated me most in the curator's story was that Michelangelo tossed the slingshot so casually over David's shoulder that it is almost invisible—emphasizing the Scripture's point that it was not force that David was relying on, but courage born of his faith in God.

I was standing in front of *David* because the opening cocktail party for this next university I was working, the Florence University, was being held in the Gallerie dell'Accademia, home of Michelangelo's masterpiece and many other incredible works of Renaissance art. Studying the statue more closely after listening to the curator made me think about the wealth of breathtaking art, architecture, and paintings on display wherever I turned in this amazing city. At times, its visual splendor sent me into the sensory overload that causes many who visit the city to suffer "Stendhal Syndrome."

I had learned about this syndrome from one of our university newsletters—according to which the affliction was a sort of "art attack" that causes a psychosomatic disorder resulting in a fluttering heart, dizziness, and—in some cases—fainting. The nineteenth-century French author Henri-Marie Behle, whose pen name was Stendhal, had experienced this effect after first seeing Giotto's famous ceiling frescoes in the Santa Croce Cathedral in Florence. In his diary he admitted to a sort of ecstasy from the idea of being in Florence, and as he contemplated all the sublime beauty, he reached the point where he encountered celestial sensations that caused him heart palpitations. "Life was drained from me," he recalled. "I walked with the fear of falling."

It appeared that since that time there had been hundreds of cases of people suffering those same effects, particularly after visiting the Uffizi Gallery. As enthralled as I was by *David* and the other breathtaking art I had seen thus far, I hadn't quite yet fallen prey to what natives of Florence call "Tourist's Disease."

Next I walked 200 yards down the narrow street to the site of our opening dinner at the charming fifteenth-century Pillazo Gerini, considered the most impressive palace in Florence for its valuable oil paintings, beautiful furniture, and heavy tapestries. The venue had been decorated *Carnevale* style with masks on the dining tables. Flames danced on top of elaborately curved table candelabras while guests wandered around to find available dinner seats in various rooms of the mansion.

On the way up the stairs to the Palazzo, I saw Susan, project manager for this university, speaking with one of the organization's upcoming global presidents, Amir. The two hadn't seen each other since a few months earlier when they had done some initial planning for a split-location university he had requested: Cairo and Jerusalem. She had shared with us that during that visit—while inspecting some of the potential desert venues—a fellow Arab had approached Amir to offer seventy camels in exchange for her. As he graciously talked the gentleman out of the offer, Susan stood to the side—somewhat stunned by this development—and decided to stay close to Amir's side for the rest of their trip.

I found this story incredulous, but Susan had told it in her usual understated and humorous manner—qualities which made everyone who worked with her love her, including me. I was serving as crew at this university and again helping with off-site activities but had also volunteered to work at social events. As I walked around dinner tables to see if I could help anyone, an Indian couple motioned me over and asked, "Are there no vegetarian plates? We are Hindu. We do not eat meat."

That night's menu featured the finest Italian cuisine but apparently vegetarian options hadn't been included. Assuring them I would do what I could, I pulled aside a red-faced waiter huffing and puffing as he headed toward the kitchen. "A couple is asking about vegetarian plates." I asked him. "Do we have any?"

"Vegetarian plates?" he responded, seemingly baffled. "I do not think so. Let me see what I can find." He disappeared into the kitchen but did not return, and none of the other wait staff seemed willing to help. Circling back to the Indian couple's table, I noticed them nibbling at the mozzarella, leaves of basil, and tomato slices in their caprese salad—and unrolling the prosciutto from their roasted asparagus. At least they had found a few things they could eat.

To make it up to them, from that night forward I made Naresh and his wife, Sonal, part of my "special attention" list. When passing them in the hallway or at a social event, I asked how they were doing; I slid little notes under their door asking about their day; and I reminded them to contact me if they needed anything. In general, I took special care of them.

As the university progressed that week, I kept discovering Florence as unlike any other place I had been before. The intimacy of the city—its beauty and history of fashion, food, architecture, art, noble families—all came together in an amazing way. One of the more interesting YPO members in the Italy chapter was an American woman named Anastazia, who had agreed to be the social chairman for the university. Based on relationships she had established over the years with local upper-crust society, she was able to gain access into some otherwise private venues for off-sites and parties.

I felt a special connection with Anastazia because, like me, she was a military "brat." Her father had met and married a Roman woman while being stationed in Italy during World War II, so she had grown up visiting relatives in both Europe and the States. While studying art history and architecture at a top-notch Boston university, she spent a year abroad and took a course in Florence where she met her Venetian/Siennese husband. Together, they had formed *The Top in the Country*, a travel company using his family connections to arrange fabulous accommodations at private Italian villas and exclusive excursions to churches and museums.

Thanks to them, there were so many fabulous off-sites available during this university that I wished I could be a part of all of them: private tours through the Uffizi and other art galleries; wine tastings; biking in the countryside, trips through churches and cathedrals; listening to Gregorian chants; trips to food markets with top-notch chefs; and even a day set apart for full-day trips to Rome, a yacht club on the northern coast, the Ferrari factory, the Tuscan countryside, or medieval and renaissance towns.

It was especially fun for me to be around Anastazia because she could relate to both Americans and Italians. All the YPO staff had liked working with her during the planning process because of her simplicity and approachability, and she was the same way during the university. Oftentimes she would join us for meals where she would explain various things on the menu. During one dinner she introduced me to truffles, and I instantly fell in love with their nutty, oaky, earthy taste.

Listening to her explain why they were such a gourmet delicacy made them that much more intriguing. Truffles had first been written about as far back as 200 BC and were also referenced by Romans, peasants, and Papacy in the Middle Ages. During the Renaissance they were adopted into French cuisine, and to my surprise, I learned that hunters used pigs to sniff them out around the roots of trees. In the nineteenth century truffles began to be cultivated and widely grown, but during the two world wars many of the tree roots around which they grew died or fell into decay. What had become a common food item in Europe prior to those years became much rarer, so they were now considered delicacies.

When one was first shaved over my butter and pasta, I was surprised to see that they were actually quite ugly and black, and for that reason, easily recognizable as a part of the fungus family. Since I wasn't paying the bill for my meals in Florence, however, I didn't realize how expensive they were and made a habit of ordering them at every meal.

I was learning during this university that I loved *any* food in Florence and was determined when I went home to expand my love of making homemade Italian sauces into a love of making homemade pastas as well. I had never seen people in any culture eat as slowly as the Italians, but it was clear everyone here wanted to enjoy their food. Anastazia told us that the "slow food" movement here had arisen just after she moved to Italy—in response to McDonald's and other fast-food American restaurants coming to the country. What Italians defined as "slow food" was called "farm to table" in California. Either way, the idea was to take time to enjoy food as an important part of life.

Walking from my hotel to the *Palazzo Congressi*—where all the education sessions were being held and many off-sites had their starting point—was always an interesting experience. The Arno River flowed past downtown and as I passed several open marketplaces, I noticed belts and scarves for sale. My co-worker Candy was the education manager for the Florence University, and on our trips around the world—as well as social events in Dallas—I had always admired the beautiful scarves she wore. When I asked how she had gotten into them, she reminded me of her semester abroad during college and jobs in some European art galleries after graduation.

"Scarves are a European thing, and you can get them everywhere here," she said. "Italy is arguably the fashion capital of Europe—

though it used to be Paris. Surely you have heard of Ferragamo shoes and scarves?" She talked about the Ferragamo business being headquartered in Florence, and their family members belonging to the YPO. Wanda Ferragamo, who in 1960 (at the age of thirty-eight) had taken over her husband's business when he died and left her with six children, was to be one of the hostesses for the "Tea with the Great Women of Florence" off-site later in the week.

I made a mental note of this as my thoughts turned to tonight's cocktail party on the landmark *Ponte Vecchio* bridge. The medieval stone, closed-spandrel arch bridge had been designed by the Dominican Friars with their sense of symmetry and harmony. Tonight it was closed to the public for a YPO cocktail party so members could privately browse the beautiful jewelry and artisan shops situated along its passageway. After that, they would be sent off to chosen restaurants around the city and one of our crew duties was to get that organized and executed.

I had learned that the *Ponte Vecchio* was the only bridge in Florence spared by the Germans during WWII. First referenced in the 10th century as a defensive structure, it had been rebuilt several times after flooding and eventually had shifted to housing tanners, blacksmiths, and butchers until the sixteenth century. At that point, a private passageway was built on top of the bridge to accommodate royalty's access between the Uffizi and the new Palazzo Pitti. But the smells wafting up to the passageway from below were so foul that the merchants were evolved to eventually allow only artisans and jewelers—which made the area more aromatically acceptable. It was a very romantic place to stroll and shop and became even more so when the lowered lights of the evening made the windows and doors across the bridge appear like suitcases and wooden chests.

My boss, Ron, was also crew for this university, and we agreed to meet up on the bridge with our next university chairman, Matthew, before doing our duty of getting everyone sent off to their restaurant choices. Matthew was hosting one of the off-sites at this university and told us he could share some interesting information

159

about the Ponte Vecchio—plus, we could talk about what he was learning from this university to apply to his upcoming university in Washington DC.

A Dallas YPO member from a prominent Texas family, Matthew had recently taken a year's sabbatical with his family in Florence— which was how he ended up helping with off-sites at this university. His father had served as a Texas senator after returning from WWII and starting an uber-successful insurance company, and Matthew and his siblings were successful in their own rights, too. His older sister Donna was married to a YPO member who had run one of his father-in-law's South American businesses and who had recently been on the YPO global board. She and Matthew had also started an investment fund and were both active in global education and charities—while their other sister was involved with finance in another capacity.

When Ron and I met that evening, we ran into Don Camp who was running around the bridge like mad taking pictures. Don asked us to pose for a photo, then leaned in toward me and whispered, "Interested in a photo shoot around the city tomorrow?"

I smiled, thinking back to our adventure in South Africa, then gave him a nod with a reminder to call me by placing my pinky and thumb against the side of my head. As Ron and I started to stroll, Susan walked toward us with Amir, along with Wanda Ferragamo and her son Ferrucio. Alessandro Pucci, whose father was another Florentine who had started a global fashion business, also walked up in his smoking slippers, leaving Ron and me to wonder how his feet handled the cobblestone streets in those soft-soled shoes.

As they got closer, Ron stopped to join their group and I stood with him for a few minutes, standing still but wanting to look into the shop windows. While everyone was talking, Matthew and his wife—along with a former global president, Bill, and his wife— joined our little crowd, and Bill maneuvered his way to my side. "Enjoying the university, Kris?"

"It's been busy, but good." I replied. "I'd like to wander around the bridge a bit before we send everyone off to their chosen restaurant."

He stepped closer. "You have been pretty busy here. Why don't you wander the bridge with me for a few minutes?" he asked, beckoning me with his eyes and motioning me to step out from the little crowd with him. He then waved at his wife, letting her know he was moving on.

Bill was always very friendly—whether I ran into him at the Dallas office in governance meetings or at any number of recent universities—and I always enjoyed our conversations. His experiences at Culver Military Academy, his time at Trinity University, and his company history gave us several things about which we could chat: the military, his adventures around San Antonio, his equipment company, or what he appreciated about YPO.

His grandfather and father had started the family equipment company and he had been a YPO global president, so it was always interesting to hear his perspective on our events. His wife had her share of friends, and I had noticed that he often left her by herself to socialize while making his own rounds. As we peered further into the artists and their stores, Bill pointed out intricate pieces of jewelry he liked and asked my opinion. I looked back at Rob, Matthew, and the group—remembering our original plans—but could barely see them now. Leaning over intimately, Bill suddenly asked, "Can I buy you a gift, Kris?"

I was taken aback. What would his wife say? But based on the way he was acting he seemingly didn't think twice about his offer. As I stood there not knowing how to respond, I noticed his wife coming toward us. She gently took his arm to lead him away to another YPO couple, and they walked further down the bridge.

Uncertain about what Bill meant by his offer, I went back to Ron who was still chatting with the group. Since he still didn't seem ready to walk around, I decided to explore the various shops on my own. At one window, an intricate hairpin caught my eye and I stepped inside to examine it more closely. The artisan asked if I wanted to try it on, and after we set it in my hair, I realized what a lovely antique it was. As I was admiring it on myself, I saw Bill wander back by with his wife and I flashed him a smile. He moved on—as did I—and Ron met up with me in the launching area just in time to send everyone off toward their restaurants.

Amidst it all, I saw Bill again leave his wife and head back to the bridge, then watched him duck into the shop where I had been. He seemed to take a moment there talking to the artisan, then I saw his eyes get large for a moment and he walked away, throwing me a resigned look as he jumped onto the bus leaving for his restaurant. Had he gone there to see about buying that hairpin for me? It was quite expensive—and I certainly hadn't expected it—though it did make me realize how thoughtful and kind he was. However, I obviously couldn't have accepted a gift along those lines. It did make me feel a bit special, though, and I wondered if this was part of Bill's charm.

I thought about the incident as I walked all the way back to my hotel, reflecting on men and where I was in terms of romantic relationships. Down deep, I still was not over Greg—and I increasingly sensed this lack of closure might be holding me back from a new romance that would bring me happiness.

During the rest of the university, I began to feel the strong influence of the fashion industry in Florence. When Candy was not handling the education program and had time to talk, we discussed scarves. She had already made a point of wearing them almost daily and shared that the *haute couture* industry had been born here due to Italian elegance and prices that were more competitive than Paris. I had always assumed Milan was the fashion capital of Italy, but now knew that Florence had produced four of Italy's most renowned designers: Gucci, Capucci, Ferragamo, and Pucci.

Every day I enjoyed strolling the markets—going to and from my hotel—especially the San Lorenzo and Porcellino Markets with their fabulous fashion wares. By the end of my stay, I had splurged on a handsome black patent leather wallet, a cream braided leather belt, and a lovely brown and red scarf with fox hunting scenes. I had a few rarely-used *Talbots* scarves at home, and decided that I would incorporate them more into my wardrobe after watching Italian women's examples all over the city.

Candy further encouraged my growing interest in fashion by inviting me to the afternoon tea with Mrs. Ferragamo, held at their company headquarters in the thirteenth century Palazzo Spini Feroni. One of her topics of discussion was scarves (was this why Candy had sent me this way?): wearing them with sweaters, tying them on purses, using them as headscarves—Mrs. Ferragamo gave many ideas. I found her an interesting, elegant woman whose family loved Florence and had invested their appreciation of classical beauty in everything the business did. My admiration increased as she shared the story of how she had taken over her husband's company and grown it worldwide.

Ferrucio, the son who had been running and diversifying the business for the last twelve years since his mother stepped down as president (though she still came to work every day), intrigued me as well. He and Anastazia were friends based on their love of restoring monuments in Florence. Today he was taking all of us attending the tea on a private tour through the Ferragamo Shoe Museum. He shared how his father had purchased this palace in 1938 to headquarter his business and how they had recently opened the museum in its basement.

During our tour, I saw Don Camp in the museum snapping pictures and realized he hadn't called me yet—so when we both got back to the *Palazzo Congressi* I walked over to his desk. After arranging a lot of his pictures, he looked up and abruptly looked at his watch. "I forgot about our photo shoot, Kris! Can I pick you up in an hour?"

After making sure I wasn't required anywhere else for work, I ran to my room and changed—throwing on a classic navy sweater with one of my new scarves—then waited outside for Don. When we zipped away on his red Vespa with me sitting behind him, I felt like Audrey Hepburn in *Roman Holiday*. Don knew all the right spots to take a great shot: looking down on the city and Il Duomo from across the Arno; on an intimate cobblestone street with my arms raised in a welcome position; lying on the ledge of a bridge with the Ponte Vecchio in the background; sitting on his Vespa with the Santa Maria del Fiore complex behind me; standing in front of the Palazzo Vecchio with its copy of the *David* statue. It was the perfect finish to a fantastic trip that had been full of fine art, food, fashion, and a fun photo shoot. All that was missing was *amore!*

Chapter 11

The Heart of Mother

A man lay face down on the street sprawled next to a crashed motor scooter. Our taxi slowed momentarily, swerved around him, and sped on. My co-worker Candy and I strained to look back, but to our horror the rest of the traffic followed suit. That poor man could be run over—shouldn't someone stop to help him, or at least get him out of the road? We didn't see any police cars or even an ambulance headed toward him.

Observing our faces in the rearview mirror, our taxi driver bobbled his head in a circle, and in a distinct Indian accent explained, "Ma'ams, why stop when you see these things? We have too many people not to let some die. It is less mouths to feed and more space for others."

He waited for us to acknowledge our understanding, but this was our first encounter with the chaotic streets of India and the famous "Indian head bobble." So, we just sat there—too shocked to respond.

I had not been looking forward to this university in Bombay, India, as I had heard so much about its poverty. On the other hand, who was I to complain given my recent trips to Florence, Italy, with its art and architecture, and South Africa with my exposure to Nelson Mandela and experience of amazing animals in the wild. But judging by this incident on the streets of Bombay, the poverty rumors seemed to be true.

A few days after receiving this assignment, I had been with a close girlfriend who just happened to be a Delta flight attendant and just might have been on a flight with Greg. She had been hearing me again bemoan the loss of my relationship with him—along with the details of the latest love interest in my life that wasn't working out. After I finished all my complaining, she had sweetly given me a Mother Teresa daily calendar.

Thumbing through the pages and reading her inspirational quotes, I had been struck with admiration for this remarkable Christian woman. Then, suddenly I had realized: Mother Teresa was in India. *I would try to volunteer for her while I was there.* But after exploring every avenue possible, I ended up downcast; her Missionaries of Charity organization in Calcutta required a minimum volunteer period of two months, and my job wouldn't allow me that much time off. So, I had finally given up on the idea and agreed instead to join my co-workers on a tour of northern India after the university ended.

Now, ten months later, I was arriving in Bombay—the commercial capital of India and the sixth most populous city in the world. Stepping off the plane, I sensed an aura different from any other I had experienced in my world travels. Everything felt distinctly "Eastern" and "exotic," yet simultaneously "Western" and "civilized." Thinking about this cultural mélange, I concluded it was the product of the country's rich history: India had birthed Hinduism and Buddhism, and by 2000 BC, Bombay was a center for both sects. Islam then reached the country around AD 700 and was introduced into Bombay in the 1300s.

166

Two centuries later, the Portuguese won control of the city and brought Catholicism. In the mid-nineteenth century, the British took control and remained a strong influence until granting India its long-desired independence in the 1940s. Studying my surroundings, it seemed those 4000 years of Eastern culture and religion interacting with 400 years of Western culture and religion accounted for the impression Bombay was making on me at first glance.

The remaining forty minutes of our taxi ride presented more disturbing scenes; more poverty, trash, and masses of people everywhere were appalling. Seemingly endless cramped squares containing cardboard shacks lined the road, with children and adults living in them and women cooking on open fires. Curious as to the smell, I rolled the window halfway down and stuck my nose out. The scent of incense and curry mingled with fetid trash was so offensive that Candy asked me to close the window. As the two of us discussed what we were seeing, the driver interrupted, "Misses, those are their homes."

The whole thing seemed unreal. How could people survive on the streets without any shelter? As we drove along, mothers thrust their infants into the front of taxi windows, begging for money or food. At the same time, I was distracted by the beauty of the women's saris—in every imaginable color and design—draped so gracefully over their bodies. Their wardrobe was a stark contrast to all the poverty and filth.

A few minutes later, the landscape began to change as we turned onto a wide avenue looking out on an immense bay. "This is Marine Drive," Candy informed me, noting that real estate prices along the esplanade were supposed to be the fourth-most expensive in the world. I had read before I came that this storied section of Bombay contained a lot of "art deco" architecture favored by the wealthy *Parsis* who had emigrated from Persia in 1920s and 30s. Locals had nicknamed this boulevard the "Queen's Necklace" because when seen at night from any elevated point along the drive, the layout of the streetlights resembled a string of pearls. As we motored along the drive, it was clear there were no beggars or cardboard shanties—just the homes of wealthy businesspeople and Indian movie stars.

After checking into the ultra-modern Oberoi Hotel, I went straight to bed because the next morning I had to begin the massive job of receiving and unpacking the conference materials followed by preparing for the registration and opening party on Sunday. After breakfast I contacted the freight manager, only to have him inform me there had been no shipment of materials. Stunned, I listened as he insisted it would be best for us to go to the customs office with my paperwork showing that my shipment had been delivered to Bombay which would allow them to locate it. I had never been to a customs office before, but it seemed I had no choice. I had to find a way to get this shipment delivered to our hotel. Everyone was counting on me.

The hotel van took us to a large Victorian building, and then the freight manager escorted me to a room with a counter behind iron bars. He spoke rapidly in Hindi to the agent, then asked me to show my papers. After the two talked rapidly back and forth, the manager told me that the Customs office would have my shipment delivered, so we should return to the hotel.

I was not convinced. "I need some kind of confirmation. I will stay here."

"You really shouldn't…there isn't anything you can do."

"But I need to," I argued, "we can't have a conference without a shipment. Everyone will be upset if they don't get their supplies. I will feel better if I stay here and return to the hotel with the shipment."

He shrugged and headed back to the van. Watching him leave, I wondered if I'd made the right decision. The man behind the counter stared at me curiously, and then a few other men walked out. Starting to feel uncomfortable, I decided to step back out of the office. As I walked up and down the hallway, I peeked into a few other offices and suddenly realized there were no women

168

in the building. But I was in dire need of my shipment, so I was going to stay put. An hour later, I asked for an update but was told they didn't have one—and that I should return to the hotel. I again refused to leave, but another hour later brought the same response, so I finally gave up and went back to the hotel.

Lunch was just ending when I arrived. Fortunately, Ron was the only one there—as he had sent everyone else out on a tour. After giving him an update, the two of us brainstormed about any contacts among our local YPO members who might be able to help, but no one came to mind. The rest of the day, I received no updates from either the shipping company or customs, and during the staff dinner I was assaulted by questions: "What's the holdup? You have done this many times before…why can't you handle it now? Kris, you know we all need our supplies to get ready. We only have three days before everything starts." I tried to explain, but no one was in the mood to listen.

The next two days I spent at the Customs office, where I got tired of hearing, "Ma'am, go back to the hotel. We will find it and bring it to you." They tried as best they could to ignore me, but I stood my ground, feeling like a sore thumb since I was the only female in the facility. Experience had taught me that waiting for something in person usually made it happen more quickly, but that wasn't seeming to be the case here.

Tensions on the team escalated—so I stayed away from all meals and social gatherings. At the end of the second full day at Customs, Ron brought the YPO international president over to show him that there wasn't anything else that could be done. But that didn't seem to help—as left more agitated than when he had arrived.

Friday, I was once again back at Customs. After a few hours, one of the men behind the desk motioned to me. "We think we have found your shipment. Go back to your hotel, please. It will be sent there."

I lost my temper and raised my voice. "I am not leaving without my shipment! You don't understand. Our conference starts Sunday morning. We have 300 international CEOs, wives, and speakers arriving, and they expect everything to be ready."

The men stared at me with their mouths open. Just then, Candy appeared with an excited look. "Kris, the shipment is here. The truck just pulled up and Ron sent me to get you." Relieved, I jumped into the cab with her and said a prayer of thanksgiving. This had been the most stressful experience in my four years at YPO, but at least it was now resolved. Once we returned, the breakdown and delivery process went smoothly—with everyone pulling together as we worked through the night. Amazingly, we were ready by the time registration officially opened on Sunday morning.

The event then proceeded smoothly, much to my relief, and during breaks I escaped the stress by strolling along the Queen's Necklace and watching the serene blue waves of the Arabian Sea. As I walked along, I thought again about the Landmark Forum and what Candy had said about it helping her work through some life issues. My research on its webpage told me that I would need to have a key life goal chosen in order to attend the event. Maybe mine should be moving on in my romantic life? Various reviews gave the organization good and bad feedback, but mostly everyone said it made an impact on their life.

My thoughts also pondered Mother Teresa and how it might have been interesting to work with her here. On the other hand, I could see how it would be a little scary given the poverty everywhere. But at least I had plans to visit a few other key areas of India, and felt it would be interesting—if nothing else.

One day during a lull between presentations, I heard someone speak my name.

"Kris," said the Indian-accented voice excitedly, "You are here?"

I turned around to see Naresh and Sonal, the Indian couple I had helped in Florence. We exchanged kisses, and after chatting a few minutes, Naresh offered, "Kris, you were so kind to us, so we would like to do something kind for you. Will you have tea with us at our home?"

Naresh saw me hesitate.

"We live only five minutes' walk from here. Why don't you come before the closing event on Friday? Sonal will dress you in one of her beautiful saris, and you can wear it to the party."

I thought for a moment about how walking into the event in a genuine sari might set off some staff gossip, but rapidly decided it was worth the risk. When else might I get this opportunity? "I would be honored," I told them.

The upcoming visit with Naresh and Sonal motivated me through all the hard work the rest of the week, and when Friday afternoon arrived I headed out along the Queen's Necklace. Following their directions, I arrived at the door of a square house—not overly large or elaborately decorated—but far above the Bombay standards I had been seeing everywhere.

Sonal warmly greeted me. "First, we must find you a sari," she said.

Taking me to her closet, she opened the door, and my eyes widened. All of her saris were delicate, hand-woven, and hand-decorated, some fashioned of regal purples and made of silk; one was bright filmy yellow chiffon; still another sari shimmered in bronze satin with intricate red patterns sewn into the fabric. They were all so lovely I couldn't make up my mind, but Sonal noticed my eyes drawn to the bronze and red sari and pulled it out. After taking ten minutes to layer and wrap the sari around my body, she expressed her satisfaction. "It is perfect. My husband will approve."

We proceeded to a sitting room where their servant had tea waiting, and lowering ourselves to the floor, assumed a lounging position. Sonal poured masala chai: black tea leaves boiled with milk and various Indian herbs and spices. I wanted to pinch myself. Was I really in Bombay—sipping chai—wrapped in an elegant sari?

As we sipped our tea, I asked Sonal about her background. "I grew up in Calcutta," she explained. "Then my marriage was arranged, and I moved here to join my husband."

Calcutta? That is where Mother Teresa worked...maybe Sonal had some connections.

"I have been trying to find a way to volunteer with Mother Teresa but been unsuccessful because of how much time they want," I confided. "Would you have any way to help me?"

She looked at me, as if surprised by my question. "Mother Teresa? My father is her bookkeeper! If you fly to Calcutta, my parents can pick you up at the airport and will introduce you to her. You can stay for as long or short a time as you want."

I got goose bumps. Sonal had responded so casually—as if it were nothing—when to me it was everything. But what would I do about the staff trip I had committed to after the conference? Should I pull out of it? Deciding didn't take long, as meeting Mother Teresa was far more important to me than seeing the Taj Mahal. "Sonal, let's make it happen," I said, smiling enthusiastically.

After joining the YPO party that evening, I approached one of my co-workers, Jeanne. "I've found a way to volunteer for Mother Teresa after the university is over. But I also committed to join the management team on the other trip throughout India. What should I do?" Jeanne was also planning to travel with the team, but I knew she was a devout Catholic and thought she might understand my dilemma.

"Are you serious? Volunteering with Mother Teresa?"

"Yes. Do you want to go with me?"

"Wow...what an opportunity. But—Kris, we promised to be a part of the other tour."

"I know, Jeanne, but this is Mother Teresa."

At that moment, a trumpeting sound caught our attention. Wheeling around, we were astonished to see enormous elephants, topped by Indian women covered in jewels, being led into the party. The elephants were draped in bright, silk cloths and their ankles wrapped with tinkling bells. The handler motioned for them to kneel—then as the women stepped off, YPO members crowded around.

I heard a voice to my side and turned to find Ramesh, the university's social chairman. All his parties had been showpieces based on his role in the Indian movie industry, but this one was over the top. Standing next to him was his wife, Sybel, and the American actress Demi Moore. She had come to Bombay with her mentor Deepak Chopra, who had interviewed her for yesterday's keynote talk. Afterward, the Bhojwanis had taken Demi shopping—which probably accounted for her presence with them tonight.

I smiled at Demi and said hello. We had met at a party the previous evening while having mehndi (temporary henna-painting of intricate designs) done on our hands. Her hands still looked freshly painted, and she was a stunning picture in a gorgeous sari with her long, black hair swept back to display a small jewel on her forehead.

Naresh and Sonal then walked up to our group. After saying hello to Ramesh and Sybel and being introduced to Demi, Naresh turned to me. "Sonal did a very nice job at dressing you," he said with approval. "Do you like the sari? And I hear you might be going to Calcutta."

"Yes," I replied excitedly. "What a wonderful surprise about Sonal's father! I had searched for months for a way to meet Mother Teresa to no avail, and now this happens. You have both been so thoughtful to me."

They moved on, and I continued to wander the party, stopping to study *Mallakhamba*—a traditional Indian sport that blended gymnastics, yoga, and wrestling grips with hanging ropes or stationary poles. Watching the death-defying gymnastics, I saw men climbing poles and balancing on top of them—or horizontally stacking themselves high off the ground while using their legs and feet to hold onto the pole behind them. The party was still in full swing when I decided to leave to get some sleep. The entire day had been such a wonderful excursion into Indian culture, and after unwrapping myself from the sari, I drifted off to sleep, thinking of meeting Mother Teresa.

The next morning, Jeanne pulled me aside to say that she wanted to volunteer for Mother Teresa with me—so now I had an ally in pulling out of the staff trip.

Once we resolved the issue with the staff, the day's pack-up work seemed effortless, and that night the venue for the staff closing party was the university chairman's home in another part of the city.

After I arrived, Ramesh and Sybel discreetly pulled me over to a corner. "Kris, you know that we're involved with Indian filmmaking. Tonight there is a special evening for the industry, and we're leaving soon to attend. Would you like to come with us?"

Flattered, I said yes—and during the car ride over, Ramesh explained more about the Bombay film industry. "It is called 'Bollywood' because that stands for Hollywood and Bombay combined." According to him, the Indian film business had started back in 1913 but in the last decade had taken the lead over Hollywood in film production. "Most of our films are done in Hindi," he explained, noting that they usually featured a love story with singing and dancing. "We used to film the singing and dancing in Kashmir, but now do that mostly in Austria and Switzerland. Every February, we also have our version of the Oscars—called the 'Filmfare Awards,'" he added. "This is the event where we are taking you."

A few minutes later, the car stopped and we stepped out into a mass of people—making our way close to the stage. A tall, handsome actor named Shah Rukh Khan, considered "King of Romance," started speaking about the 1995 film he starred in, *Dil-volley Doo-lanya Lay Ji-yeengay*, which was one of the highest-grossing Hindi films. Tonight, it had been nominated for ten different awards.

As a clip from the movie came up on the screen, I realized it was a love scene, but much more understated than American films. All the romance took place between the eyes. The male actor gazed at his lover with much desire, and she returned his look even more longingly. The music grew passionate. A minute or two of this continued, but with no kissing. The clip ended and the crowd cheered. Leaning over to Sybel, I asked, "Why was there no kissing in that scene?"

"Indian movies are like that. There are no passionate scenes. Everything takes place between the eyes of the lovers."

Thinking back over the last two weeks in Bombay, I had noticed an innocence to the people—as if they had not been hardened by exposure to graphic violence or sex. After a few more clips were shown and awards given, Ramesh said, "We'd better leave. The crowds will be crushing."

But it was too late. As I tried to follow Ramesh, the mass of people separated us and swept me along. Suddenly I lost sight of him and became panicked. Pressure from all the hot, sweaty bodies squeezed the air out of my lungs. Miraculously, a hand grabbed me and I realized it was Ramesh—who pulled me through the maddening crowd, out the gate, and into the car where Sybel was waiting. "Crowds can be so unpredictable in India," Ramesh said, shaking his head.

After they dropped me at the Oberoi, we said our goodbyes. I had come to love them and their graciousness to me. The movie crowd, though, had thrown me for a loop and I wanted to find someone to talk with about it. Then I thought about tomorrow's trip to Calcutta with Jeanne and realized our time on the flight would provide an opportunity—as well as get us set up for whatever adventure awaited us there. So, I headed up to my room, finished packing, and fell fast asleep.

The next afternoon we landed in Calcutta. As we picked up our luggage, we noticed many people standing, sitting, and lying outside the gates. But they did not appear to be there to greet anyone; they were all begging, and many appeared malnourished. The sight of so many human beings suffering like this tore at my heartstrings. Only a few hours before, I had been staying at a luxe hotel on the Queen's Necklace and rubbing shoulders with Bollywood movie stars decked out in gorgeous saris and jewels. Now I had entered a city known for its abject poverty and appalling slums.

Uncertain what to do, Jeanne and I looked around for Sonal's parents—then a short, older Indian couple approached us, introducing themselves as the Agarwallas. "We knew who you were straight away," they said with a smile. "You were the only white girls exiting the plane."

After a short drive to our destination, they parked across the street from the Motherhouse—the headquarters of Mother Theresa's Missionaries of Charity—and then walked us into the nearby Bely Guest House where they had booked us a room. Once we checked in, Jeanne and I went back over to the Motherhouse and promptly bumped into a handsome Brazilian priest in a frock. "*Olá*, ladies," he greeted us in a thick Portuguese accent, "Are you here to serve?"

We nodded. He introduced himself as Father Miguel and told us he'd been assigned to the mission for a month, then went on to explain the daily agenda. "We start by celebrating Mass at 6 am. After that is chai and breakfast, then assignments are given out. Mass is open to all, and I'll be leading it tomorrow. Will I see you there?"

Jeanne was accustomed to going to Mass, but it had been a while for me. Given my Catholic upbringing, I knew the rituals and could follow along. Plus, he was officiating, and I thought it would be worth it just to see him behind the altar. "We'll be there," we assured him.

We headed back to our room which wasn't exactly YPO standards, but—compared to the poverty surrounding us—was very comfortable. The next morning the sun was peeking over the horizon as we headed to the Motherhouse where we were hoping to catch a glimpse of Mother Teresa. We had been told she came to morning Mass if she was in town—and we knew she was here because the Agarwallas had promised to introduce her to us in the next day or two.

"Top of the mornin' to ya," a dark-haired woman seated next to us announced in a pronounced Irish brogue, "this must be your first day." We noticed she was one of the few non-habited people at Mass. Most everyone else was attired in a home-spun, blue-striped "Missionaries of Charity" sari. But before we could strike up a conversation, Father Miguel began the Mass.

Everyone seemed attentive despite the early hour, but we had a hard time concentrating. Our eyes scanned the room for the one person we most wanted to see, but we were disappointed to realize that Mother Teresa wasn't there. Halfway through the service, as Father Miguel asked for prayer requests, we heard the rustle of a sari. A voice spoke from the back of the room and turning quickly, we glimpsed the tiny figure of an older woman. Someone whispered, "That's her...Mother. She just walked in." We soon learned that everyone called Mother Teresa "Mother."

When the service ended, the Irish lady next to us again started talking. "This place is full of sisters, brothers, and volunteers," she said. "Those of us not of the cloth are 'volunteers' who stay for a few months." She noted that many volunteers were from Ireland. "They feel a special affinity with Mother because the first order of nuns she joined was in Ireland, and that order was instrumental in bringing her to India."

One of the nuns giving directions approached us. "Ah, you are Jeanne and Kris," she said, nodding. "I am Mother Teresa's head nun, and the Agarwallas asked me to watch for you. There are many places you can serve—the orphanage, tuberculosis sanitarium, leprosy colony, and a few other projects around the city." She paused a moment. "The Khalighat Home for the Dying is nearby, and they are always in need of help. Why don't you start there? I'll let the Agarwallas know that you'll be back in the afternoon."

We then followed another nun and as she led us to our assignment she explained the history of the home. "It's situated in an abandoned Hindu temple, and in 1952 Mother got permission to use it as a hospice. It houses destitute people without families who are in the last stages of AIDS, leprosy, malnutrition, cancer— almost anything—and allows them to die with dignity."

Following her up the front steps and into the building, we passed a man without any legs who was sitting on a cot and repairing woven cloth. He looked at us and smiled. From there, we were led down a hallway into a room filled with women lying on plastic-covered cots, most of whom were emaciated and too weak to move. Volunteers were turning them over or propping them up, and several women who had soiled themselves were being gently cleaned.

"Come over here," motioned a nun on duty. "Who are you, and why are you here?"

"We have been given this as our first day's assignment."

"Ah—you." she pointed to Jeanne, "Come help massage this woman's skin. Do you see how cracked it is? Most of these patients are in misery, and their bodies are dried up. Just rubbing oil into their skin will give them relief." Motioning to a woman who was clearly in pain, the nun poured oil into her hand and carefully rubbed it into the sole of the woman's foot.

Jeanne looked at me somewhat hesitant, but I was already being directed toward a woman who had just emptied her bowels. A volunteer gently shifted her sideways, taking a rag to wipe off her bottom. "Watch that volunteer clean her," the nun ordered me, "then see if you can find anyone else to help in the same manner."

I did as instructed and the morning passed quickly. In addition to massaging and cleansing the women's bodies, we cleaned floors. The method was simple: Throw water on the floor, mop it, then push it down the drains. Also, rugs had to be beaten. One of the nuns signaled us to do it, so we pulled the bulky, heavy rugs up the stairs to the roof and—throwing them over the wall—used wooden sticks to beat the dust and particles out of them. The sun was blazing and sweat poured off our bodies. Gazing down at the streets, however, we didn't see anyone else sweating—even though they were draped in layers of saris. Maybe they were just used to this oppressive heat?

By two o'clock we were exhausted. Another volunteer escorted us back to the Motherhouse, where we sat down to wait for the Agarwallas to finish their office work. A few minutes later, the door flew open, and Mother scurried by with a very purposeful air. Mr. Agarwalla poked his head out and asked, "Ladies, would you like to join us for a meal?"

Jeanne and I were so worn out that we forgot we hadn't eaten since breakfast—which seemed a lifetime ago. We eagerly agreed and hopped into their car for the short drive to their house, where they served us our first home-cooked Hindu meal. Vegetarian foods were placed in front of us, including dishes made from chickpeas, okra, and potatoes. There was also naan bread for dipping into spinach mixed with cream cheese and Indian spices. As the meal progressed, we followed the Agarwalla's example of eating with the right hand, using all but our pinky fingers.

While we ate, the Agarwallas explained their belief in eating only vegetarian meals. "How can we eat meat from a cow that, in another life, might be me or my brother?" they asked us. "Every living thing is just a form of energy that has been transposed from another form of energy. Reincarnation is very powerful!"

I listened intently, rejuvenated by the delicious meal. Curious, I ventured, "You are devout Hindus, and I know that your religion is different in many ways from Christianity. Yet, Mother is a Christian—how is it that you have become such close partners in this outreach?"

"We are more than partners...we are friends, and we greatly admire her work," they responded. "We respect each other and our religions, but we do not understand the Christian concept of 'prayer.' We have seen Mother pray for things and then they literally happen. It is very unusual."

Sensing a story or two coming on, I drank some tea, took another bite of naan, and settled in to listen.

The Agarwallas then related that twenty years before, there was a war in Sri Lanka and Mother's heart was broken for all the victims. "She told us she was going to visit the war zone and had asked her God to help her set up a refugee camp within a short time. We told her it could not happen, as these are the most bureaucratic countries in the world. She looked at us and said with great passion, 'My God answers my prayers.'" According to them, the next day she left, and while she was away, someone stopped by their home with medical supplies, asking if they knew anyone who could use them. "We were amazed at his offer—given what we knew about Mother and her prayers for a camp in Sri Lanka—and accepted on her behalf."

The Agarwallas continued their tale, telling us that when Mother returned to Calcutta, they went for their usual volunteer duty. While there, she shared that after she had arrived in the war zone, a military person approached her to say they were leaving the area but wondered if she could use their camp quarters. She immediately accepted. "We then shared how we had received medical supplies, to which she replied with a smile, 'I told you—my God answers my prayers.'"

Jeanne and I understood the "prayer" concept in general, but these extraordinary prayer requests were everyday life for Mother. Mr. Agarwalla then told us another story, saying that a few years later, just as they were leaving their house for their volunteer day, someone dropped off a large supply of tea bags. "We did not need them ourselves, so we took the bags with us. When Mother met us at the front door and saw what we were carrying, her eyes widened and filled with tears. 'How did you know the Mission was out of tea? I was just on my knees praying for God to send us some!'" Mr. Agarwalla shook his head, saying that he and his wife could not explain these unusual occurrences.

Later that afternoon, Jeanne and I followed the Agarwallas' suggestion to visit the Indian Museum. We discovered it was the oldest and largest museum in Asia, and its most prized possession was the ashes of the Buddha. This museum also housed one of the largest bug collections I had ever seen, and although the displays reminded me of the British Natural Museum, there was no air conditioning. How did everything stay so well preserved?

Leaving the museum, we explored the May-dan—Calcutta's largest park—on the way back to the nearest Metro station. We had been careful not to eat or drink anything off the streets, but the hot chai for sale was tempting. If it was boiled, could it be bad? We took the risk, enjoying its spiciness. Walking further, we came to the Park Street Metro stop. At its entry was posted Ghandi's list of seven sins:

Wealth without work
Pleasure without conscience
Knowledge without character
Commerce without morality
Science without humility

Worship without sacrifice
Politics without principle

I stopped to write them down. As I finished, Jeanne motioned for me because the subway was approaching. But when we started down the stairs, we heard a voice. "Ma'ams, do you want a ride?"

Turning, we saw a young man with a rickshaw behind him. We debated for a second. "Do you know where Mother Teresa's headquarters are?"

"Of course, ma'ams, and for you I charge only twenty rupees. I am a very good puller."

We quickly did the math, and realized he was offering his services for *fifty cents*. We climbed aboard, and he took off. Riding along, we could hear his hard breathing and feel his strong effort. The sound of his running on his two legs made a curious rhythm, and we could feel the vibration of his feet as they pounded the ground. As we exited the rickshaw, we both paid him five dollars and watched his eyes light up. This was more than he could make in several days—and would probably also pay the monthly rental fee on his rickshaw.

Before retiring that night, we stopped in at the Motherhouse to check tomorrow's assignment. Sister Mary Nirmala suggested we split our next day between the orphanage and leprosy colony. I loved children, so that part seemed perfect; but I had only heard about—but never been around—lepers.

The next morning after Mass and breakfast, we were on our way toward the orphanage when I felt a small sting on my arm. Looking down, I saw a purple splotch. Suddenly I felt another sting on the side of my head and saw red dripping down to my shoulder. Fearing that someone was shooting at me, I looked at Jeanne—only to see she also had colors splattered on her body.

Starting to worry, we caught sight of four boys laughing and pointing at us as they ran away. We chased them but they disappeared around a corner, and then we heard more shots coming from behind us. Stopping in confusion, we spun around and saw another crowd of boys taunting us. Frightened, we ran down an alley—but it turned into a dead-end and we were trapped. The boys chasing us were only ten or twelve years old, but it was clear they were enjoying their dominance in the situation. They began pushing against our bodies and touching us inappropriately.

Out of nowhere, a young man broke through the crowd. "Get away, get away!" he shouted as he shooed the boys off. Then he turned toward us. "You okay? Boys pretty wild, yes?" He spoke in broken English with an American accent but had a distinct air of authority. He had easily taken control of the boys, and it was clear they respected him.

Introducing himself as Robert, he explained that today was Holi, a religious spring festival celebrated by Hindus. "There are many rituals involved, but the main ones are lighting bonfires the night before, then chasing people the next day with colored and scented water or powders." He advised us we would need to be careful and change our clothes because we had so many stains on them.

We had been listening to him closely, but his comments on our appearance reminded us of our morning's assignment. Running back to change would give us even less time at the orphanage, so we decided to keep going. Besides, the orphans might appreciate all the colors. Thanking him for rescuing us, we then admitted that we were now lost.

"I know where the orphanage is," he said. "I'll take you there. I go every once in a while, but don't work there." As we followed, he told us that he had come to Calcutta six months before while on break from Dartmouth College and stayed, wanting to find a way to help. "The poverty of this place really overwhelms you," he sighed. "I just hang on the streets with the kids. There are a bunch of us living on Sudder Street in backpacker dorms a short walk from here. We all feel the same way about the city."

I asked if he planned to go back to Dartmouth.

"I don't know yet. I'm the fourth generation there, and my father expects me to finish and join his law firm. Right now, I just want to stay here and help."

Robert seemed lost and overwhelmed, trying to figure out his life. Maybe this was a way of rebelling against a wealthy upbringing and controlling parents? Or maybe he just had a sensitive heart and was trying to figure out how he could make a difference? I remembered reading that Mother had gotten her start in this city in somewhat of a similar way. For some reason, he piqued my curiosity, and I wanted to know more about him and where he was living.

He interrupted my thoughts by pointing out we had arrived at Sishu Bhavan—Mother's home for abandoned children. He was about to leave when I asked if he would mind showing us the Sudder Street dorm. Knowing that we were planning to visit the Leprosy Colony later that day, he offered to meet us back at our hotel around 1 pm and guide us to the train needed to get there— with a short detour to see his dorm on the way.

At the orphanage, we were greeted by a nun who led us to a room full of toddlers in cribs, with one adult attending to them all. The second they saw us, the children all stood up and stretched out their arms—desperately wanting our attention. The attendant motioned us toward them. Looking around, I glimpsed one tiny baby girl with haunted eyes clinging to the side of her crib. I reached down to pick her up and felt her melt into my arms as she lay her head on my shoulder. Jeanne chose another little girl, and as she picked her up the rest of the children began crying. They all so desperately wanted to be picked up; it was too much for my heart! I tried to put my little girl down to pick up another, but she clung tightly to me. I wondered how being abandoned like this would affect all these children as they went through life.

The nun came over and pulled the child from my arms. "You can see that it is very hard for me. There are twenty children in this room, and I am the only one to take care of them." I felt for her and for the children but didn't know what to say or do. The emotional pain of these little ones was so overwhelming. Jeanne gently reminded me that we needed to be at the leprosy colony soon, and that we still needed to clean up. Sadly saying goodbye, I wished I had time to come back here—but we were leaving tomorrow. I wondered if there was anything I could do that would even make a difference? It seemed impossible.

Rushing back to the hotel, we quickly showered and changed in preparation for our meeting with Robert. When we walked downstairs, he was there waiting. "The Ghandiji Prem Nivas Leprosy Centre is an hour outside the city," he informed us. "The train leaves every half hour, so we'll need to walk fast to get there if you still want to visit Sudder Street on the way."

He led us a few blocks away to a large section of cheaply advertised rooms. A few college kids were hanging about, and he told us that, like the families who lived and cooked on the streets, they had small "squares" they rented. Following him into his "square," we saw his sleeping bag set on it. I wondered how he lived in such a tiny space. But everyone here was living like this and seemed to really want to make a difference around them. It reminded me that this idealism to change the world was common among college students. We looked around for a moment, then followed him as he encouraged us to head toward the station.

Robert waited with us for the train, advising us to be aggressive about getting on and finding seats. "Everyone will be pushing and shoving; don't let them intimidate you." We heard a train whistle blow, and saw the engine approaching with people hanging out the doors and windows of all the cars. When it came to a stop, Robert helped us on board. Left on our own, we discovered the train was so packed that there wasn't a place to sit—so we stood. As the train slowly chugged away from the station, we noticed vendors pushing their way down the aisles selling hot tea and sandwiches.

185

We finished the ride in silence, deep in our own thoughts about what we might experience at the leper colony. The train arrived in Titagarh, and we stepped off, pushing our way through the crowd. Standing over to the side was a nun in the standard issue white sari with blue stripes. "Jeanne and Kris?" she asked. We nodded. "I'm Sister Mary Prima. Come this way."

As she led us toward a group of buildings, she explained the history of the Centre. "Years ago, there was much crime in this area, and Mother's heart went out to the lepers who were isolated here. So, she opened a mobile clinic for them, then added more and more buildings. After the city saw that her efforts were reducing the crime, it gave her a narrow strip of land that extended six miles along the railroad tracks." Sister Mary added that The Centre had now grown to house about 1000 lepers, 75 percent of whom were cured and worked at spinning, weaving, carpentry, tailoring, and making artificial limbs. The other 25 percent were in a separate area undergoing treatment.

Stopping in front of a gate, she rang a bell. A man in his mid-twenties came to the gate and let us in. "Hello, Svupun," she said. "How nice to see you at the entry. Are you taking a break?"

He nodded his head yes, smiling shyly, then looked at us. "This is Jeanne and Kris, and they've come for a tour."

He extended his hand, but I hesitated. I was pretty sure that leprosy wasn't communicable, but the "untouchable" stigma was still at the back of my mind. Sister Mary noticed and laughed—telling me not to worry—so I shook hands with him. "Swapan is one of our many success stories," she confided as we continued into the building. "He was cured and decided to stay, and even married another cured patient. He now runs our weaving division, which is a big responsibility since we make all the cloth used by our Order around the world. That includes clothing, bedding, towels, curtains…everything."

186

As we walked through the facility, we saw people concentrating on their tasks. Many of them stopped to look at us curiously, so we smiled at them and were happy to see them smile back. After our tour of the production center, we sat down with Sister Mary for a tea break. "Why did we only see healthy people?" I asked. "Where are the others still being treated?"

"They are in the clinic, which is off-limits to all but staff and patients," she replied. "In addition to them, we have many others who come to have their wounds dressed and receive medication. I hate to rush you, but we need to get you back to the station. The trains get packed very quickly, and you soon won't even be able to get on."

During the trip home, we could barely stand. It was unbearably hot, and the smell of body odor mingling with strong overtones of curry overwhelmed our Western noses. Bare bodies pressed against ours, as many of the commuters were shirtless. The journey seemed endless as the train kept making stops.

When the train finally pulled into our station, we tried to step forward but found ourselves stuck in the crowd. It reminded me of the situation at the Bombay movie awards with Ramesh. Feeling alarmed, we began to push and shove our way toward the exit—and barely made it onto the platform as the train began to take off. Hearts pounding, we turned to each other and breathed a sigh of relief. We no sooner entered the lobby of the Bely Guest House that we were given a message from the Agarwallas asking us to come to the Motherhouse as soon as possible.

Filled with anticipation, we rushed to meet them—and found them at the front door waiting for us. "Come. Now is your chance to meet Mother." They led us into the lobby, where several American journalists and other guests were standing around. Scanning the room for Mother, we saw her over to the side talking with some of her nuns. When she saw the Agarwallas, she walked over. She was so tiny, hunched over, and looked older than her eighty-five years.

Her face was a mass of wrinkles, but her sparkling eyes commanded attention, radiating intelligence and energy.

"These are your two guests?" Her words carried a heavily Eastern European accent.

"Yes, Mother. This is Kris," the Agarwallas introduced me as I extended my hand to her in greeting.

"You're Hindu?" she said in surprise. "Your hands are painted with henna!"

I had forgotten about my painted hands. "No, ma'am, I'm Christian," I assured her. "They were painted at a social event with the Agarwallas' daughter last week."

Reaching into her pocket, she pulled out two Virgin Mary medallions. Praying a blessing over them, she placed them in my hand. "You'll need these."

She turned to meet Jeanne and it didn't take long for her to discover that she was a devout Catholic. She, too, was handed a medallion—but only one.

"Mother, may I take a picture of you with the girls?" asked Mr. Agarwalla.

She looked askance at him and reluctantly agreed. One of the nuns leaned toward another in surprise, and we overhead her say, "Mother doesn't like pictures. Why did she say yes?"

We weren't sure what to do, but Mr. Agarwalla pulled out his camera and motioned us toward her. One of the journalists standing nearby saw what was happening and stepped into the picture just as he was snapping the shot, then asked if she could have a copy. He firmly said no, making it clear that her behavior had been inappropriate.

Turning to Mother, Mr. Agarwalla thanked her and said he would see her in a few days. He and his wife then walked us back to our hotel and told us goodnight. We thanked them and gave them a hug—realizing that since we were leaving tomorrow, we might not see them again. I was so grateful for all they and their daughter had done for me.

My thoughts then shifted to Mother. I had felt a sense of "toughness" about her. She was a leader and very ambitious, evidenced by all she had achieved. In fact, she could have been a YPO member, given the 600 missions she had established in over 120 global locations, and the 4000 sisters who had joined her Order. But I hadn't felt very comfortable in her presence; rather "defensive" was more of my feeling, given the way she had challenged me about my mehndi without knowing how it came about. She had just seemed to assume I was Hindu.

In contrast, the psychiatrist Victor Frankl again came to mind, as his demeanor was gentle and accepting and his effect on me had been profound. To be fair, he hadn't lived his entire life around extreme difficulty—apart from his time in Auschwitz and Dachau. Mother had chosen to live a life of poverty among the physically suffering and set up her first facility as a place for dying people to be pulled off the streets. She met them with compassion and let them die with dignity, and she had been doing this now for decades.

Trying to draw a comparison, I decided that Mother's focus was on death, whereas Frankl's was on life. Mother didn't necessarily encourage people to stay alive—rather, she gave them a place to die and tried to make their final days comfortable. However, suicide prevention was one of Viktor Frankl's strongest passions—starting with his work in medical school with Austrian suicidal adolescents. Within two years, that suicide rate was reduced to zero and from that point forward, he worked on preventing suicide—even doing so in WWII prison camps. I wanted to ponder all of this but needed to think about it later when I had time. Everything right now was too overwhelming, and with so much poverty here in India I was still feeling it impossible for me to make a difference.

It then dawned on me that I could at least ask if there was something I could do. So, after dinner, I walked over to the Motherhouse and tracked down Sister Mary Nirmala. "Jeanne and I are flying home tomorrow," I told her. "Is there anything we can do from the States to help out here?"

"Stop by here on your way to the airport," she suggested. "I will ask Mother and have an answer for you then."

We packed the next morning, and I spent my last two hours at Khaligat caring for the dying patients. Stopping by the Motherhouse on the way back to the hotel, I found Sister Mary Nirmala. "Did Mother have an answer?" I asked.

"Yes," she said, "she asked me to give you this list."

Looking at the hand-written items, I saw things like bandages, cold compresses, aspirin, and syringes. I promised to see what I could do.

Jeanne and I said our goodbyes to each other at the airport. She was headed back to the States, whereas I was making a couple days' stop in a sleepy hamlet outside Frankfurt to visit my parents. The entire flight I felt guilty, thinking back to the immense suffering I had just left. I was sitting in Lufthansa coach class, but it now seemed like an opulent luxury. I could easily relate to Robert and his confusion about returning to Dartmouth.

My mind also drifted back to my mission trip in Papua New Guinea before starting with YPO and my desire at that time to do something in a third-world setting (three of our group had returned within a few months to the exact same mission). I again thought about those natives and their happiness despite their poverty (maybe because of their unawareness of anything but their home?) and how that set an example of simplicity and gratitude. There was also poverty in India, but the people were not happy in their condition—and perhaps for that reason, my desire to work in this environment was not as appealing. As much as I was ashamed to admit it, I just wanted to be back in my well-to-do world where I felt more comfortable. Was that because of my years of work at YPO? Or because the poverty here was so overwhelming?

While wondering if mission work would appeal to me again in the future, my few days in Germany were engrossed in reading *Freedom at Midnight*, a book about Ghandi and Indian independence in the 1940s. That author, Dominique LaPierre, had been one of our YPO speakers in Bombay, and his book contained such a great perspective on India that I wished I had read it before the trip. Thinking back to how I had originally felt about the Bombay assignment, I vowed to be more open to any future venue. This one had proven in the end to be a truly divine adventure—and it might not yet be over as I was determined to find the medical supplies Mother had requested.

After arriving home, I felt the usual let-down with my return to ordinary life. Mother Teresa's list went with me everywhere, but I could not come up with any ideas on to how to get the supplies. Two days later, my phone rang. "Kris, it's Jim. Do you have any plans tonight?"

Jim was a good friend and church mate. "No, not really. I'm still a bit jet lagged, though."

He continued, "Tonight is a Young Professional's League meeting downtown. I know it's late notice, but I have an extra ticket. Do you want to come?"

I didn't really feel like going out, but Jim's company was always interesting—plus I would probably know a few other people at the meeting. It was to be held at the top of one of the beautiful downtown buildings, so there would be a lovely view of the city if nothing else. "Sure, I'll see you there," I replied.

Arriving a little late, and it took me a minute to tune into the speaker. Dr. Martin Lazar was a distinguished neurological surgeon who was talking about how he and Jane Goodall had founded Medisend International in 1990 with the humanitarian mission of shipping medical supplies and surgical instruments to developing country hospitals and clinics. My mind swam for a minute as something sounded familiar. Then, it struck me: *I needed medical supplies for a clinic in a developing country.* Mother Teresa was praying for the list she had given me. How could this not be an answer to prayer?

Well, I thought to myself, *I won't know unless I ask Dr. Lazar.* So, after his presentation I walked up to him, and with trembling hands showed him Mother's list.

He scanned it and said, "We have all of these things. Call my office tomorrow morning and we'll get it started."

I was stunned. This seemed almost too easy. That night when I went home, I was so excited I could hardly sleep. My first call the next day was to Medisend, and they confirmed what he had told me. "You'll have to ship it yourself," his staff member told me, but we will need the names and addresses of her Calcutta clinics for our records. We have had too many shipments 'lost' in transit, so that is now required."

I hung up the phone. On the one hand, it was amazing that they had all these medical supplies Mother wanted, but how was I going to ship it? Given the recent problems with the YPO shipment to India, I knew how expensive and difficult the process was. And how would I pay for this?

I thought for a minute, then called FedEx; maybe they would give me a discount? "I need to ship something to India," I told them. "May I speak to a supervisor?" I had learned that supervisors were often the best way of dealing with complicated issues. When a supervisor came on the line, I explained to her about my trip and the supplies Mother Teresa had requested. Hoping against hope, I asked if they could give me a discount on shipping.

"A discount? We'll do it free of charge…this is for Mother Teresa."

Once again, I was astounded. Now I had the supplies and a free way to ship them; I just needed the addresses of the clinics. I faxed Mr. Agarwalla, explaining the situation. Hitting the machine's "send" button, I recalled our discussion about Mother's belief in the Christian God and how He answered her prayers. I wondered what they would think about this answered prayer!

The next day brought a return fax, and as I read it my excitement waned. "Kris, you have such a great heart," he had written, "and thanks for doing all of this. But we never allow people to ship supplies into the country as they are often stolen at Customs and sold on the black market. Wait until you come again to visit and then bring them in your luggage." Then, laying out the addresses of her clinics, he signed "A. G. Agarwalla."

Disappointment swept over me. All this work—and now none of it mattered; Mr. Agarwalla had vetoed my plan. Over the next few days my heart grew heavier, and the sealed boxes full of Medisend supplies near my desk were a constant reminder of what I had not been able to accomplish. I had been so close to answering Mother's prayers—only to meet what seemed an impossible obstacle.

At the same time, my conversation with the Agarwallas about God's faithful answers to Mother's prayers played repeatedly in my mind. I had grown up believing in the power of prayer and seen it firsthand in my own life. Getting to meet the Agarwallas, their daughter, and Mother Teresa were all answers to prayer. My chance meeting with Dr. Lazar was another answer to prayer. So, why this sudden setback? It wouldn't work to stow all these supplies in my luggage, as I had no plans to go back to India.

Then I realized that the successful shipment of the supplies would be another answered prayer. And it wouldn't be just my prayer, it would be mine and Mother's. I recalled the Scripture verse, "If *two* or more of you agree together…it will be done for you."

With renewed dedication, I called FedEx and gave them my information and the name of their supervisor who had promised the free shipment. That very evening, the supplies left for India on their truck.

I sent another fax to Mr. Argarwala: *"I appreciate your concern but have decided to send the supplies. I have prayed about it and fully expect the boxes to make it into your hands."*

Now I had to play a waiting game. A week passed with no word. Week two passed. Shouldn't I have heard something by now? At the end of the third week, a letter arrived in the mail with a return address from Calcutta. I opened it to find a note from Mr. Agarwalla: *"Dear Kris, I just thought you might want to read the note Mother Teresa sent to Medisend."*

Stapled to his note was another note: *"Dear Sirs at Medisend. Thank you for the medical supplies sent through the hands of Kris Jaeckle of the Young Presidents Organization. Please keep the love of God strong in your hearts always. God Bless You All, Mother Teresa."*

I burst into tears—both emotionally overcome and yet so relieved. It had been a nail-biting three weeks, but now I knew the medical supplies had made it; I had done what I could in some small but meaningful way to help Mother Teresa in her mission to care for those suffering and dying.

As the days passed, the happy ending of my medical supply story inspired to me to make prayer even more present in my life. I could have given up when I received Mr. Agarwalla's fax. But I had trusted my instincts. My perseverance in the face of tremendous obstacles had proven to be difficult but ultimately worth it. And I felt matured in the process of prayer—both from the results in asking for something that was seemingly impossible—and in staying firm in my belief through a "dead end" of what had seemed to be working. My "faith" muscle was getting stronger, and I began to share this story with people around me—who often expressed amazement. They often also wanted to hear more about this amazing God who answered prayer.

My confidence in Him and myself was growing. I had gone to Calcutta in hopes of helping Mother Teresa, but in the end, she had given me a much greater gift than I had imagined.

Chapter 12

It's Just a Car

I was sitting at my department head's desk waiting for my annual review. She walked in, closed the door, and sat down. Pulling out a few sheets of paper, she shuffled through them nervously, then stopped and looked directly at me.

"Kris, you've been here for four years."

I nodded.

"You've been through quite a few universities, and the issues with your fellow staff —not the *members* but the *staff*—have caused all of us a lot of stress. I still don't understand what the problem is, but I must listen to their complaints. So, I have a proposal to make."

I sat forward, wondering what could be coming. It was true that YPO members—not co-workers—always seemed to call me a friend. But they weren't around much, whereas I had to deal with co-workers day-in, day-out. Some semblance of this pattern had been true all my life, though it had usually shown up in age differences of friends. For sure, the job seemed to have given me a bout of ulcers, and sometimes I would suffer small dizzy spells after I had been through a stressful global event. I had thought about quitting a time or two, but then I would be assigned another interesting location and decide to stay. Plus, I would ask myself, what else could I do? What other job did I want? I had been on the way to getting certified to teach kindergarten when I first took this job at YPO but given the extraordinary life experiences I had encountered during this job, I wasn't sure I could go back to the idea of being a teacher.

My boss interrupted my thoughts. "I have been asked to offer you an opportunity to leave your job—with a six-month severance package."

Looking at her with questioning eyes, I realized she wasn't finished so I remained silent and let her continue.

"There is another position here available—and if you decide to stay, I could see about putting you into that job. It might be a bit easier than the universities because it deals directly with members, and you wouldn't be part of a six to eight-person internal team. But this position is more national than international. Why don't you think about it and let me know your decision by next week?"

I returned to my desk, reeling. *Leave YPO?* She had caught me so off-guard with her announcement that I had not asked much about the other job option.

The next few days, I confided in several friends to get their opinions as I gave serious thought to what I should do. One friend whom I considered very wise enforced praying about the two options. She also reminded me of all the difficulties that had been involved with my current position and the fact that I didn't seem happy most of the time at YPO.

Agreeing with her suggestion, I prayed and struggled to think through both options. On the one hand, six months' severance was generous and would give me plenty of time to find another job. But the more I thought about it, the more I decided to try going the direction of a different job at YPO. Maybe I could make it work?

The following week when I informed my boss, she smiled. "I knew you'd make that decision. I just wanted to give you the freedom to leave. In your new role as a seminar coordinator, your first assignment will be working for Jeff, who is chairing the Parent-Child Mountain Adventure. He is a really nice guy."

Energized by the possibilities of my new job, I immediately connected with Jeff via email (communication had sure changed since I had come to work for YPO!) and he offered to take me to lunch in a few days when he would be in our building for a meeting with a regional director.

When the day arrived, I was surprised to see a head pop over the divider between my desk and the receptionist. "Hi, Kris! I'm Jeff. I'll swing by and get you when I'm done with the meeting. Will that work?"

I was taken aback, as most members were more reserved. Jeff also had a Texas twang that sounded a bit cowboy-ish. I was in for another surprise when he picked me up and led me to his car, a sports utility vehicle. I had never seen this type of enclosed truck-like vehicle before. "I love this Ford Explorer," he announced enthusiastically. "I go everywhere in it because it can handle all kinds of roads, seat my whole family, and is great fun to drive."

On the way to lunch, he asked me how I had been assigned to his seminar and I opened up a bit about my recent change in positions, sounding a bit sad. The more he listened the more I let it all pour out: my difficulty with other employees, my shock at the resignation offer, my time of decision-making—although I left the part about praying out of it. No one at YPO—that I knew of—was the least bit spiritually oriented. Besides, talking about my particular faith might be inappropriate given the many different religions within our global organization.

When I finished my saga, he abruptly exclaimed, "Well, praise the Lord! You are an answer to prayer."

I about fell over. I had not heard someone talk like that since church during my high school years—especially at YPO. A tingling sensation ran through my body—the one I felt when there was a sense of the divine around me. My instant reaction was that he must be on a similar spiritual plane as mine, and I felt my heart leap. Jeff was so open about his beliefs; maybe he was the answer to *my* prayers—or at least a confirmation that I had made the right decision to stay.

Over lunch, he explained that the seminar we would be working on together was what he called the Parent Child Mountain Adventure, or PCMA for short. He told me how it met every summer at a camp in Colorado called Wilderness Ranch, owned by a Christian organization called Young Life. According to Jeff, the event featured a week of trekking through the mountains and sleeping under the stars—all led by Young Life counselors—but wasn't the standard "evangelical outreach" normally conducted by their organization. If, however, spiritual matters came up during the week, spiritual conversations could take place. "And that is how Young Life works anyway," he finished.

I thought twice about what he had just mentioned: camping under the stars…a whole *week* of it. I was used to five-star hotels in glamorous locations with fabulous foods and exotic activities. I had not camped out since I was—what—twelve years old? Although I had been excited about meeting Jeff, I was now concerned about what these "seminars" were about. And, given Jeff's country accent, I wondered what I had gotten into. He was not the most polished person I had met—though he was on the leadership board. Did the non-international parts of YPO involve more people like him?

As our lunch went on, I learned that he was from Wichita Falls and had gone to Oral Roberts University, then joined YPO after he took over his father's pest control business. Following that, he had gone to executive graduate school at Harvard.

I instantly felt a connection. I had also attended Oral Roberts my freshman year, and my parents had met and married in Wichita Falls at Sheppard AFB back in 1964.

"Ah, Sheppard AFB," he remarked. "It's done a lot of good for our town."

From that point forward I felt comfortable with him, and our plans were soon underway for what promised to be a fun PCMA. As the seminar drew closer we talked more on the phone, and I couldn't wait to meet his wife—who seemed very sweet whenever we had chatted. Jeff also had three children I was looking forward to meeting and said his house near Wilderness Ranch had an extra bedroom—so I could stay with his family there during our set-up days.

About two weeks before the event started, Jeff called me to discuss a potential change of plans. Since he and his family needed to attend the YPO board meeting in Maui just before the PCMA started, they would have to fly directly to Gunnison to be there for the seminar's start. The problem was that their car would still be in Texas, so he wondered if I might meet them at the DFW Airport before they flew to Maui and then take two days to drive it to Colorado. "I'm happy to treat you to an overnight at the Broadmoor Hotel in Colorado Springs on the way out there if that works for you."

Drive his car to Colorado? This was something I hadn't done before, and I wasn't sure if the powers-that-be would approve. Jeff had been so friendly with me from the beginning—and we had bonded so well—that he probably hadn't thought twice about it. I, on the other hand, wondered what would happen if I got into a wreck or something. And it could bring up rumors—yet again— about my getting too close to the members to whom I was assigned.

201

After telling him I would have to ask my boss and get back to him, he laughed and replied, "Nah...don't worry about it. If you get any flack, I'll take care of it. All I want to know is if you're okay with doing this."

I thought for a minute. "Would it be okay if I brought someone along with me? I wouldn't want to fall asleep while I drive." My friend Kim was a flight attendant and could probably go with me—then fly home on an employee pass from Colorado Springs.

"Great idea!"

Kim was indeed available and willing to drive a long day with me. So, after I met Jeff and his family at the airport and he handed me the keys to his beloved SUV, I drove it home. I noticed that it seemed really big in comparison to the other cars I passed on the highway, and its heaviness made lane-changing a bit more difficult than it was in my little Nissan.

At that time, I lived with two other girls in a mid-century ranch home—and in addition to our double garage, we shared an attached carport. We traded parking spaces off on a monthly basis and right now was my turn with the carport, so I carefully squeezed the Explorer uphill into it. There was just enough room to slightly open the doors on either side.

Kim met me early the next morning. We loaded our bags into the back of the SUV, and I pulled down hard on the heavy tailgate until it latched. Jumping in the driver's seat, I turned the key in the ignition but all I heard was a clicking noise. I stopped for a minute and then tried again only to hear the same noise—which I knew could be the sound of a starter not getting any electricity from the car's battery. Had I left on the lights when I parked—and possibly drained it? I wouldn't know until I raised the hood to look into the front of the car, but there was no room to do that because of where it was parked.

I turned to Kim. "It looks like the battery might be dead. Do you think you could help me roll it down the driveway a bit so that I

202

have room to raise the hood? If I put it in neutral and keep my hand on the brake as we roll backward, we should be fine."

I tried not to be nervous, but I had never done anything like this before. Kim was worried too. "This car is huge and heavy. How will we keep it from rolling backward out of control?"

I assured her that we would go slowly. She set herself up on the passenger side with the door open and held onto the car. I did the same on my side—pressing my hand on the brake—then switched the gear shift to "N" and felt the car gently roll backward. I immediately pressed on the brake and the car stopped.

"Okay," I said, "it seems to be working."

We started again, and this time I let it roll backward more quickly. I suddenly heard a "crunch" and felt the car jerk to a stop. My stomach did a somersault. I was quick-thinking enough to shift it back into "P," felt it stop, then looked around. Behind me was a large metal pole holding up the carport. I had forgotten it, and sure enough the vehicle's door had hit it and now had a bend on its door frame.

Oh no, I thought in a panic. What to do? What would I say to Jeff, who had trusted me with his car? Even more important: What would Jeff say to me? Could I hide this bend? Would the door even close? Kim walked around to my side and saw what happened, and her expression mirrored my horror. I tried closing the door and it did just fine, which gave me a small feeling of relief. "Kim, what do I do now?" I asked.

"I don't know what to tell you, Kris, except that if you want me to ride along, we need to get going. If we don't get there in time, I won't make my flight in the morning. The good news is there is nothing else to run into, so let's get it down the hill and get it jumped."

We finished rolling it, connected jumper cables to the car, and got it started. The headlights also kicked on immediately confirming that I had left them on.

We headed on our eleven-hour drive west, chatting about what had just happened. I kicked myself for being such an absent-minded person. Had I simply paid attention, I would have turned off the headlights. Had I looked around before I started rolling it backward, I would have seen the pole. Oh well—there was nothing I could do about it now except worry how Jeff would react.

We finally arrived at the Broadmoor and settled into a beautiful room. Kim fell asleep quickly, but I tossed and turned, fearful of what was going to happen with Jeff. All too soon the alarm went off, and I took Kim to the airport—though I dreaded dropping her off because I would then be by myself and have to face Jeff. Would I be fired? The three-hour drive from Colorado Springs to Gunnison was miserable. My brain was buzzing with anxiety as I thought about what could happen to me.

My breathing shallowed as I neared Gunnison and I remembered that the elevation here was higher than Colorado Springs. I thought about the next week and wondered how I would survive six days camping under the stars with no showers or beds. That alone had me stressed out, although Jeff had assured me it would be fun. Then, reality set back in about what had happened. I so wanted to do a great job for him—given how kind he had been to me and had cheered me up when I met him.

Pulling in front of his house, I tried to gather my courage. My trembling hands had a hard time opening the car door, but I finally did so and stepped out of the car. Walking around the house, I found the front door and knocked on it, but there was no answer. Continuing to walk around the side, I sighted Jeff—who was by himself.

His eyes brightened as he asked, "Hi, Kris. How are you? How was the drive?"

"Jeff," I said, talking quickly, "don't say anything to me. I need tell you something terrible. Will you walk over to your car with me?"

Looking puzzled, he followed me. Opening the driver's door, I showed him where the frame was bent and explained in a rush how it had happened. "I am so, so sorry. I don't know what else to say." I stopped momentarily, looking at him, then started to cry.

He let me calm down, then he put his arm around me and gently said, "It's just a car."

I couldn't believe it. That was it? Apparently so, because he immediately changed the subject, reminding me of the need to pick up soon-arriving members at Gunnison Airport. Then we went over the schedule, starting with tonight's gathering at the ranch and Jeff giving a briefing about the seminar events. He also reminded me that we would have a Young Life staffer or two there to join us during that time.

Out of the blue, he pulled out a ball cap with a long braid hanging down both sides. "I have a really fun idea that I will do while we greet everyone," he said with a grin. "This is my Willie Nelson cap. It always shocks people when I wear it, and this is the perfect crowd to try it out on."

I wasn't exactly sure what to say—or how the group would react—so I decided I would stay quiet and watch him. When we began picking up members, everyone appeared a bit taken aback when Jeff introduced himself and shook their hands. They stayed apart from him—and kept their children even further away. They might have expected such a thing from the Wilderness Ranch staff, but not from a YPO Board Member!

As we drove back to Jeff's house to do a quick change for the evening, he told me the first evening was always inspirational. Held around an open fire, this get-together involved goal setting, ice-breaking, and bonding…and would set the tone for the whole week. I was still wondering how he would show everyone that he wasn't Willy Nelson.

After we all got settled at the dinner tables, Jeff walked around and talked with everyone in the group, all of whom still appeared a bit wary of him—and he seemed to notice it. He then walked over to the fire, grabbed a branch and stoked the embers. Without warning, he took the cap off his head and scratched his scalp. Everyone was watching him, and they seemed surprised.

Starting to laugh, he said, "Well, everyone, I really love my Willie Nelson cap. Is anyone else here a fan?"

The tension instantly dissolved, and the event went perfectly from that point forward. I survived sleeping under the stars and washing in the stream during the week; the mountain scenery and wonderful Young Life staff made it all bearable. And I had a newfound respect for Jeff because he never again brought up the damage that I had done to his Explorer during the entire ten days we were together. Needless to say, Jeff became my new favorite member.

Chapter 13

A Gift Unlike Any Other

As I had learned working with Jeff, chapter-level YPO members could be quite different from international board members. I learned just how different they could be on another assignment—a two-day event on Mergers and Acquisitions to be held in Dallas—which had an ominous beginning.

My co-worker Sandra, who had already been assigned to the event, included me in an email requesting to cancel a planning call because of a staff meeting. Oddly, she had chosen to schedule this call despite her advanced knowledge of that meeting—so she almost seemed to be making a point of having more control than Mike, the member chairman. I responded to the email with an offer to go forward with it—saying that my schedule was free. Not replying back via email but rather walking by my desk—she wished me a "good luck" with her eyebrows raised. Since I had just been added to this small event, this would be my first encounter with him. All I knew was that he was a high-powered attorney from Los Angeles and a bit difficult to work with. When the time came for the call, I reached out to Mike and was told by his secretary to "stand by."

We finally connected, and within a few seconds of talking I found Mike subtly intimidating. Although he spoke softly, his comments were cutting and all I got was an earful of complaints about our office's lack of service and Sandra's unavailability. Before we ended the call, he told me he appreciated my reviewing the logistics of the event with him—then followed it with a comment about it not really mattering since it was Sandra he needed.

I hung up wondering what I could do to make a difference in his attitude about the upcoming seminar. Mike certainly wasn't a positive motivator, but I hoped that I would make a difference by being on the team. I pondered sending a gift of some sort—saying something about the fact that we were looking forward to giving him good customer service—but realized there wasn't any room in the small budget to allow for it. I decided to ask our executive director for the money, and he allotted $150. I didn't share my "Mike gift idea" with Sandra, as she was yet another fellow employee who made it clear that becoming friends was not something that appealed to her.

After thinking a few days about what to send, I decided on an unusual flower bouquet—signing it, "In anticipation of a great seminar from Your YPO Planning Team." Waiting to hear something about it from him or Sandra, I got nothing. And on our next call, there also was nothing. He did, however, acknowledge her presence; but when she told him she had another meeting in ten minutes, he went back to complaining about her lack of availability. Every time she tried to focus on the seminar and all its details, he circled back to his favorite subject of her lack of availability. Finally, she flashed me a "hands up" sign, told him goodbye, and went off to her meeting.

Now it was just Mike and me, and he changed the direction of the conversation. "Kris, I got an interesting delivery of flowers a few days ago, and it said it was from 'my YPO Planning Team.' I had a feeling that Sandra wasn't a part of that...did you send them?"

His remark made me feel like I had done the right thing, so I enthusiastically replied, "Yes—I did. Did you like them?"

"Like them?" he bellowed. *"Flowers?* I gave them to my wife who works down the hall. Kris, if you want to send a man a gift, you send something *masculine*...not something *feminine*. You might want to remember that for the future. Feminine gifts are chocolates and candies and flowers. Masculine gifts are things like scotch; an autographed football from someone like Roger Staubach or Joe Namath; a golf club; dueling pistols; or something along those lines. Talk to you next time." With that, he hung up.

I slammed the receiver down. I rarely got angry, but this man was too much. I had already gone above and beyond to make things better, but he couldn't be pleased! How would we make it through the seminar if he was going to be like this? I briefly thought about sharing my feelings with Sandra, but then I wondered if Mike's constant complaints were why she had asked for another person on the team. She probably wanted a buffer, given his shark-like behavior, and maybe she thought I would make a good decoy.

Still boiling, I wasn't sure what to do. He had been such a jerk, but—darn it—I didn't like to fail in the area of great customer service. Then a thought came to mind: I had tried flowers and that hadn't worked...maybe I would do for him during this seminar what we did during our universities: Give him room gifts. There were only two nights for which I had to figure something out, and he had given me some ideas, hadn't he? I had a bit of money left from the extra funds the executive director had given me, which could easily cover one of his requests: a bottle of scotch. An autographed football would be another possibility, but who knew how much that might cost?

I spent a few days racking my brain about an autographed football. There *had* to be a way to make that happen given all the

YPO connections out there. Hadn't Roger Staubach been a member of some YPO chapter? He had a very successful real estate company right here in Dallas, so someone must know him.

The following weekend as I was waiting for a table during brunch, someone tapped me on the shoulder. I turned to see a tall, handsome man I recognized from Jeff's Parent-Child Mountain Adventure at Wilderness Ranch. I could not recall his name, but the waitress suddenly called "Robert Shaw," and he turned to look at her. That issue was resolved, and I jumped in with, "Hi, Robert. How are things? Did you and your daughter enjoy the event?"

"We did, Kris. Thanks for all you did in taking care of us."

As we continued to casually chat, I remembered that he had something to do with the Dallas Cowboys. After he finished what he was saying, I asked, "You played for the Cowboys, didn't you? What is your company now—I've forgotten."

"I did play for them. I was their center for a bit. Now I am in real estate."

Real estate? Could it be Roger Staubach's company? This could be just the connection I needed. "Robert, do you happen to know Roger Staubach? I have a member chairing a meeting in a few weeks—here in town—and he has been asking about an autographed football from Roger. Would you have any way of helping me make that happen?"

"I think I could help with that," he replied. I tried to contain my excitement as he continued with, "Call my assistant on Monday and she'll get you set up."

Following his instructions, I rang his office on Monday morning and his assistant was very helpful, asking to whom I wanted the autographed football dedicated. "'Mike Blueton'...thanks. But do you mind me asking how he can make this happen so easily? Are Robert and Roger good friends?"

"They are partners who are currently working on a project in Uptown Dallas," she replied. "Should we have the ball delivered to your office?"

I told her that the office was fine, then hung up. This autographed football was going to *wow* Mike, I felt certain, especially since it would be autographed specifically to him.

A few days later when Sandra and I checked in at the Crescent Hotel to get things set up, we saw Mike arrive. I was surprised by how handsome he was, and his eyes sparkled at me while he greeted us. Then, he promptly went to the front desk of the hotel to start complaining about how his car was handled—and where it was parked—by the valet service.

I realized that was how Mike did business. He immediately threw the hotel staff into a tizzy and kept it going. Nothing the hotel did was good enough—he could always find a flaw and make them work harder. And rather than stand up to him, they just tried harder and harder.

Somehow we made it through the set-up day, double-checking all the details. Mike seemed to have a magnifying glass, and the more he found wrong, the more things seemed to go wrong. I knew I had to get him out of the way, or the entire seminar would go south.

As I followed him around, I wondered how I could do it...then finally decided to just be up front with him in the morning. Wasn't it *my* job to take care of logistical details? And wasn't it *his* job to smile at the attendees and lead the whole event?

At the end of the day, we sat down to catch a quick breath while he went off to the opening dinner. I started to share with Sandra my room gifts idea, then again, decided it best to keep to myself. I didn't have to worry about this evening, anyway, because the hotel was going to give him their standard room gift (champagne and chocolates). Then again, he would probably have some complaint about that!

During breakfast on the first full day of the seminar, Mike incessantly followed hotel staff around, complaining about every little thing that wasn't perfect. I waited for my strategic moment to chat with him and found an opening right after the speaker started that morning. I caught up with him, a bit nervous, and started a conversation. But instead of bringing up the subject I wanted to, for some reason I switched to another one. "Mike, you have the most amazing silver hair. How long has it been that way?"

He looked at me quizzically—as if wondering why I would chase him down to bring up his hair. "That is an interesting story." he replied. "It started changing in my early twenties, and I thought about having it colored. Then, I noticed that everyone thought I was much older and seemed to have more respect for me than other people who were my age. So, I just left it that color." He started to walk away again, but I caught his arm.

Taking a deep breath and starting again, I said, "I see that you are keeping a close eye on all of the logistical details. Since that is why I am here, would you mind if I took care of that? It would allow you to sit down and enjoy the seminar—and you could let me know if you notice anything that needs to be done."

He was taken off guard and struggled to keep his temper under control. After a moment, he smiled and said, "Okay, Kris—deal."

A bit later, he went over to Sandra and started complaining to her. She listened, then seemingly ran off to take care of whatever was needed. I felt for her but couldn't change how she was deciding to do things.

During the day, I checked in with Mike every few hours. If he asked me to correct something, I decided to use the Stephen Covey "emotional bank account" principle to resolve the issue. I had read about it his *Seven Habits of Highly Effective People* book—and also heard him speak about it back in Taipei—and had found it to be very practical and positive. Uncertain whether I had given enough

212

positive feedback to make this work, I concluded that I had and decided to give it a try.

After the first complaint he gave me to handle, I found our conference services manager and told her how wonderful the Crescent was, how amazing the food had been, and how attentive the staff was. *Then* I brought up Mike and the miniscule issue needing attention. She looked a bit frustrated when I mentioned him, so I told her I knew how difficult Mike could be—giving her permission to lean on me if necessary. She looked at me, much relieved.

In the meantime, Sandra and the hotel staff were growing more and more intimidated. If he saw me, however, he would sit down and pretend he was listening to a speaker and flash me one of his great smiles. That evening, after we sent the attendees off to their dinner, I asked the concierge to deliver the bottle of scotch I had purchased. I did not attach any kind of note (that made it more of a mystery) and went to bed wondering what would happen.

At breakfast, he pulled Sandra and me aside and asked, "The strangest thing happened last night – a bottle of really nice scotch was delivered to my room. But it didn't come with a note. Do either or you know anything about it?"

I didn't reply, and there was a moment of silence. Sandra looked at me with questioning eyes and when I didn't comment, she took credit. "Did you like it, Mike?"

"It was nice, but it wasn't my favorite brand." He then turned away and walked to the front of the room to introduce the morning's speaker.

That whole interaction upset me a bit, but I was pretty sure Mike suspected that the scotch had come from me.

The second day of the seminar flowed a bit more smoothly, and I grew more confident about keeping Mike from his usual intimidation tactic. Catching his eyes as he started in about something he didn't find up to standard, I would immediately have the conference services manager fix it and then approach him. From what I could see, the hotel staff were outdoing themselves, and the attendees with whom I spoke said they felt the event was top-notch.

The last thing to get through was the evening's closing dinner, and I had already double-checked the details. I had chosen a sophisticated meal, starting with gougères and bibb salad with radishes—feeding into beef bourguignon. So far, Mike hadn't complained about my meal choices...but who knew about tonight?

When the dinner was over, I gave the football to the concierge—asking for an 8 pm delivery. I tried to relax by having a pedicure at the hotel's spa, followed by shrimp scampi on linguine at the hotel's Italian restaurant. I sipped on a glass of wine during dinner—hoping it, too, would help me unwind—but couldn't get over feeling nervous (and excited) about tonight's special gift.

Recalling his reaction to the flowers and scotch, I wondered if he would have a complaint about the football as well. Maybe he would say that *Roger Staubach* wasn't the right autograph. This was one of the two names he had mentioned, but maybe he preferred one to the other. Then I caught myself and realized I was being sucked into his game—I had pulled strings to make this football happen, and I was grateful. If he didn't like it, it would have to be his issue.

After falling asleep, I was awakened by a phone call. I stared at the hotel clock: 11:30 pm. Who could be calling at this time of night?

"Hello," I cautiously answered.

No sooner had I finished my greeting than I heard Mike's voice.

"Oh, my God, Kris. Oh, my God. This is *so* amazing, and it even has my name on it! Did you send this?"

"Mike," I asked, still struggling to wake up, "Are you talking about the football?"

"I've never gotten anything like this before…not in my whole life!" he choked.

Giving him a moment to get control, I wondered how much of this was emotion and how much was alcohol. I also wondered if criticism was about to come. But there was just silence, so I followed his lead.

I heard a few sniffles, then he said, "I asked if you sent this."

I was unsure as to what to say. But I had to say something, so I replied that it was.

"Why would you do something like this for me?" he asked. "People don't usually do kind things for me."

"You had told me what you thought were masculine gifts when you criticized the flowers I had sent. It was a bit of a challenge, I guess."

"Really?" His continued hesitation made it clear he was thinking, which gave me a moment to say just a bit more.

"Mike, you criticize everything. Here at the hotel, they are trying so hard to do their best for you. But nothing seems good enough. Maybe people would want to give you more gifts if you were a bit more grateful?"

Again, silence. So, I ended the conversation with, "Good night, Mike. I hope you sleep well."

When the conference ended the next morning, Mike shook my hand and told me what a great job I had done—then left. Sandra was nowhere to be found. Figuring she had already gone back to the office, I cleaned up what was left and put it all into my car.

On the way home, I passed a top-notch car dealership and thought about how many times I wanted to stop in there. I was appreciative of my current car; it had been given to me in a very divine way as a result of my church group praying for me—but the miles were getting high and I had been pondering a new one. While

I thought this dealership's brand was beautiful and sporty, I was aware that it was out of my price range. For some strange reason, though, something told me to swing in.

I spent some time there talking to a salesman about a vehicle I liked—but wouldn't commit to buying it. The more critiques I made about it, the more he defended the model. He seemed to be deferring to me. Finally, he said, "Why don't you just take it home for the evening?"

That surprised me. No one had ever offered me the keys to a luxury car for a free night—but why not accept? So, I took him up on his offer, and the longer I was in it, found it to be nicer than anything I had ever driven. While driving, I also pondered whether my whole back and forth with the salesman had brought out a bit of Mike's attitude in me. Then again, all I had done was act confident and criticize. Had I learned something from being around Mike?

The next morning, I decided I needed to walk away from the whole thing. My current car came from the parent company of the vehicle I was "trying out," so what could the price difference between it and this vehicle really be about—except for name brand? When I returned to the dealer and told the salesman that I wasn't interested—in a confident and firm way—he brought his manager over.

"Did you have any issues with the car?"

"Well, it was nice," I admitted, but then laid out a list of what I had found wrong with it.

I expected them both to be indignant, but the opposite happened: The sales manager asked if I would like to take it home for another evening. Uncertain they were serious, I accepted their invitation.

The longer I drove the vehicle that day and evening, the more I liked it—but still knew the price was too high. So, I brought it back again, talking to the salesman in an even more forceful way about it and laying out a few more criticisms. He seemed unable to counter my objections, and once again, consulted his boss—who walked over and initiated a new conversation. "We like to have exceptional customers, and you look to be that kind of person. How can we sell you this car?" he asked.

I talked primarily about the cost being too high, and he did a few calculations on a pad of paper. He then offered me an unbelievable price. His salesman looked at him a bit stunned—as did I—until I caught myself. I was learning to play tough.

"I'll take it," I said confidently, and walked away with a beautiful, pearl-colored touring sedan. The hardball tactics I had learned from Mike had enabled me to purchase my dream car—and I had learned a bit more about standing up for myself in the process.

Chapter 14

Working for a Rock Star

Shimmering pink sand lapped the turquoise waters of the Atlantic under a bright summer sun as I zipped along between the Southampton Princess and Reefs Resort. The sight was so dreamy it was all I could do to keep my eyes on the road—the *right* side of a very narrow road. I had arrived on the island of Bermuda to run off-site activities for the YPO university here, and the trip back and forth between the two hotels offered spectacular views to the south of East Whale Bay—as well as a peek to the north at the cast-iron Gibbs Hill Lighthouse that had been operating since 1846. A little past the bay sat Horseshoe Beach, the most famous of all beaches on the island for its long crescent of coral-colored sand set against jagged volcanic rocks.

Getting used to driving on the opposite side of the road took me a try or two and reminded me of being in South Africa (the last place I had driven with this road setup). However, this time I was cruising around on my very own scooter—the most popular mode of transit for tourists. Still a territory of Great Britain, Bermuda struck me as an ideal honeymoon spot because of its romantic aura. Lush tropical blooms of oleander, bougainvillea, hibiscus, and poinsettias lined the roadways. Houses were painted in pastel shades of yellow, green, blue, pink and peach, creating the effect of a watercolor painting. White terraced limestone roofs added to the island feeling, even though I learned they were not just for show but to help collect valuable rainwater for the island's water supply.

I had just been brought back to the "Universities Department" and offered this assignment of managing the Bermuda University off-site activities. Although I had secretly hoped to coordinate educational aspects of universities, handling activities was interesting and I wasn't going to complain—especially since my off-sites chairman for Bermuda was John, former CEO of Pencil Supply.

At our preliminary university meeting in Dallas, John had introduced his wife Patty. He then explained that she would be the one to make it all happen due to his demanding business schedule (CNN had recently been by his side for a whole day after he was named "CEO of the Year" by *Financial News*). After looking at her across the table and seeing her smile back at me, I felt confident this new assignment could work out. I always had to believe in people to want to work for them, and she and John seemed "believe-in-able."

Off-site adventures took a lot of organizing, and this university involved families. So, there would have to be activities for all ages—set up for families as well as individuals. I thought back to my experience two years earlier in Maui involving children, but that was a daily schedule that didn't involve choices. Parents attended classes while their children were educated through activities taking place during the same time slots—whereas off-sites were activities involving the entire family and utilizing a variety of experiences. Given that scenario, families had to choose ahead of time what off-sites they wanted to do on certain days and times, then turn in their choices. And because there weren't many spaces for a lot of the activities, a computer "lottery" then randomly made the final selection and assigned the spaces.

We all knew this process could become complicated because members got upset if they didn't get the activities they requested—as they would often try to manipulate their way into slots they wanted. Manipulation tactics included yelling at us; being syrupy-sweet; calling the Executive Director and complaining about our "lack of professionalism;" the list could go on and on—so that would now be a big part of what I would have to handle, too. I would also have to help choose an on-site Destination Management Company (DMC) to coordinate the logistics of the activities. If we chose the right one, it would be a godsend.

During our initial meeting, I discovered that John also played in a rock band and was now making the move into the music world full-time. His torn jeans and white t-shirt gave him the appearance of a rock musician, and his New York accent seemed to match the world he was stepping into. After our initial meeting ended, Patty had to stay for some other meetings and asked me to drop John at the airport. On our way, I ventured to ask why he was choosing to become involved in the music industry now that he was stepping down at Pencil Supply.

"I have always loved music—especially rock music—and it all happened up on the stage with my rock band, Eraserhead, during one of our Pencil Supply conferences," he replied. He went on to share that after a few years of phenomenal growth, he had let Pencil Supply buy his first company, Office Club, then and took over merged operations as president. Incredible growth had continued over the next few years until he had a realization about his future during a Pencil Supply annual conference. "One of the evenings, my band was scheduled to play. As they were introducing us, I heard, 'Here he is: CEO by day and rocker by night.' I realized at that moment that I didn't want to be a CEO by day and rocker by night; I wanted to be a rocker by day *and* a rocker by night. So, I decided to step down."

John went on to say that he had spent the next few months at home until Patty finally told him to find something to do. So, he got the idea of starting Music Lesson Headquarters—somewhat along the same lines of Pencil Supply—except that it would be about music. His new company would feature recording studios and demo rooms as well as offering lessons in addition to instrument sales. "It was a little like Guitar Center, except that I designed it more for novices," he said. "I threw in $10 million of my own money, got a few Wall Street investors based on my Pencil Supply reputation, and have been going strong for the last eighteen months. In fact, our Dallas store is our nineteenth location to open. The goal is to open sixty locations."

John then suggested that I visit their home in Boca Raton while Patty and I were working together—as it might be a bit easier for us to plan if we were closer together. Patty and I did work feverishly over the next few weeks on the project—and I spent some of that time at their house. While there between our work sessions, I learned about South Florida by running around with her while she did her errands. We dropped off and picked up the kids from school, shopped at local markets, checked in on John at his new headquarters, made dinner for the family, sailed on their beautiful boat, and spent time with their children.

Several times while I was there, John invited me to go jogging with him early in the morning. Patty was all in favor since she didn't want to get up, so I put on my shoes and joined him. Our runs gave me time to ask him more stories of what he had learned in life, and one interesting story he recalled was learning how to stand up to people while working years before as an ambulance driver in Long Island. Another story he told me was about an employee who taught him about prioritizing his family—back when he was just starting Office Supply. "We were all working 24/7 getting everything set up, and I was pretty demanding. There was one particularly nice, hard-working guy on my staff who would mention his family and how they were his priority. One day when we were working long into the night and talking about coming in early the next morning (which was on the weekend), he told me he would probably not be coming in—as he had plans with his son. I hassled him a bit—expecting him to change his mind—but he didn't. In fact, he firmly but kindly said 'John, my family is my priority, and I need to spend tomorrow at home.'"

The man's comment had impressed him a great deal. "I thought about Patty and my son Carl—who was just two or three at the time—and the point I had made to Patty about keeping me a priority after he was born. Was I doing the same for them? I started backing off a bit from work, though just a little bit then. And, to my surprise, the company still grew—to the point of my being able to sell it off to Pencil Supply in just a few years."

I reflected on my father, who had always made it clear that our family was his priority. That hadn't always been true—as he was determined from the time he was a little boy to become an Air Force general. When he met and married my mother as a young captain, it was clear that work was the priority. But after he had a "spiritual encounter" with a jogging friend—and as a result committed his life to God—he switched his priorities from "work, family, God" to "God, family, work." I always knew that if I needed him, I could call his office and they would track him down—even when commanding a large, nuclear military base. We all felt like we were his first priority, so I could relate to what John was saying and told him so. I also thanked him for giving me some of his time while he was running—as it was teaching me things.

Our first trip to Bermuda was mainly to get a feel for the island and to choose our DMC. We listened to four different companies present us with their ideas and give us sample activities. These activities included learning about the town of St. George and its history as one of the oldest colonies in the British empire (it had been founded—and continuously inhabited—even before the

Pilgrims founded their colony in Plymouth, Massachusetts, in 1620); visiting one of the oldest aquariums in the world; beach activities; cave exploration; snorkeling and scuba diving (thank heavens I had just certified in SCUBA); swimming with dolphins—the list went on and on.

As Patty and I pored over the lists of possible activities, we discussed how many people should be allowed to attend each activity and how many times it should be offered during the six days. Activities were all expected to have some kind of "special" aspect to them that qualified them as "YPO activities."

We each made notes on each DMC proposal, compared their prices, how many good ratings they had from other groups, and how well we personally connected with them. We finally chose *Select Sites* run by Chris and Starla Williams, a recently-formed company, which handled transportation, events, recreation—basically everything. When we left with our decision made, I felt it a good first planning trip.

Getting to know Patty impacted my life. In addition to our travels to Bermuda, she came to Dallas once or twice. She could have booked a luxurious hotel suite while she was with me, but instead was gracious enough to stay in my little house with my three roommates. I thought this was amazing, given her position in life and the first-class treatment she was used to. But she was a most approachable person and talked about how much she enjoyed my house and my company. It seemed I was the center of her universe whenever we were working together, and I began to understand John's feelings about her and how she empowered him.

As it grew closer to the university, things became more stressful as usual. I had often suffered an upset stomach when I worried about things at YPO, and it was happening again. My cousin-doctor mentioned that this might be ulcers—which were now easily treated based on a recent discovery that they were caused by a gastrointestinal bacterium. After a positive test result, he got me started on the right drug and for the first time, my stomach discomfort started to lessen.

That helped immensely, but it didn't deal with the root cause of my problem—constant stress from my job. Handling Bermuda off-sites would be the most high-pressure position I had taken on thus far with YPO. The responsibilities included working with the DMC, making sure the crew launched all the activities each day, handling the lotteries, dealing with feedback from members and their families, reporting to Patty and John, making sure the transportation was all set up—the list went on. Was I ready?

Patty and I arrived on the island a week before the university started and were working feverishly on set-up when Starla, the owner of the DMC, arrived looking upset. She pulled me aside to say that rumors had erupted about a "refusal to drive" protest from some of the island transportation companies—including the ones we were using for our off-site program. She reminded me that we didn't need transportation until our activities started in another two days—and that tomorrow's registration day and opening party probably wouldn't be affected since all of those activities were on hotel property. Then she circled back to the fact that this situation could ruin the entire university—it was a really big deal.

I felt a strange numbness come over me, then started walking around in circles in my office while Kelly, our off-sites assistant, tried to figure out something to say. Finally, she handed me a glass of the Bailey's Irish Creme she had brought along. "I am so glad you have to deal with the members, Kris. I get to stay in the background and make the details work," she said, adding, "and it will somehow all work out."

It was all I could do to acknowledge her. And I appreciated the Bailey's—though I had never in my life had an early afternoon drink. While I sipped the creamy caramel-flavored liquid and chewed on the ice over which it was poured, I felt calmer. Patty arrived soon after with Starla, who was now suggesting on the availability of

225

island taxi drivers. Susan, the event project manager, came five minutes later and listened to the idea. She was her usual positive self and encouraged us to go full steam ahead, so Starla ran out of the office to go to work.

My mind still reeled at the thought of disappointing 1000 members and their families who had paid their money and signed up for all our activities. They were already arriving on the island and asking questions about everything; we even had a desk set up to give information about the various off-sites and where their departures would be. But there would be no departures without transportation (unless it involved hikes or bicycle rides)!

While I liked handling desks and interacting with members (and had done this at off-sites desks for other YPO universities), a terrible feeling was growing over me as I evaluated all of this until suddenly I was totally lost. I could feel my heartbeat increase, then couldn't stand up anymore and leaned against a wall. I was having a panic attack—unable to speak—so I went into a private room where I just sat down and breathed. I had never felt like this before—but then remembered reading something about "shock" and wondered if this was what I was experiencing.

Kelly came to ask me a question, and then, seeing all the blood drained from my face, turned back around to handle our desk and answer questions. At that moment, I realized all I could do was pray—and did so fervently—asking God for help while evaluating all the things that could go wrong in this situation. After a while, Kelly took a break from the desk and came to find me again to see if I was okay. I still wasn't able to talk, so she again went back to the desk. A bit later Patty came to find me, asking if I had heard anything from Starla. I hadn't, and I could see that Patty was stressed out too. Since I didn't seem to have any answers, she went off to find John—who was a great motivator—to see what he thought.

The rest of the day was a blur, and I didn't feel of use to anyone. This stressed me out even more because it was my first off-sites project and seemed to rapidly be turning into a disaster. The next morning, however, I was at least able during registration to have all our information set up to answer questions for arriving members. They had their schedules and asked various questions about switching dates and times—as well as asking if other activities had waitlists. I answered the questions as best as I could—mentioning nothing about the transportation—and tried to keep a smile on my face.

Patty kept checking in at the desk between wandering around with John and interacting with all the arriving members. He didn't seem the least bit worried—but I had learned this was his personality. He had been through much more in his life than transportation strikes in Bermuda. By this time, the university chairman had found out what was going on and was trying to think of other options as well. We all hoped (and I kept praying) that Starla would find an alternative form of transportation quickly.

After registration was over and the guests were attending the opening party, we sat down to brainstorm again. Starla had sent feelers out in every direction she knew but didn't have any answers yet. She had been able to put enough taxis together for the next morning's 7 am activity launches, then we would again have a break before the afternoon activity launches started at 2 pm. At this point, the taxi idea seemed the most feasible solution, but the drivers still had to accept the proposition and we knew they would all talk among each other after the morning launch.

I kept praying and was up by 6 am to be sure everything was ready for the 7 am launches. Some very cheery native Bermudian taxi drivers showed up and were waiting by 6:45 am, and the few members and their families who showed up for the activities looked groggy. I had heard that last night's party went well (and ran late), so they may have found it difficult to get up. Everything went smoothly for the morning's launches, then we were back to waiting to hear if the taxi group would accept our transportation request. We had no idea how much the whole thing would cost if the taxis accepted; our budget at this point was blown. We just needed transportation!

That afternoon had six launch times, and two to six different activities would be leaving at each launch time with anywhere from four to sixteen people. Some taxis could do drop-offs and then swing back around to do more launches—and for some activities, several taxis would have to be employed to take the larger groups of people. It would take a tremendous amount of coordinating, and Starla was creating extensive lists and charts to make it all work out. By 11 am, we still didn't have a solid answer—and my stress level grew again. I still felt the after-effects of the "shock" I had encountered yesterday, though now there was also a feeling of helplessness as I continued to pray. I also thought back to my ulcers, wondering what all this tension would do to my stomach?

John and Patty checked in several times between morning educational classes—with him being calm and positive, and Patty, like me, biting her nails. About noon, we heard from Starla with a confirmation that the afternoon had just been coordinated and the starting drivers would be at the hotel fifteen minutes before the launch. Almost afraid to see what would happen, I showed up and saw plenty of taxi drivers, but also confused-looking members. They were used to seeing vans and large vehicles with YPO signs in their windows—not local taxis.

The crew did its usual job of lining up and loading people, and it seemed to flow smoothly. At the end of each launch time (and while coordinating our next set of launches), we would catch each other's eyes and express amazement that everything was working so far. After the 4 pm launch, Patty, Starla, and I gave each other hugs and collapsed in exhaustion. Starla checked in with the head of the taxi group, and they agreed to take on the project. We all breathed a sigh of relief and started coordinating the next day's launches.

The rest of the week had a few hiccups—given the smaller-sized cars for some of the larger-populated activities—but it all eventually worked out and we were grateful.

Friday night's closing party took place on Horseshoe Beach, and I noticed a lighted stage all set up for the surprise band. The committee was wandering around and greeting everyone, and John walked by in a YPO Bermuda-logoed t-shirt with his arm around Patty—who looked like her usual casually attractive self. Their son, Carl, was out with a new group of friends he had made during the university, while their daughter, Lauren, had chosen to hang out with me. I did a "lay of the beach" while thinking about how we had become friends between my working at their house and Patty bringing her on a planning trip. We were both in beach attire—me in a beautiful new coral-colored bathing suit and wrap from the hotel boutique.

Fires had been set up on the beaches, and some families were already gathered around them. Other members were in circles chatting with each other, gesturing, or slapping each other on the back while their kids were off playing beach volleyball. As we walked past them, I asked Lauren if she wanted to join, but she grabbed my hand and pulled me to walk on with her. Drawn by the smell of grilled beef, we stopped at a food station to pick up a hamburger and some lemonade.

Then, the sound of tapping drums started, and a tenor voice sang something like *sunlight plays upon her hair*, followed by a lower-pitched voice singing, *I'm picking up good vibrations*. People stopped what they were doing and turned to look at the stage, beginning to wave their arms and shake their hips. It seemed to be the Beach Boys, and I immediately wondered if John with his involvement in the *Rock n Roll Hall of Fame* had any influence in getting them here. Then, thinking about what that might cost, I pondered it possibly being a "copy band." Next I heard the song "Fun, Fun, Fun 'til her Daddy Takes the Tbird Away" followed by "I Wish They all could be California Girls" followed by even more of their hits—with

229

everyone laughing and dancing. At some point, the band introduced themselves as a copy band—so that resolved my idea—but it didn't really matter because they were so good. The evening was definitely memorable, and after everything that had happened I was able to smile at long last and sigh with relief that my job was done.

The following night, we held the usual post-university private committee/staff party. Everyone shared feedback and celebrated the end of the event, but this time it was a swimming party held at a committee member's private home on the island. It was a fun and relaxing evening, and once again, I enjoyed time with Lauren. Susan, the event project manager, took the time to tell me what a nice job I had done—and that she was glad the transportation issue had been resolved so well.

I knew that Susan had recently married a Dallas minister, and was open to spiritual ideas—so I shared with her how much I had prayed about that situation and was grateful that it had worked out. It also gave me an opportunity to share with her what had happened with Mother Teresa's request for medical supplies, which seemed to touch her deeply. Before she turned to talk to the university's social chairman, she said, "I have a feeling you'll do a great job on your next assignment in New Zealand."

Chatting with Susan helped me reflect on how my life had changed since I had attended my initial Landmark weekend (called a "Forum") the year before, and then the advanced course during the Bermuda University planning process.

Chapter 15

My Landmark Moment

B ack in South Africa when my co-worker Candy had first shared
the idea with me of attending Landmark Forum to help with
my personal life—as well as in India when I strolled the Queen's
Necklace thinking about it—I had pondered what "official goal" I
would set for the weekend if I went.

Since then, I had talked about attending Landmark with my
college friend, Karen, who was very insightful and wise—having
already been through marriage, childbearing, divorce, re-marriage,
and had also built a strong career with her sign language capabilities.
In contrast, my romantic life was still at a standstill and Greg was
still coming to my mind even though it had been over six years
since we had separated. And the seeming lack of anywhere to step
up to within YPO—as well as a lack of idea where to go outside of
YPO—seemed to create another standstill.

Karen gently kept me focused on trying Landmark, and we
both thought about what goal I would set if I chose to attend. She

suggested I ask myself what I wanted to accomplish—then listen to the very first thing that came to mind. Making time a few days later, I followed her instructions and waited in as much silence as I could garnish. Sure enough, "marriage" came to mind, so I registered for Landmark and named that as my goal.

The weekend was interesting from the very beginning. There were about 200 people in the room, and they seemed diverse in terms of age, ethnicity, and educational level. It also seemed everyone was more intellectually-oriented than emotional—and that appealed to me. There were absolute rules about talking, phones, and break times—as well as a lot of pressure to attend the entire seminar to reap the "full benefits." Additionally, there were people designated as "monitors" around us—which made everything seem very controlled during the three consecutive days and one evening it ran.

The leader of the weekend came across as strong and direct. She said that whenever she brought up a Landmark principle and someone wanted to give their thoughts on it—or had any questions—they could come to the front microphone and have a discussion with her. People were also free to just listen because the conversations she was having with the microphone participants would impact everyone in the room. She asked us to try to stay "present" and listen—rather than analyze—as *listening* was often the way people got insights about themselves. I had an immediate struggle with that because the first thing my brain did in any situation was to analyze it from every angle possible.

She then promised that we would all get some kind of "breakthrough" in our life. And although she couldn't promise when or how it would come, she said it would be related to our established goal. She also suggested that during the weekend, everyone call those with whom they had unresolved tensions and take responsibility for their behavior—as that could be another way that a breakthrough could happen.

The first basic Landmark principle she brought up were three sets of letters that affect life: "WYKYK," "WYKYDK," and "WYDKYDK." She drew a large circle on the board and drew a small piece of pie in that circle, then said, "WYKYK is *what you know you know*: like you know your name or where you live." Next, she drew another line creating another small piece of pie within the circle and said, "WYKYDK is *what you know you don't know*: like you don't know astrophysics, or you didn't know a relative who died before you were born." Then, she pointed out that a majority of the circle was left outside those two small pie slices, noting, "WYDKYDK is *what you don't know you don't know*: and all of that has a huge effect on your life." According to her, that big piece of the pie was the focus of our time together—which was something powerfully affecting our life but about which we were totally unaware. She compared it to an iceberg with a massive section underneath the water with only a small part of it exposed. Most people, she argued, thought the iceberg was small based on that tip they could see above the water, unaware of the huge chunk of ice below.

Another principle she presented was that all situations contained two things: facts that *happened* versus the *interpretation* of those facts. She called those interpretations "stories"—and pointed out how much people confused the two. A woman came to the microphone to discuss the principle as it related to angry feelings about her mother. While talking about her mother's behavior toward her over the last thirty years—and listening to the simple questions the leader asked about whether that was her mother's behavior toward everyone—the woman suddenly got an insight, realizing that what she was saying about her mother was simply a story (and thus her interpretation) since her mother just *was* who she *was*.

This prompted me to think about being more accepting of members of my own family. Although it didn't seem to have anything to do with my "marriage" goal, this small insight encouraged me to listen more closely to see what else I could learn. The leader then brought up the idea of "coming alive," which involved being pulled out of the "mud" of where we were with no seeming future anywhere around—and suddenly seeing new possibilities for our lives. She also discussed being "present" at all times rather than focusing on the past. This turned my thoughts toward what was happening with my job and the fact that so many more things could open for me in ways of which I wasn't even aware. Perhaps if I were more open, then all those walls I seemed to see around me might fall—and other options become possible on the horizon.

This approach reminded me of the scene in *The Sound of Music*, where the Reverend Mother tells Maria (after she flees the job she has with Captain Von Trapp) that when "God closes a door, He always opens a window." I started wondering what might happen to me if He opened a window, and whether I was willing to explore such an opportunity.

I also became aware that much of the Landmark discussions centered on belief systems. I personally disagreed with their suggestion that beliefs were simply "made up." While I knew that there were many cultures and beliefs around the world, I was convinced there were universal beliefs. If there weren't such beliefs, I didn't feel the world could operate effectively—and this pointed toward a divine Being with a higher level of intelligence and morality who shared it in such ways as the *Ten Commandments*. But I didn't focus too much on the belief discrepancies I was pondering—mainly because there were many excellent points being made about forgiveness and acceptance. Plus, I was enough of a critical thinker to look past the differences.

As the weekend progressed, more and more participants seemed to be having breakthroughs with a strong sense of love/euphoria sweeping over them. I watched as they made phone calls to tell people they loved them and/or ask for forgiveness for things they had done. By the end of the second day, I was following the logic of Landmark but hadn't experienced a breakthrough. On Sunday, I wondered if I would have a breakthrough at all but was told that it might happen during the break time before we reconvened on Tuesday evening for our last session together.

While chatting with Candy at work on Monday, she told me that she did not have her breakthrough until a day-and-a-half afterward when her brain had time to work through everything from the first three day-long sessions. That night I awoke around 2 am with a sudden insight about my behavior and knew that I needed to call some of my family members and apologize for my lack of acceptance of them in the past.

A feeling of incredible joy and love came over me, and I began to think about who else I should share my Landmark experiences. I already knew I would share it with Karen, but then my mom came to mind. I figured she might get some good breakthroughs by going through Landmark—and since she was a counselor, it could be added into her "hat" of resources.

As happy as I was about all my sharing, I realized I was disappointed that I had not gotten any insight as to my goal of getting married. Then, I thought about what I had learned about being present and wondered if I should work on "just being okay with life the way it was." I was always so obsessed about marriage; maybe it was time to accept the way things were. This seemed like a new kind of "emotional muscle," so I decided to try to focus on strengthening it as one of the outcomes of the weekend.

During that weekend, I had been encouraged to attend their "advanced" course. I had been too busy to attend over the next year given all my new job responsibilities, but one day the schedule of advanced courses caught my attention and I noticed it being offered in Atlanta around the time I would be returning from a Bermuda planning trip.

I hadn't been in Atlanta in a while and always had an open invitation to stay with Brooks, a lawyer for whom I had worked (if he wasn't out on assignment somewhere with the Marines). When he acknowledged that his place was available during that time—and I found a layover flight that would work—I signed up for the course.

Setting a goal was again a requirement, and I pondered "letting go of Greg" as one option given how often he came up in my mind—even while I was dating other men. Perhaps I had not experienced a breakthrough in my marriage goal because I was still emotionally tied to him? I also wondered if my initial Landmark weekend had helped me release emotional baggage in other areas—which was maybe what had led to my job promotions.

Thinking this through, I realized I had learned a great deal from running YPO seminars—which had allowed me to step into my new off-sites position with even more responsibility. And in addition to managing off-sites, I was also now managing an assistant. Still—I wanted to go the direction of marriage, so I swung back around to the thought of "letting go of Greg" and set it as my goal.

The few weeks before the course had passed quickly, and I grew excited as I headed for the Advanced Course. After landing in Atlanta, I jumped on the subway headed north toward Brooks's place. While the train traveled above and below ground, I saw parts of downtown I used to ride past while commuting to Georgia State University to finish my college degree back in 1989. My degree had been in marketing, but looking back now I didn't see how the classes I had taken were of any help with this job (or my first job in the law industry, for that matter)—though at least I had a graduation certificate to put on the wall. The subway ride also reminded me that I had started my elementary education certification before leaving Atlanta, with plans to finish it when I got to Dallas. That had never happened, though, given how busy YPO had kept me.

My business degree also made me think of all the YPO members I had met who had never gone to university—they just had passion for an idea and made it happen. That also made me wonder if college degrees really made much of a difference (except maybe in the areas of law or science)? Since my talents seemed more about

236

teaching and supporting people, I wondered what a good college degree for me would have been...or what would have happened if my "gap year" had been before I started college rather than when I graduated. Greg had pushed me to finish, and in some senses, I was grateful that I hadn't "thrown away" four years of study.

While settling into Brooks's place before the course, I thought about contacting Greg for a get-together—since Landmark was about reaching out to broken relationships in a positive way. The course again ran Thursday through Sunday, then—after Monday off—there was a final evening on Tuesday. So, maybe Monday would work. But how to contact him? And was he even in town? I wasn't sure how to handle the whole thing—or even if I was brave enough—so I put the idea on the back burner and decided to deal with it during the seminar.

This course was like the first one I had attended with long hours and short breaks. This time, however, we were assigned to groups. I tried to be open to what I could learn about myself while listening to the facilitator and interacting with my group, but all that was on my mind was Greg. Throughout the seminar, we were encouraged to reach out to people with whom we had "issues"—and wasn't that why I came to the advanced course in Atlanta? Wasn't this all really about Greg?

With suggestions coming toward me about reaching out to him, I thought about calling his home number; if I called and his wife picked up, I could just hang up—right? But if he picked up, there would be some chance of meeting. When I got back to Brooks's house that evening, I discussed it with him (since he had been through it all with me back when it had happened). He suggested we meet at his house, then nudged me to call him.

The next morning on a break, I found one of the community phones and dialed Greg's number. I ran my fingers nervously through my hair as it rang, then I heard a familiar voice answer the phone.

237

"Greg?"

"Yes?" he replied.

"It's Kris. Kris Jaeckle. How are you?"

I heard a pause, then he responded, "Hi, Kris. I'm good. How is your dad?"

Of course, he would ask about Dad; Dad had been his commander and the reason we met.

"He's good. He and Mom are stationed at Ramstein Air Force Base right now in Germany."

I heard silence again, then he replied, "Good. I'm glad they are well."

I gave it a moment, then got my courage up with, "Hey—I'm in town attending a seminar and I wanted to catch up. Would you have any time on Monday to get together? I am staying with my former co-worker Brooks (I knew he would remember Brooks), and he said it would be OK to meet at his place. He's home right now from some Marine Corps Reserve duty."

After more silence, I heard Greg say, "I'm home from a trip right now, so Monday would work. My wife would need to be okay with it, so let me just ask her."

I heard some voices in the background, then he came back with, "How about 2 pm? And can you remind me of Brooks's address?"

After we finished arranging the details, I hung up the phone and took a deep breath. My heart was beating so hard I could hear it, but at least I had finally done it. It had been six or so years since we had talked—and now it might just happen.

Monday came around and I tried to stay calm. Brooks took me to breakfast and tried to coach me on how to handle the situation. After that, we both stayed busy around the house while we waited. Thinking back over the weekend course, I wondered if I had learned anything. Maybe something would come out after today's meeting? I knew that the biggest thing I wanted was to ask Greg's forgiveness—as I felt I had treated him so badly during our relationship.

At 2:15 pm the doorbell rang, and Brooks answered it. He let Greg in and then left us in his living room. Looking at Greg, I realized he hadn't changed looks-wise. Before he could say anything, I told him I wanted to ask for forgiveness for the way I had treated him. He responded that it wasn't necessary...that we had both had our problems. Then looking at me intently, he said, "I miss you so much."

That took me aback. I had not expected him to say that after so many years. I told him I missed him too, then tried to explain a bit about Landmark as well as my job with all its travels. I wanted him to pick up on my career success—since he had always encouraged me during our relationship to push toward a top-notch career. I also remembered that it had been something he had told me he admired about his wife back when they were dating.

Greg expressed interest in my travels and what I was doing and then looked at his watch, saying he had to go. I shut the door behind him, not quite sure what to think. That night, I went out with some old girlfriends to discuss the meeting, and all of them urged me to just let him go (as they had years before during our traumatic breakup).

Lying in bed that night, I thought about the day and my visit with Greg and fell asleep with him on my mind. I dreamed that we were back together—and that it was as simple as forgiving each other—then realized that it was over because he had moved on. I woke up feeling sad but somewhat relieved that I had achieved my goal. Was I ready now, at last, to find the man of my dreams? All I could do was watch what manifested itself in my life as a result of seeing him one last time—as well as get ready to do my next assignment in New Zealand.

Chapter 16
Do It Afraid

"Dad, I need you to pray for me."

Dad was my role model. Prayer was a way of life for him, and he prayed for everything that he was involved with in the moment: sick dogs, broken microwave ovens, marriages in trouble, lost rings; nothing was too big or too small. He had even prayed for a dying man in the hospital bed next to him after having been admitted with a kidney stone. His tales of flying supersonic B-58 bombers (and subsonic B-52 bombers and electronic warfare C-47s in Vietnam)— as well as the stories of his life in general that he shared with us— made it sound like he was always on some kind of adventure.

Those adventures included stories of life in the military corps while attending Texas A&M College; tales of "Sucks", the squadron dog in Vietnam who rode the bus to work every day with the troops, flew on B-52s and barked to let the pilots know that enemies were approaching, and stole Dad's chicken while it was being barbecued on the grill; and of his life growing up in downtown San Antonio as one of eight children in a devout Catholic family. One of the stories that always made me laugh was about him serving Mass as a young man, swinging a loaded thurifer a bit too high, and accidently releasing its incense on the crowd.

The reason I was asking for his prayers was because I was about to try my first bungy jump. I was assigned to off-sites activities for families coming to the YPO University in New Zealand—and had discovered the country was a land of adventure sports that seemed to inspire visitors to do wild and crazy things. Just as had been true of Bermuda, my job included visiting New Zealand beforehand and sampling potential activities—similar to what I had done with Patty—and one of the big things to do in this country was bungy jumping.

Located in the South Pacific to the southeast of Australia, New Zealand was made up of two islands. Since Maori natives had inhabited it since the 1300s, it had a Polynesian culture adapted to a slightly cooler climate. After a Dutch explorer in the 1600s discovered the islands, the British circumnavigated and mapped them in the 1700s. Both visitors and immigrants then tracked onto the islands, attracted to the pristine state. Its abundance of natural beauty was made up of a diversity of landscape: rolling hills, majestic mountains, lakes, fjords, amazing harbors…the list went on.

On my first planning visit, I fell in love with the incredibly nice and efficient people—whose culture seemed a mixture of South Pacific and British—and the wonderful sounds of their words (though you definitely didn't call them Aussies despite the similarities of accents). I also loved being around what had—until recently—been its most important agricultural industry: sheep. These creatures seemed so sweet and fluffy—bleating as you walked by—and were everywhere. In fact, New Zealand had the highest density of sheep per unit area in the world—and jokes were abundant about the greenhouse gases (methane, to be specific) on the island from this wooly population.

This university would be a bit like the South Africa one a few years earlier in that it was broken into two parts: Families could choose to spend their first three days on adventures in either Rotorua, Christchurch, or Queenstown...then everyone would converge on Auckland for the last three days' educational classes. The member to whom I was assigned for this event was a wonderfully cheery Kiwi named Murphy. He had already chosen the global event firm Abercrombie and Kent (A&K) as the DMC—which was a different experience from what I had just experienced with Starla's startup firm in Bermuda.

On my first planning trip, we started in Queenstown (known as the "Adventure Capital of the World") for a few days to organize things for both that city and Christchurch on the South Island. I had taken a quick southward trip to Stewart Island for a peek at the *hoiho* (yellow-eyed penguin) and *korora* (blue penguin; the smallest penguin species in the world), and we were able to see both of them waddle and dive. Off in the distance, I watched in amazement as two whales jumped out of the water and dove back in—a movement called breaching. I had seen dolphins swim and jump while in Bermuda (and it was awesome to swim with them there), but their size made it seem like a natural move. These whales were massive, yet somehow they were able to perform this acrobatic maneuver so gracefully.

Our trip had involved a two-hour drive to Invercargill and then an hour's ferry ride across the Foveaux Strait. Since it was still winter here in the Southern hemisphere—and this island was almost as far south as the tip of South America—it struck me that I had never been *this* near to Antarctica, though the fifty-degree temperature didn't seem that chilly.

Despite the fascinating visit, my mind was focused on getting back to Queenstown for a potential bungy jump. My interest in trying this sport had been piqued because A.J. Hackett was advertised as one of the keynote speakers for the university. His biography mentioned that he had built the first commercial bungy jumping site on a bridge outside Queenstown in 1989 after having done it himself off the Eiffel Tower.

Tim, my handsome, accommodating, and friendly (again, everyone here seemed genuinely friendly!) Abercrombie and Kent guide had taken me to see the penguins. He was also now showing me all kinds of other activities here on the South Island: parasailing, river rafting, mountain biking, heliskiing, and jetboating...just to name a few. In the midst of it all, I had gotten up my courage to ask if I could try bungy jumping. His response was, "I could probably fit *The Ledge* here in town into our schedule. But are you sure you want to do it? It's pretty scary stuff, Kris."

"No worries," I replied, using local lingo, "I think I can handle it."

He was able to squeeze in an appointment for two hours later, and I went back to my room to change clothes and call Dad for prayer.

"You are doing what?" he sounded incredulous when I told him what I was going to try. "Why would you want to do that?"

"You would do it, wouldn't you?" I asked.

"No! Why would I jump off a ledge? The cord could snap...or something."

"Well, I'm going to do it, so will you please just pray for protection?"

He said a quick, simple prayer for me, and we hung up. Tim was waiting outside, and I hurried to the car. On the way over, he shared that he wasn't exactly a bungy expert and so hadn't done the Ledge—even though he had set it up for a lot of tourists.

We headed up the side of the mountain on the gondola to *Skyline Queenstown*. The Remarkable Mountains were beautiful as we climbed, and Lake Wakatipu, New Zealand's longest fjord lake, appeared an opalescent blue due to its glacial depth and clarity.

I was tingling with excitement (or something) the closer we got to the top, but Tim remained quiet. I pondered the feel of the elastic bungy cord around my ankles, hoping my leap would have the same sensation as jumping off a bridge. The scenery was certainly spectacular.

As our gondola continued ascending, I asked Tim about the history of bungy jumping. According to him, it was a ritual started by Pentecost Island natives in the country of Vanuatu. Women who lived there—one of eighty islands in Vanuatu—had supposedly started the idea by attaching vines to their ankles and jumping from trees to escape from men who were chasing them. The native men soon took to doing it—building tall wooden towers from which they jumped—and eventually this vine jumping became a rite of passage called *Naghol* to prove their masculinity.

When Vanuatu was conquered by the British and French, the missionaries who arrived in the early 1900s were horrified to see this activity, calling it "land diving," and persuaded the natives to stop it. However, the missionaries never reached a southern section of Pentecost Island, so it continued there. In the 1970s the ritual was both written up by *National Geographic* and performed before Queen Elizabeth. Then, when Vanuatu received its independence in 1980, the ceremony was publicly reinstated and is now a major reason people visit the island.

Tim continued with his history, explaining that two members of Oxford University's "Dangerous Sports Club" had decided to try their own version of bungy jumping from the Clifton Suspension Bridge in England after reading the *National Geographic* article. A.J. Hackett came into the story at this point in that he happened to be speed skiing in Britain when he saw a video about the Oxford jumpers, and that inspired him to try it. After doing so, he and a partner (along with Auckland University scientists), designed a special cord to accommodate these kinds of jumps.

Although they found a few jumping locations in New Zealand, they pondered where a jump would most catch the attention of the world. While speed skiing in France, the Eiffel Tower's height and prominence inspired him, and he and a dozen or so of his team found a way to sneak up and attach their newly designed cords. At sunrise, Hackett successfully jumped from the top and the rest was history. His stunt gave him the idea of starting a bungy jumping business, and he built his first site near Queenstown on a bridge in 1989—which had a 300-foot drop just above a river. His newer build here on the Skyline, called *The Ledge*, featured a drop-off of 1200 feet.

"He'll talk about all of this in his keynote speech," Tim concluded his story.

I tucked that away in my mind so that I would be sure to hear him—and maybe even meet him. "So," I asked, "how is this jump I will be doing from The Ledge different than the one off the bridge?"

"Well, two things: first, it is here in town, so you'll get a gorgeous view of Queenstown and its mountains, known as the Southern Alps; and second, you'll get a look toward Milford Sound as we make our way up." I knew about the European Alps from being around them in Switzerland, but these "Southern Alps" had been named in 1770 by the British explorer Captain Cook when he discovered them on the southern island of New Zealand. They spanned one-third of the area that the European Alps did—with their highest peak reaching 12,316 feet.

"If you really want to jump, this is the only one we can make time for, as the other one is further down the Kawarau River in a canyon," Tim noted, bringing my attention back to the issue at hand. "The longer drop off makes it seem scarier—though the bungy cords at both locations are about the same length of around 150 feet. This jump stops you way above the ground, while the other stops you just above the river—unless you ask for a "head dip" which gives you more of a ground rush. We're here; let's get off."

We stepped out of the gondola and over to the bungy's entry walk. This consisted of a few connected tunnels from the side of the mountain to create space for a drop-off—but not many were needed, given the steepness of the mountainside. Tim followed me to the entrance of the jump, saying he would wait for me there.

"You're sure you don't want to do this with me?" I asked.

"Nope," he answered confidently. "But the jump is on us. I even paid for a video to be shot so you can remember it forever, Kris."

I didn't feel the least bit scared. It had to be similar to what I had done when hang-gliding recently in the Engadine valley of Switzerland, right? And both places were gorgeous, so I focused my attention on their beauty. I walked through the tunnel and met up with a friendly jumpmaster named Sue, who asked if I was ready to get set up for the jump.

"Let's do it!" I said, waving and flashing a smile over to Tim.

Sitting me down, she explained that after getting me securely bound, she would walk me over to the edge. From there, she could encourage me in case I got scared to step off.

"Get scared? No way; I am excited to do this!" I insisted.

"Great, then let's get you set up! Do you want to be bound at your ankles and have a harness around your chest for support—or just be bound at your ankles? It's a bit scarier if it is only around your ankles."

"Oh, just around my ankles. I don't think I need anything else. I really want to feel the rush."

She checked out my clothes to be sure they were snug, then started the work on my ankles. She twisted and tied and pulled and yanked. When she finished her work, she showed me a D-shaped, spring-locked link called a "carabiner." She used it to attach the bungy cord to the ankle binding, then had me pull on it to be sure it was secure. She also asked me to feel the cord, showing how it was made to "give" a little—since I had been concerned about my rebound at the end of the fall. She also explained that A.J. Hackett's bungy cords were made from exposed latex threads; other commercial operators used a tough, outer cover over their threads resulting in a harder, sharper bounce. I re-envisioned myself hanging upside down at the bottom of the fall based on this newly acquired knowledge. This should be just perfect!

Looking over at the magnificent mountains—some with snow on their peaks—I got a sense of how high I was. One thing I loved about higher altitude, no matter how it was attained, was the perspective it gave me. *Perspective* was good—a universal force—and its force applied to everything in life if one took time to stop for a minute and utilize it.

"Are you ready?" Sue asked, disrupting my thoughts.

"Let's do it!"

I turned to wave again at Tim with confidence. He waved back.

Putting my hand on her arm for steadiness, we walked over to the jump-off point—with my taking mini "shuffle-steps" due to my bound ankles. When we finally got there, I peeked down to the ground and saw that it seemed really far away. Had I thought about it being such a long dropoff? I also noticed the rocks around the safety person at the bottom as he waved at me; did I really want to be smashed against them if my cord broke? Suddenly, I felt fear rise within me—so I shifted my eyes back out to the horizon. I saw the mountains and beyond—which was a view that I liked better. I could hear my heartbeat increasing. There was nothing for me to hold onto, and I became aware of my unsteadiness. Instantly, my hands went toward my chest to grab something...and there was nothing there either. Maybe this was why she had asked me if I wanted a chest harness? The move was subconscious...and it was interesting that my hands went toward the center—and most key part—of my body.

I heard her next to me saying, "Spread your arms out to either side. You'll hear me say, '5, 4, 3, 2, 1,' and you can jump. Are you ready?"

"I...I think so." I said, but now I wasn't feeling so confident. I spread my arms.

"Okay...5, 4, 3, 2, 1...and *jump*!" she instructed confidently.

I didn't move, except to bring my hands back to my chest. There was nothing there to grab, so they immediately went upwards and found a metal bar. Both hands gripped it with all their might.

"You know, Sue...I think I maybe want to try to do this tomorrow. Why don't you unhook me?"

This was perfectly in line with my love of procrastination. I had thought I wanted to impress Tim by doing this, but now I didn't care. I just wanted off this ledge.

"Kris, if I unhook you, you won't come back tomorrow. So, I am just going to let you stay there for a minute until you are ready to jump."

"No, I really think I will come back tomorrow," I assured her, feeling my hands grasp even more tightly on the bar above me, "I am good about keeping my word." I felt sweat beginning to form on my neck.

"Just try breathing slowly for a moment," she said calmly. "It will help you. Let me know when you are ready, and I will count for you again."

It was clear she was not going to let me out of this. I was trapped. I wasn't sure what to do next, but then I remembered one of my favorite Scriptures, though heaven knows I hadn't memorized it for this purpose. I started speaking it to myself: *I can do all things through Christ who strengthens me.*

I spoke it a little louder, then started repeating it. I noticed one of my hands starting to rub my stomach. As I kept speaking, I felt my other hand go to the top of my head. They both kept moving: back and forth across my head—and round and round over my stomach. I wasn't sure why my body was doing this; it made no sense. I did know that this was probably the most stressed and scared I had ever been in my life. Then, another Scripture, *God has not given me a spirit of fear—but of power, love and a sound mind*, came out of my mouth. I noticed my brain doing this speaking without my even purposely thinking about it. On the other hand, it had been ingrained in me since I was young to find appropriate Scriptures to speak—and to keep my focus on God—in hard or scary situations. I had also grown up listening to talks about all of this. Maybe this was why it was happening unconsciously?

An amazing calm suddenly came over me. Sue noticed some kind of shift because I heard her start to count: "5, 4, 3, 2, 1…"

I felt like I was in a trance…and I wasn't sure I had ever been this calm in my life.

"…jump!"

My foot stepped off the ledge. The other one followed it. I felt my upper body begin to pitch forward, and then I could feel myself go through a horizontal position on the way toward flipping upside down.

There was still no sense of fear. In fact, my brain—in a very calm state—seemed to say, "This is it? It's not scary at all." It almost began to be a let-down.

Then I realized that the biggest fear in this whole situation had been *making the decision to jump*. The actual jump itself was nothing. Thinking through this as I continued to fall, I didn't even realize I had reached the end until I started to pull back upwards with a little bit of gentle, long bobbing. I could see the rocky side of the mountain next to me, and as I descended, one of the staff reached for me and pulled me toward him. Holding me by my arms against his chest allowed for my legs to gently come down, and then for my feet to touch the ground. Once I was standing and steady, the ankle cord was removed.

I could feel my heart rate still racing and figured it would take a few minutes to calm down. After all, this had been an adrenaline-rush. Tim came running toward me. If he had heard me talking to myself and what I had said, he didn't mention anything; he just hugged me and told me how impressed he was. What it really was for me, however, was a life-changing event that would affect me from that point forward. I had learned to "do things afraid." I had learned that the scariest part of any situation was *taking the first step*.

The whole experience stayed on my mind as we headed up to Auckland on the North Island. Based around two large harbors, Auckland was a beautiful city, sparkling clean and full of boats bobbing in the harbors. The Kiwis there and elsewhere in New Zealand were incredibly warm and friendly but also very efficient. The more I thought about the whole country, the more I decided how much I loved it—but especially Queenstown set against the backdrop of the mountains. It just seemed *perfect*.

My time growing up in various locations had taught me how cultures often matched their climates. North Dakota was a great example; it was a cold climate and took a while for people to warm up to you—but once they did, you had friends for life. Atlanta was the opposite in that it was a warm climate whose people were your best friend from the moment they met you—but you never quite knew what they were saying behind your back. Then, a theory struck me: Maybe the Kiwis were hospitable due to the South Pacific climate. But they were also just across the "water" from Australia—which could account for their English efficiency.

The rest of the planning for New Zealand went well, and when the start of the university approached, it was just before Christmas. It was hard to leave my family during the holidays, but when the staff all arrived and settled in Auckland, the committee met us with a surprise Christmas dinner. After that, we broke into the three initial locations for the families to experience adventures—with me heading to Queenstown.

Excited for the members to arrive, I was also glad to have Sam and Rachel—our executive director and his wife—on my team here in the "Adventure Capital of the World." Already in love with this scenic spot, I shared with arriving members the "adrenalin rush" I had felt from my bungy jump—and encouraged them to try all kinds of different things. Once they began their activities, we watched them go for more and more "rushes," and then reminded them that *this* was why it was all called "adrenaline adventures."

With everything going well and some activities having "open" spots, I tried to give Sam and Rachel opportunities to try things—though they didn't seem interested in bungy jumping. And we were getting great feedback on tandem skydiving, so I encouraged them to try it. After they came back excited about the experience, I wondered if I could "sneak it in" before heading to Auckland for the second half of the university. I got everyone else packed up and shipped off, then used my remaining half day to try it out.

NZONE Skydive was the company we had chosen for this adventure. They had been the first to offer tandem skydiving seven years before and had nothing but rave reviews about their service. The whole experience took three hours (though the skydive itself was a thirty-sixty second freefall, followed by a float the rest of the way down). After a twenty-minute ride from downtown Queensland to their setup building on a sheep farm, we were assigned to our tandem skymasters, geared up for the fall, and shown the plane they would use: a Cherokee Grand Caravan airplane.

While dressing us in gloves, a hat, goggles, and a jumpsuit (they told us it would be chilly while we fell), they had told us how skydiving all started: Andre-Jacques Garnerin, a French Revolution POW in Hungary, had dreamed of a way to escape his high prison walls. Three years later, he was released, and on return to Paris, he put his idea into action—eventually becoming the first official aeronaut of France. When he traveled to London to perform his skydive, he did his first jump over Grosvenor Square, inspiring a popular ballad:

Bold Garnerin went up

Which increased his repute

And came safe to earth

In his grand parachute

Listening to this story brought back memories of my stay at Grosvenor House, and I tried to imagine anyone parachuting around there. My thoughts were interrupted as our skymaster explained that although it still took quite a bit of training and practice to get certified in skydiving (like scuba diving), in 1983 someone had concocted the idea of doing it in tandem—which revolutionized the industry and opened it to the public. First jumps no longer required training—just the ability to be strapped to someone and fall in *very* close proximity to them.

The guy I was assigned to was quite the Aussie, with a fun personality and lots of leading comments about how close together we would physically be. He asked what order I wanted to be in for the jump, and I told him last—so we were the first ones on the plane. We headed towards the back and he sat down, spreading his legs, then pulled me back toward him before connecting us at the shoulders and hips. At that point, I realized what he meant about our intimacy.

I tried to ignore all that, though, as everyone else piled into the plane and we headed out the bumpy private runway into the skies. Our ascent gave us more and more amazing views of Lake Wakatipu and the Southern Alps, and when we reached 15,000 feet, the door to the front right of the plane opened and the first tandem couple slid forward and dropped out. Feeling jittery because of this jumping height, I thought back to stepping off The Ledge—and how much I had to coach myself to do it. At least here someone was attached to me and could push me out if I got scared, but I could still feel my fear rising. After watching everyone else jump, my jumpmaster encouraged me to push on out—but I didn't move. He again asked if I was ready, and I made myself nod but didn't move. Finally, he nudged me forward enough to get us to the door, then pushed us a little more forward, and *out we went!*

The jump shock wore off, and another shock came over me as the freezing cold air hit my face. Then, I realized we were falling at a very fast pace with *nothing* stopping us—and this was really fun! I started to laugh uncontrollably (feeling my teeth start to freeze), then found I couldn't stop. One of the other free-falling skymasters dove toward us and high-fived me, then dove back away. All around me was the *whoosh* of rapid air and spectacular scenery—except that the ground below was rapidly growing larger and larger.

Suddenly, I felt a "bump" and was jerked upward (that was different from bungy jumping's soft "catch" on the descent!), and then there was some swaying and dead silence as our descent rate changed to a much slower pace, and we began our float downwards. I remembered that this would be about five minutes and settled in to enjoy it. The scenery was magnificent, and I focused in on that. What *didn't* New Zealand have in terms of beauty and graciousness? I suddenly realized my teeth were still chattering and wondered if it was from the cold or the fear?

A minute later, my skymaster reached for my arms and placed each of my hands into the handles above us, showing me that pulling on one or the other affected the direction in which we floated. As we approached the landing spot, I noticed some sheep in the distance but was distracted by how fast we were still going— and wondering how we would hit the ground without hurting our legs. My partner said loudly into my ear, "Hold your legs up and I will hit the ground with mine. We'll slide for a second or two, and when we stop you can lower your legs."

With the ground approaching rapidly, I thought about what he had told me—but was still scared about a hard hit. I remembered seeing people who rolled when they hit the ground and how it seemed to help the shock, but that wouldn't work with a parachute attached—so I could only hope I would be able to do what he asked. He reminded me again to raise my legs just as we hit ground, and to my relief it all worked out perfectly.

Once we stopped and he detached himself from me, I stood there hearing my heartbeat and thinking about what an amazing experience the skydive had been. I also wondered if I shouldn't have done it *before* bungy jumping since it had involved the help of someone else. But what did it matter now? I had just finished my second adrenaline rush experience. What else could I do in this amazing country?

After arriving in Auckland for the second half of the event, I again sensed a different sort of energy compared to Queenstown; it still had that "fresh" sort of feel—although it was less rugged and adventurous. I got all the activities coordinated and launched, including tours of historical museums and art exhibits, sailing, biking, canoeing—even visits to mystical caverns lit by glowworms. Rap jumping was one adventure about which members were raving, so after the university was over a few of us decided to try it. I figured this third "adventure" would make me an official "adrenaline junkie."

Rap Jumping advertised itself as "running down a building," and Auckland's venue was the twenty-story downtown Novotel. Looking at pictures to get a feel for how it worked, it seemed like "backward rappelling"—something that Tom Cruise might do in one of his action- movies like *Mission Impossible*. The Australian Special Forces had originally invented it in the 1960s as a way of descending a tall building while using an assault weapon to fire at the ground. Then, in the 1980s, one of their members realized it could be put into commercial use and opened a Rap Jumping experience at the top of a hotel in Cairns, Australia.

Jane and Steve from the marketing department had decided to join me, and we made our way to the Novotel roof. We were all a bit apprehensive, though—to me—twenty stories (somewhere around 300 feet) didn't seem *too* high compared to the bungy jump and skydive I had done from 1,200 and 15,000 feet, respectively. I put on my bravest air, given my new "Do It Afraid" motto, and assured them that it would be a piece of cake.

"This is a very safe adventure," the lead jumper encouraged everyone as he briefed us to start, explaining there were many backup systems in place: fixed anchors hammered into the top of the building that attach the descent ropes; experts holding the ropes on top of the building to guide us down and experts holding the ropes from the ground ("brake people") who could stop us if anything went wrong; carabiners that held all parts of the system together; and figure-eight *descenders* that connected our carabiner to the rope to allow for easy and smooth descents. "Once you are in the system, the slightest touch of your fingers to the ropes will stop your descent immediately," he concluded.

He then took us over to the side of the building to point out the *brake people* who waved up at us. While looking over and down, I felt that now-familiar fear of long, uncontrolled descents creep up on me (why would it not go away?), then reminded myself that I had done two other things like this before. I was glad Jane was there, as she was another of my favorite fellow-staffers who was fun, sweet, and would always drop whatever she was doing to give me a listening ear. Steve was as adventurous as me and very ambitious; he had recently taken over the entire marketing department after having started his job at the ground level just a few years earlier.

Our guide led us to the preparation bench where gray helmets were fit snugly over our heads, red harnesses secured around our waists and legs to form a "seat," then appropriately sized gloves and traction boots chosen and donned.

"Who wants to go first?" the lead jumper asked.

Jane and I looked at each other and stepped back. Steve looked at us a bit disparagingly and stepped forward. We watched him walk to the edge of the building, get attached to the system, grasp the rope with his gloves, then allow himself to be tilted forward from the harness in the center of his back until the lead person released him and he disappeared. We walked toward the side of the building in hopes of seeing him, but it took a moment before he was in sight about halfway down. We watched him jump away from the building once or twice at that point, then finish walking to the ground and get unhooked. He turned up to look at us, made a sign that it was "no big deal," then motioned us to "come on down."

Jane and I both heard, "Who's next?" and we looked at each other without moving. Finally, she stepped forward, hooked up, and began her facedown descent. I pondered again what I was doing. This was the closest to the ground of everything I had tried and had the most controls attached—which should make it the easiest—but everything within me told me *not* to do this. Why was I mentally struggling? Hadn't I already done two other things like this? Then, I heard it was my turn. I walked over—not very confidently—and the lead jumper took my hand, re-checked my gear, and clicked me into the rope system.

"All you have to do is hold still while I lower you forward to a horizontal position, then we'll let you start walking to the ground," he gently encouraged me. "We'll be holding you from up here *and* stopping you from down there, and it will all work. Once you're over the side, you can squat like a duck all the way down, walk, jump—anything you want to do. Go ahead; you can do it."

I once again realized there was no "out" for this situation (why did I keep doing this to myself?), so I stepped to the building's edge. I felt the rope's tautness and his hand holding the harness at the center of my back as he leaned me forward. During the last two adventures, this was the point at which I had let go and fallen, but not here. I was still held in place even though I was facing the

257

ground. It was almost as if the fall was in slow motion—except there was no fall.

The fright of taking my first step led me to take a squatting position (he knew what he was talking about when he made that suggestion!), then I tried a step or two—followed by squeezing the ropes with my gloves. The descent stopped immediately (as promised), and my confidence increased—it was just that the position was uncanny. Whoever walked down the front of a twenty-story building facing the ground? There was just no logic to it. In my mind, I should be falling, but I didn't *want* to fall. My brain was on overload trying to handle it all.

Closing my eyes, I took another breath or two while feeling the wind blow softly over me and the sun warm my body. Hearing encouraging cheers, I opened my eyes, focused on Jane and Steve next to a *brake person*, and tried another step. Pushing down into the building with my feet allowed me to stand taller, then I inched forward a step while holding tightly to the rope. Feeling that work, I took another step—then another. I tried going a little faster but squeezed again on the rope to be sure it was working and came to an immediate stop. Feeling that safety net again, my confidence grew even more. By now, I had passed four windows—which probably meant four stories—and I thought about how to go down the remaining sixteen. Should I try a jump or two? Wasn't this called "rap jumping"? When would I ever have this kind of opportunity again?

I started walking more quickly—then sped up enough to try a slight jump. It worked, and I tried another and then another. Squeezing on the rope again, everything stopped, and I felt my heart thumping (that poor heart; all these unnatural adventures!). How to finish my descent? Noticing there were now just a few windows left below me, I decided to keep it slow the rest of the way (no more adrenaline needed). Soon I reached the street and was released—getting warm hugs from Jane and Steve.

As all the activities in New Zealand ended and we prepared to fly home, I felt the adrenaline rush wane and the focus return to my romantic life. There had been no one to think about in that area during this university, but then again there had also been more than enough excitement to keep me occupied. The same had been true in Bermuda due to a different kind of excitement—both had been overwhelming. Was all of this happening because of my Landmark work? Seeing Greg again? Or was it just because of increased responsibilities at work? I continued to ponder it all over the long flight back to Dallas, wondering if I were finally ready for romance—a real romance, where I could be fully committed to another man. Only time would tell…

Chapter 17

Dinner at Tiffany's

Hovering above the World Trade Center at the southern tip of Manhattan, I thought back to how I had gotten here. I had just finished helping at the YPO New York City University—and it had been a hectic but amazing experience—but when was a YPO event *not* amazing in some way? My feelings about the city were very different than when I first arrived, and the dramatic skyline view from up here added to my growing sense of amazement.

Flying over Governor's Island on our way to "Lady Liberty," we had taken off from the New York City Heliport on the southeast tip of Manhattan. As we approached the familiar copper-turned-green, twenty-two-story statue with her flame held high, the helicopter had slowed and hovered for us to get a better look. After a moment there, we sped over toward the famous Ellis Island of immigration with its beautiful baroque-style Main Building—then the pilot ascended and increased in speed until we were here at the tip of Manhattan, hovering.

Next, we headed up the Hudson River until we reached the George Washington Bridge, then banked toward the East River. Central Park loomed below us, and its perspective was remarkably different for me from this vantage point since all I had seen of it was its southern edge while launching activities from our hotel. We finished out with a run down the East River, back to the Heliport, and stepped off. That full circle around the Big Apple summed up the whole week for me.

The experience had begun with my walking into the Plaza Hotel, and I had stopped for a moment to gaze at a tip of Central Park on the other side of 59th Street. Never having been in New York City, I was curious to see the legendary green space. Comparing it in my mind to London's Hyde Park, it didn't quite have the same feel. The road leading across to it appeared grimy and dirty—in fact, there was a grungy look about almost everything in this city.

Even LaGuardia Airport, where we arrived, had seemed unclean. People were pushy and walked right in front of me—as if I wasn't there. They walked close together too, as if there wasn't enough space. I had experienced crowd crushing in India, but the feeling here was different. The incredible speed people were moving here hadn't happened in either Bombay or Calcutta. And the atmosphere was nothing like London where the people were friendly and courteous.

The bus ride from LaGuardia to Manhattan took us past endless blocks of tall, non-descript grey and brown buildings—many with kids playing basketball behind fences. Trash was everywhere, and the roads were full of bumper-to-bumper cars all honking at each other. What was the appeal of this city, I wondered? Was there any beauty to it? Why was Manhattan so world-famous? I had looked forward to helping with off-sites for this university, but now I was regretting my decision. I just hoped that when I got settled into the Plaza, I would see a different picture than I was seeing now.

Crossing a bridge with a little island underneath it, we continued into Manhattan and merged onto street called "60th." After going a few more blocks, I saw the famed twenty-one-story, chateau-style hotel sitting at the corner of 5th Avenue and the southeastern corner of Central Park. Built in 1907, it reminded me of the Grosvenor House in London. Both were square and tall, though the Grosvenor was larger, whereas the Plaza was taller. I would soon find this to be true all over New York City: small parcels of precious land were used to construct tall buildings. It was easy to understand why some people joked that someday this little island would sink. The only other place in the world with more skyscrapers was Hong Kong, but it was built on three and a half times the amount of ground.

My former boss Ron was the project manager for this university, and after evaluating hotels around the city, had contracted with the Sheraton on Sixth Avenue. Then the university chairman changed—and with that came a demand for a different hotel: the Waldorf Astoria. Breaking the Sheraton contract resulted in financial penalties, but the Waldorf did seem an appropriate hotel for the city, so plans moved forward. Then the university chairman changed again (although I had never known of a university chairman changing even once), this time to a NYC chapter member named Kimberly—a real estate powerhouse in the city—who demanded yet a different hotel.

Ron, whose personality matched his incredible organizational skills, tried to explain to Kimberly the financial consequences of breaking another contract, only to be ignored as she contracted with the Plaza herself. From that point forward, the two kept their distance, but I didn't get a chance to hear much about all this because I was busy with the Swiss global board meeting and no longer reported to him.

My friend Candy was again in charge of education and reported to a well-connected member from California. The two had worked together to assemble a list of topnotch speakers, landing an impressive name or two by offering honorariums—something

YPO wasn't known to do. Then again, many things about this university seemed different. I had hoped to work with the speakers at this event but instead been assigned once again to working off-site activities.

Barb, whom I had met early in my YPO career, was coordinating the activities. She had moved to Dallas with YPO when its headquarters relocated from New York City, but after a few years, returned to her hometown of Punxsutawney, Pennsylvania, and was now being used on a consultant basis. I enjoyed seeing her again, and we caught up for a moment before she introduced me to Nathaniel, the off-sites chairman, and Deborah, the destination management coordinator.

Nathaniel immediately captured my attention. There was something charismatic about him, and it was difficult to pay attention to anyone else at that moment. Forcing myself to focus on what was being said, I learned there was a wide array of activities that included early morning visits to the Fulton Fish Market; private wine classes at places like Windows on the World at the top of the World Trade Center; cooking classes with Peter himself at Peter Kump's Cooking School; tours of museums around the city; midnight ride-a-longs with policemen on their beats; helicopter rides around the island; informational walks through the oldest parts of the city; guided walks through the New York City Flower Market—and much more.

Barb had prepped me that both Nathaniel and Deborah knew the city well, and that anything and everything possible to do was offered in some way, shape, or form. Perhaps this breadth of activities *was* the appeal of NYC. As I listened to Deborah talk, I tried to guess her accent—though my attention remained on Nathaniel. When I asked about her background and how she had gotten this job, Deborah replied that she knew the city well from working for the *92nd Street Y*— mentioning the name as if I should know it. I racked my brain as she continued, "I grew up in Tunisia but then lived in Israel. When I got here, the Y hired me and I worked my way up to their head of travel."

Seeing my puzzled look, Barb explained to me about the *92nd Street Y* being the top Jewish cultural and community center in the city—if not the world. Then, after she and Nathaniel spoke quickly about some details, he turned to talk to me. He emanated elegance and confidence, but his intelligence was the most striking thing about him. I instantly knew I wanted more time with him to see what I could learn (or was it that I was attracted?) and wondered if this week would afford me that on a personal level.

After he left, Barb told me that he had majored in economics at Harvard at the undergrad and grad level, but there still seemed to be something about his intellect that I found unusual—not arrogance, but perhaps ease or confidence; I couldn't put my finger on it.

After our meeting, I explored the hotel. Fresh flowers were everywhere, and I strolled through the German-looking *Oak Room*; the *Palm Court* with mosaic floors, the *Plaza Restaurant* and *Champagne Porch*; and looked inside the *Edwardian Room* that had apparently been open, off-and-on, just for men. I knew from a guidebook that the Plaza Hotel was also famous as the home of Eloise, the charming little girl in children's books who had many adventures here. The playwright Neil Simon had also used it as the backdrop for his comedy *Plaza Suite* about three different couples who have life-changing experiences in the same room.

After getting settled into my room, I checked in with Candy to see what she was up to, and she invited me to join her to check on a venue—with a quick stop at Bergdorf Goodman. I figured this could be another "first" for me, as I was curious to see it.

After exiting the Fifth Avenue hotel doors, we stepped into a crowd walking the way we needed to go. We made it about a block, then she waded through the stream of pedestrians to the right and turned to enter a sophisticated storefront. Following her, I was glad I was decently dressed because I felt a "stuffy" air inside—then understood why when Candy mentioned that the store was owned by Neiman Marcus. As I walked around, I got that *Neiman's* feel—but unlike its store in Texas there was not a trace of friendliness from the staff. Once Candy finished looking through the scarf department, she announced that she was ready to go and we headed back out to Fifth Avenue.

Joining the crowd again on the sidewalk and picking up our pace, we continued to walk toward 57th Street, where she pointed out the famous Tiffany & Co. off to the left. As we crossed 56th Street, Candy explained streets here decreased in number going south—and that twenty blocks equaled one mile. I was wondering how far she wanted to walk when she abruptly stepped to the curb, raised her left hand, and a yellow taxi pulled over. She quickly opened the door and slid into the backseat—motioning me to follow—then told the driver she wanted to go to Bryant Park.

Acknowledging her request with an Indian accent, the cabbie took off. We didn't go very fast (horns were blaring everywhere), and after inching southward he finally turned to the right on 42nd Street—pulling over to let us off. The meter read $2.50 but Candy paid him $5, whispering to me that people always paid at least $5 for a taxi ride in New York City. We walked up a short flight of steps into a clean, open area with people sitting around tables, and she led me through glass doors into a French-looking restaurant called Bryant Park Grill. Leaving me on the patio, she suggested I order a glass of iced tea and look over Bryant Park while she quickly checked on the nearby New York City Public Library for one of her speakers.

Taking her advice, I ordered and then observed the scene below me in Bryant Park. Bordered on every side by streets, this green space in the heart of the city was beautiful, unlike my opinion thus far of the rest of Manhattan. Looking a few more blocks to the south, I caught a glimpse of what I thought was the Empire State Building with its 103 stories rising into the skies.

Candy returned fifteen minutes later, and after grabbing me, she again hailed a cab—directing him to go back to the Plaza through the Theatre District. As he drove with the traffic, honking and swerving, she pointed out Times Square. This section of the city appeared large, brassy, and colorful. I noticed Madame Tussaud's (hadn't I seen one in London too?), and when we reached 8th Avenue, Candy pointed to theaters advertising *Phantom of the Opera* and *Les Misérables*. I thought of London's West End where she and I had walked several times—and where I had seen both of those musicals.

Quietly observing as we turned to the right, I saw more bright colors, lights, litter, taxis, and people walking en masse. At the end of the street, we came into Columbus Circle, an interesting, busy intersection at the southwest corner of Central Park. Again turning right, we were soon back at the hotel. As we exited, I noticed the Pulitzer Fountain—named after the man who established the Pulitzer Prize—who designed this little section of New York City to be like the Place de la Concorde in Paris.

Registration day of the university arrived, bringing many people by the off-sites desk. Watching Nathaniel and Deborah in action, my admiration grew for their teamwork. Nathaniel was also considerate, ensuring we all got breaks, as well as stepping in diplomatically whenever members had complaints or demands. Sensing that getting to know Deborah might be a way of getting to know Nathaniel better, I helped her any way I could.

Out of the blue, Mike—the Mergers and Acquisitions chairman in Dallas for whom I had gotten the Staubach-autographed football—showed up at the desk and seemed to be arguing with Barb about an off-site he had requested. When I saw him, I walked up and asked if I could help. Nathaniel was nearby and I thought they might enjoy meeting, so I pulled Mike over and introduced Nathaniel.

Mike looked at me a second as if trying to remember who I was; then, after seeing my nametag, it dawned on him. A calculating look came over his face. Introducing us both to his wife, he came around to my other side—leaving her to talk to Nathaniel. Flashing a smile, he told me how great it was to see me, then followed it with "Kris, you know that 'midnight ride with a cop on his beat' off-site? Is there any way you can get me in it? That is the only activity I really care about. And I head out early, so the only nights I would be available are Monday and Tuesday."

He again flashed his charming smile. I thought a moment, conscious that what he was requesting was one of our most popular offerings—with many people on the waitlist. Realizing how quickly he had formulated his special request upon seeing me, and reflecting on our interaction in Dallas, I decided this time I was the one who had control. "I don't know, Mike," I replied, "as there are so many people on the waitlist. Check in over the next few days and I'll see what I can do."

The week proceeded to be the usual crazy-busy, so I wasn't able to take part in too many of the off-site events. I also had to keep up with my Switzerland project, leaving me no time to explore much of the city. Mike also checked in several times, but neither Nathaniel nor Barb would confirm anything for me—especially since it was against YPO rules to allow "special privilege" for off-sites choices.

The last time he checked in, however, the magic tickets appeared—and he walked off very happy. Stopping at the desk before leaving the next morning to speak with Nathaniel, and I heard him say how interesting and different this ride with had been compared to doing it in his hometown of Los Angeles. Nathaniel nodded, and they exchanged cards—especially when Mike talked about his connections to Berkeley and UCLA. Mike then stopped to thank me, and grabbing his bags, had a bellman hail a taxi for him.

Watching Nathaniel interact with Mike, I thought about how much I was enjoying getting to know Nathaniel better, even though I never really saw him for longer than a few minutes here or there because he was always on the move (New York culture again?). I had found him to be levelheaded and cerebral, and other than Deborah, there weren't many women around him. I wondered why he was still single given all his accomplishments, personality traits, and good looks. He was also the youngest member of YPO I had met so far, and joining wasn't easy in New York City—given the high-powered people everywhere. This only added to his mystique, and I could feel my attraction to him growing by the day.

The more I hung out with Deborah at the off-sites desk, the more I liked her too. I had a special love for Israel, and she talked with me about her experiences living there after she left her birthplace of Africa. She also told me a lot about the 92nd Street Y and Nathaniel's involvement with it, as well as his attraction to Orthodox Judaism. That piqued my interest as another subject to bring up should I ever get some alone time with him.

Deborah suggested I might find it interesting to visit the Y, but after a week here, my mind was already thinking more seriously about what an adventure it might be to move to New York City. Considering how much I disliked the city when I arrived, it seemed surprising to even consider the notion. But I had now seen samples of so many things to see and do in the city, and it was obviously a sophisticated place full of traveled people—a definite melting pot of cultures—much like living on Air Force bases. I was also intrigued by the history of Manhattan going back to the Dutch in the 1620s.

The Metropolitan Museum of Art was the venue for the final university evening event, and I volunteered to work it with hopes of getting a walk-through. Its façade featured enormous two-story classic pillars with half-round glass windows above them, and well-lit red banners hung from either side of its main entry doors. To me this museum seemed huge, running from 80th to 84th Street and far back into the park.

The dramatic, tall-ceilinged Great Hall had an octagonal Information Desk laid out with wine, champagne, and martini glasses—and was staffed by formally dressed bartenders. Lit candles flickered around the glasses and on cocktail tables that filled the hall. As members entered, they mingled at the cocktail tables before heading into the various privately open sections of museum on the way to dinner inside The Temple of Dendur. Somewhere above us, I heard piano music, but I was too busy checking people in to be able to figure out where it was coming from. Nathaniel popped in (again unaccompanied) and waved at me as he tablehopped.

Once we checked everyone in, we were given permission to wander the museum with a drink for another hour or so before it closed. So, I grabbed a glass of champagne and headed down a barrel-vaulted gallery filled with Greek and Roman sculptures from the fourth- to sixth-century BC. Past that I found myself in a large, open courtyard enclosed by pillars with a tiled floor and glass roof. This gallery was filled with even more sculptures from the third century BC to the fall of the Roman Empire. I had seen many of these types of statues in London and Paris (and some newer versions of them in Florence), but classic art tied to history always appealed to me. I ambled along slowly—enjoying the beauty of the art—and then paused in front of "Young Hercules" and a sarcophagus featuring the "Triumph of Dionysos."

Hearing the tinkling keys of the piano again, I turned back toward the Great Hall and followed the music up the stairs. Its volume grew as I turned to the right, and then I noticed an entryway to a hallway of European paintings. After peeking inside, I decided to enter and discovered a long, narrow gallery—this time seemingly full of Rodins—and then came upon a startlingly sensual painting. "Pygmalion and Galatea." The French artist Jean-Leon Jerome had depicted a nude, perfectly bodied female sculpture coming to life as its sculptor, overcome by her beauty, wrapped his arm about her body and passionately kissed her. Entranced with this erotic painting, I stood there—conscious again that my life currently had no romance at all.

Suddenly I heard a voice behind me. "Kris, are you enjoying that painting?"

Turning around, I discovered Nathaniel smiling at me, looking handsome and elegant in his dark business suit.

Caught off guard, I blurted, "Yes—they seem so taken with each other. Right now, I have no man in my life, and it makes me long for a relationship like that."

Now why had I told him that? There was a moment of silence between us, then he changed the subject to the museum collections. After chatting for a few minutes, he said he had to get back to the dinner, but as he turned to leave, suddenly whirled around again. "Are you free tomorrow night for dinner? Will you be staying around that long?"

My heart skipped a beat. "Well, I am scheduled to leave tomorrow since I am due in Switzerland for a board meeting planning session. But I could see about flying out the next day instead." Thinking quickly, I added, "I can probably talk Ron into letting me have a room here one more evening."

"Wonderful," Nathaniel replied. "Let's confirm in the morning when I stop by the office." With that, he sped off toward the dinner in the Temple of Dendur while I tried to think about what I would wear—and say.

While we were packing up our materials early the next morning, Ron asked if I wanted to take a helicopter ride early that afternoon with him, and I jumped on it. I also mentioned the need to stay another evening to meet with someone before heading to Switzerland, and he confirmed that I could have one of the leftover hotel rooms. Nathaniel checked in and suggested we meet in the hotel lobby for an early dinner—noting that I should wear comfortable shoes so he could walk me around town a bit.

Now I was doubly excited about my final day in New York City: an aerial tour of Manhattan followed by dinner with Nathaniel. On the cab ride to the heliport—while looking at all the streets and buildings—I thought again about how much my opinion of the city had changed to the point of thinking about moving here. It certainly wasn't a beautiful city, but the energy level was addictive—unlike any other place I had ever been. Would I really like it here? Was it my kind of place? I decided to add these questions to the list of topics I wanted to bring up with Nathaniel this evening.

As I dressed for dinner, I went back and forth in my mind about what to wear. Black seemed *chic* in this city, but I didn't have much along that line. Besides, black wasn't really my personality. I did have a two-piece dark teal, floral-patterned suit with a pair of matching high heels—but how far I would be able to walk in them? In the end, I settled on that outfit.

We had talked about meeting around 5:30 pm, so I made sure I was down in the lobby on time. 5:30 pm passed, then 5:45 pm. My heart sinking, I turned to head back upstairs when I heard his voice as he rushed into the lobby, apologizing for being late. He then asked if I wanted to walk a few blocks, since he thought I might enjoy the King Cole Bar at the St. Regis.

As we started walking down Fifth with the flow of the traffic, I asked Nathaniel if he had ever seen the movie "Breakfast at Tiffany's." He nodded, and then suggested we walk past the store since it was near the restaurant where we were headed. Without warning, he darted across Fifth Avenue to the other side, assuming I was right behind him. I increased my pace to keep up with him, noticing that everyone seemed to do this (not paying attention to traffic signals) but keeping their eye out for breaks in the rush of cars and buses.

Once we got to 57th Street we turned left, then walked halfway down the block. There it was all lit up: Tiffany & Co. I couldn't help but stop to peer into one of their windows at the elegant jewels on display. All of a sudden, I felt like Audrey Hepburn—playing Holly Golightly—mesmerized at the thought of a man loving me so much that he presents me a ring in one of those small robin-egg blue boxes tied up with a white satin bow.

"Are you ready to go?" Nathaniel asked, jolting me back to reality. I pulled myself away from my romantic fantasy to follow him. We turned right on Madison Avenue, and I enjoyed the slightly less frenetic feel of that street. Even more expensive shops appeared one after another, and I struggled to catch the names since we were walking so quickly. Turning back toward Fifth just two more blocks south, we found a traffic opening and we crossed to the other side— just in front of the twenty-story St. Regis Hotel.

As we walked past the doorman under the black-and-gold canopy and through the gilded revolving door, I entered what appeared to be a small version of the Chateau de Versailles. Nathaniel explained that the St. Regis was—arguably—the fanciest and top-rated hotel in the city, built by John Jacob Astor in 1904 as a companion to his Waldorf Astoria further down Fifth Avenue. He had built it as the highest hotel in the city—as well as taller than all other mansions in the area. When Astor died, it went into the hands of his son, who eventually sold it off. A few other companies had owned it, but the Sheraton had restored it recently, spending $100 million. I gulped when I heard that amount. But this *was* New York City.

We arrived early enough to find a seat at a candle-topped table in the King Cole Bar, known for the cocktail it made famous: the Bloody Mary. Neither of us were interested in one, so we ordered a glass of wine and looked over the menu. I stopped to look up a minute at the mural of a king and his royalty behind the bar. Following my eyes, Nathaniel explained that it was based on the nursery rhyme "Old King Cole," and Astor had paid a large sum to have his own face painted on the king's body, which prompted me to laugh.

When the waiter walked up with our wine, Nathaniel suggested we order the Tuna Tartare and Mushroom Risotto, and I agreed. As we waited for our food, Nathaniel asked me what I thought about New York City. I reflected a minute, then told him my opinion had changed since first arriving. I asked whether he liked Boston or New York City better, and he related what he appreciated about both—especially their educational aspects. The more he talked the more I was drawn to him, and my opinion about his intellect and culture continued to increase. And as we sat there, I didn't want to talk—I just wanted to listen to and look at him, hanging on his every word.

I finally ventured to ask if he thought I would enjoy living in the city. He responded that it took some adjustment, but that he considered Manhattan his hometown—given that his business and YPO chapter were both in the city. He did mention that he also spent quite a bit of time in Boston—which prompted me to bring up the Cantons, to whom I was reporting for the upcoming global board meeting in Pontresina. They were from Boston, and Dan was this year's international president. After we discussed the upcoming board meeting, Nathaniel graciously offered his assistance if any help was needed. At this point I hadn't seen his name on the attendee list, but I tucked away in my mind the possibility of getting him invited.

When our entrees arrived, I switched the conversation to spirituality, and Nathaniel talked about how much his faith meant to him. Remembering my observations about Deborah and her "culture" versus her "faith," I listened to his thoughts about God and his relationship with Him. He admitted he'd always had a passion for growing spiritually and enjoyed time at Hebrew University in Jerusalem as a visiting research fellow.

He inquired where I had gone to college, and I mentioned my three undergraduate schools. I also shared that after my years of traveling with YPO, I was now pondering getting a master's degree in international affairs—perhaps at Columbia or Tufts—given their well-rated programs.

"That would probably be full-time," he noted, adding, "so are you thinking of leaving YPO? If you get into Columbia you would probably enjoy the city. And you already know Deborah and me now, so you would have friends here."

That thought excited me, both for the education and adventure involved and for the fact that it might be an invitation to get to know him better. I peppered him with questions about living in New York City: was it expensive, hard to live in, easy to make friends, too hot or cold? I knew he lived somewhere near Fifth Avenue around the Plaza, but when it came to his personal life, he was evasive. He had been open about almost everything with Deborah, but I knew they had been friends for a long time. She was also older than him—and they were professional associates— whereas I was more his age and single.

I decided to back off and turned the conversation to pursuing a graduate degree. "This is an amazing city academically—just because there is so much everywhere," Nathaniel assured me. "It might be a great step for your career. Why don't you go ahead and apply?"

"I need to finish out the board meeting," I explained. "But I guess I could apply for a fall admission."

"Well, good luck—and let's stay in touch," he replied, putting his napkin down and motioning the waiter for the bill. After escorting me back to the lobby at the Plaza, he hugged me goodbye and again said to stay in touch. I felt a little thrill run down my spine, and as I watched him walk off I realized I needed to make a major change in my life. The time had come to apply to graduate school.

Chapter 18

Rockapella in the Alps

" I'm desperately searching for waiters who can sing a cappella," I begged the person on the other end of the line. "In Switzerland—Pontresina to be exact."

I was on the brink of tears. In all my seven years at YPO, I had never faced a mission as impossible as this one—and I had only ten days to pull it off. For the last week, I had been racking my brain and calling everyone I knew who might be able to help me, to no avail. This might be the one time I failed to deliver, and it would be epic because the demand for these singers had come from the very top: Dan, global chairman of YPO, wanted them for a special moment he planned for the YPO global board meeting's closing dinner in Pontresina, Switzerland.

His wife Sandra, a gorgeous redhead, had told me about her husband's unusual request during our first planning meeting together in Dallas. We had enjoyed each other's company at a YPO spa event the year before, and our reunion in a hotel lobby to chat about the board meeting brought on a big hug. Then, almost immediately, she started chattering away. "Won't this be fun—a board meeting in Switzerland? I love the St. Moritz area. The YPO university there in 1990 was the first one our family ever attended, and it was awesome."

Enjoying her enthusiasm, I replied, "I've been with YPO for seven years and helped plan all kinds of universities and seminars. I'm currently working on the family university in New Zealand in December–and that one will be pretty exciting."

"Why do you say that?" she puzzled.

"Everything is an adventure there—so many wild and crazy things to do. And once you try something daring, even more daring opportunities beckon you. I actually did a 1200-foot bungy jump on the South Island last month."

"Wow!" Sandra gasped. "I'm not sure I'd want to do that. Paragliding or hiking, maybe. Have you done anything else through YPO that has profoundly affected you?"

I thought carefully, then shared my Mother Teresa story. I hesitated because it involved God, and unaware of her spiritual leanings, I didn't want to be offensive. On the other hand, everyone loved and was inspired by my story, so I decided to forge ahead.

When I finished telling her how I had found the medical supplies Mother Teresa had requested, Sandra became teary-eyed. "That is an amazing story, Kris. I struggle with the *God* part of it because, despite my prayers, my sister-in-law died a horrible death from cancer. But listening to your story encourages me to try praying again."

I smiled, remembering that my morning wake-up prayer had been, "God, please use me powerfully today." It seemed my prayer was being answered.

After shifting our conversation back to the global board meeting, Sandra announced that Dan had one specific requirement. "He loves a cappella music and has re-written the lyrics of two songs from his favorite singing group called 'Rockapella' to honor the incoming international president. So, we need you to find some people who can sing a cappella and get them the lyrics. Supposedly there are singing waiters in that part of Switzerland during the summer. Can you check on it?"

"Sure," I said.

"Oh, and I have a tape with the two songs Dan wants them to sing—with the lyrics he wrote," she added, fumbling around in her shoulder bag while talking. Finally, she pulled the tape and typewritten sheets out and handed them to me. She then made a second request that was her own idea: an "encouragement board." She explained that it would be something like a big bulletin board with family-named envelopes pinned to it. When members thought of kind things to say about other members, they could write a note and drop it into that family's envelope.

"I haven't heard of anything like it at previous family events," I said, "but it sounds like a great idea. What if we had notepads with the YPO global board meeting logo made just for this purpose—and included them in the registration packet?"

"That's exactly along the lines of what I was thinking!"

We chatted a bit more, then a concierge walked up to remind her it was time to go to the airport. While separating, we agreed that our next planning meeting would be held at the event's venue, the Grand Hotel Kronenhof in Pontresina. I shared that our YPO chief events director, Susan, would join us—along with Joseph, an American YPO member living in Switzerland whose business involved running teen activity camps in the country. He had agreed to meet us in Zurich, and suggested that we include Linda, an American who lived in Pontresina and had helped organize the 1990 St. Moritz Family University, in the planning process.

A few weeks later, Susan and I landed at der Flughaven Zurich—minus Sandra, who had decided to meet us up in the Alps. The airport was my first taste of Swiss culture, and it struck me immediately as the most organized and quiet airport I had ever seen. A tall silver train that ran underground from our arrival gate to the main terminal featured sounds of running water and mooing cows, and scenic pictures flashed on the walls as we sped on our journey.

Once we gathered our luggage, we took an "S-Bahn" to the Zürich train station—and exited to the Bahnhofstrasse, a beautiful walking area. I had read that the city boasted the best quality of life in the world, and this gave credence to that claim. Clean and modern, yet with a European street-sized intimacy, the area was full of stylish people walking at just the right pace.

Joseph was to meet us at Cantinetta Antinori, a Tuscan restaurant near Teuscher, the famous Swiss chocolate shop. As we strolled the seven blocks to our rendezvous point, we took in the vista of snow-capped peaks in the distance, the streets banked in fresh flowers, international finance offices, and high-end fashion stores—with amusing, full-sized sculptures of cows scattered here and there.

On entering the restaurant Joseph flagged us to his table, then greeted Susan Swiss-style with three kisses. She turned on her usual charm, offering her cheek starting with the left one; then, he then turned toward me and offered the same greeting. Over lunch, Joseph explained he was originally a New Yorker, and after graduating with a degree in accounting, had gone to work for IBM in Switzerland. When IBM shut down his office, he found a way to stay in the country by setting up summer camps for kids. The business had grown enough to allow him a YPO membership, and the organization now used his services to coordinate their global teen camps.

Joseph suggested we finish our lunch with just an espresso because he had a surprise for our dessert. After paying the bill, he ushered us down the street to Teuscher, where he bought each of us one of their signature champagne truffles—one of the more than 200 kinds of chocolates they created. The second I bit into the bonbon I knew it would become my lifetime favorite chocolate.

The Dom Perignon cream center was covered first in dark chocolate ganache, then with either a milk chocolate coating dusted with powdered sugar...or a dark chocolate coating dusted with cocoa powder.

While indulging in this dreamy confection, I wandered around the flower-filled shop and learned that Dolf Teuscher had started the company in the Swiss Alps in 1932. He invented the champagne truffle, and eventually moved the company into Zurich's old city center. By the 1970s, Teuscher was flying their sought-after chocolates to customers around the world on a weekly basis.

As we headed back onto the street and toward Joseph's car, we passed another colorful cow sculpture, and I couldn't resist asking him why Zurich was *so into* cows.

Joseph smiled. "Switzerland loves its cows, many of which you'll see on our drive to Pontresina," he responded. "But these sculptures are an art exhibition called *Land In Sicht* (which roughly means, 'Country in View')." It seemed a prominent Swiss window store dresser, Walter Knapp, had the idea of making sculptures of his favorite animal so that they could be placed in public areas around the city, and commissioned his son Pascal to design them in three different poses: reclining, standing, and grazing. At the request of the Zurich Tourism Association, he had several dozen made of fiberglass and asked local artists, businesses—and even schools—to decorate them. "The exhibit has been so successful that they have had to make more cows," Joseph added. "They are thinking that by next summer, there may be more than 800 of them on display around Zurich."

Heading out of the city toward the Alps along 3W, we followed a lake for a while and I noticed a stream of expensive cars passing us: Rolls Royces, Aston-Martins, Bentleys. Joseph saw what I was noticing and said that, given the history of the Engadine Valley, it was normal to see these high-priced autos because they were on their way up to the glitzy resort of St. Moritz. He continued to explain that, situated at the base of the highest peak in the Eastern Alps (*Piz Bernina*), St. Moritz was a popular destination of the international Jet Set and upper class. He noted that its fame began in 1864 when St. Moritz hotel pioneer Johannes Badrutt invited some British summer visitors to return in the winter. He promised them that if they didn't like it, he would reimburse their expenses; but if they did enjoy their visit, they could stay with him as long as they wanted.

The British took him up on his challenge and stayed, kick-starting the tourism movement in the Alps. St. Moritz had hosted the Winter Olympics twice, but had also become a summer destination, offering golf, polo, cricket, sailing, and windsurfing. "The village is now called the 'Top of the World,'" Joseph said.

Although Pontresina was only five miles away from St. Moritz, YPO had chosen it as the venue because of its historic Kronenhof hotel, which was more understated and the right size for a more intimate gathering. I had done a little homework before coming and learned that the name Pontresina was derived from "Ponte sarasinae," meaning, "a bridge built by a man named Saraschin."

Peering out the car window, I suddenly noticed an enormous building on top of a mountain in the distance. Joseph informed me it was Sargans Castle, one of 600 ancient fortresses in the country. "Sargans is older than Switzerland itself—founded in the thirteenth century," he said. "Its six-floor medieval culture museum is one of the most visited in Europe."

He and Susan shifted their conversation to his company's youth counselors and where they would be housed during the board meeting. I kept my eyes on the scenery, which was so breathtaking—a bit like the southern island of New Zealand with its mountains and adventurous city of Queenstown. What made this different was that the European Alps spanned a full 750 miles over eight countries—with Switzerland basically in the middle—and featured the much higher peak of Mont Blanc at 15,780 feet.

We climbed higher toward the 6,000-foot elevation of Pontresina and the scenery grew even more dramatic. I caught sight of many herds of contented Swiss cows and understood now why "alp" referred not to the *peak* of a mountain, but rather the high mountain pasture where animals are taken for grazing during the summer months.

Joseph slowed to allow me to look at some of the cows grazing by the sides of the road. Lowering my window, I heard something like tin cans "ringing" at various pitches. Then I noticed that the cows had collars with bells on them, and some of the bells were beautifully decorated.

Joseph could see my fascination, so he explained that there was a whole history behind cows and their cowbells. Back in the Middle Ages, this custom had started with large collars made from a mixture of wood and leather. Bells were now made from all kinds of metal—but the majority came from sheet metal. "There are also all kinds of meanings behind the bells," he observed. For example, the sounds they make may indicate the age, sex, or species of the cow. The size and decor of the bell could also reflect the prosperity of the cow's owner. Once a year, at the end of the summer, owners adorned their cows with flowers and necklaces during a festival called "Alpabzug," which was a processional from the Alps back to their home farm after grazing in the higher mountain meadows.

Entering Pontresina, we pulled into the Grand Hotel Kronenhof where Linda was waiting. Attractive and petite with long brown hair, she was in great shape—probably from taking advantage of all the winter and summer sports opportunities in the area. Walking through the hotel it was immediately obvious why it was named the Grand Hotel Kronenhof: its neo-baroque style was indeed grand as well as elegant, reminding me of the classic hotels on the Champs Elysees in central Paris.

The hotel had originally been founded as a postal stop in 1848, and for the following fifty years, various architects had continually worked to enhance and upgrade it. The result was a six-story white chateau nestled in the heart of the Alps, with a green copper roof and gold trim. Listed as the best-preserved Grand Hotel architecture in the Alps, it was also known as the Grand Dame of European hotels.

I dressed down for dinner but still wore a scarf and some shoes from Florence. I had heard (and had seen in Zurich) that the Swiss enjoyed Italian fashion—not surprising given that, as the crow flew, Italy was a mere ten miles away!

Marcus, our hotel contact, had hors d'oeuvres and candles waiting for us on tables when we arrived. The sun was sinking behind the mountains with just a sliver of the moon showing. After drinks were served, he gave a short description of Pontresina, telling us that its altitude was 5900 feet and its municipality—almost exactly in the middle of the triangle formed by Zurich, Milan, and Munich—was home to the highest mountain in the eastern Alps—Piz Bernina. Although locals had ascended the mountains in this area, a noted Swiss climber had scaled Piz Bernina in 1850—and that began the gradual build-up of summer alpinism. The WWI and WWII eras slowed it, but one thing that kept business going here was the Kronenhof's famous wine shop—as well as the 1928 and 1948 Olympics held in nearby St. Moritz. Pontresina also had its own airport in nearby Samedan—the highest airport in Europe.

Sandra and I had a few goals for this first planning meeting: to hear Joseph's idea for the youth program; explore some general early morning and afternoon activities for members, their wives, and/or entire families; and establish some ideas for evening social events. So we spent the next few days with Linda exploring the area, which was a great break for me from all of the New Zealand planning. Unlike the friendly Kiwis, the Swiss were a bit more reserved. But I knew the Swiss centuries-old reputation for efficiency and perfection—as seen in their Swiss watches—would make them great to work with. My "Air Force brat" background had also taught me to adapt to new cultures, and it was one of the things I enjoyed in my job with the YPO.

Hiking and bike rides were a given, but we still sampled one or two of each possibility. Our first night's meal was at Muottas Muragl, a destination Linda felt would be great for the opening social event. Perched on the side of one of the most famous mountains in the area, Muottas Muragl featured a restaurant called Panorama for its 360-degree view of the Engadine's Lake District. The restaurant was only accessible, however, via a funicular ride, which started at Punt Muragl and rose 2400 feet.

Riding it would be my first time on a funicular, and the incline looked steep. I wondered how fast it would go and what it would feel like. As we waited in line to start the ascent, Linda explained that funiculars were based on physics. In a way, they combined the technology of an elevator (a cable pulling a car up) with the technology of a railroad (a car on a track). They had first been invented in the 1500s in Salzburg to lift heavy goods into the town's castle, and by the 1800s were being used to carry skiers to tops of mountains. "This particular one is over one hundred years old," she noted as we stepped aboard.

We heard a whistle blow, then felt the car begin to move up the mountain. Looking out the windows at the valley, Pontresina and St. Moritz grew smaller as we rose higher and higher up to the restaurant. The ten minutes it took to get to the top was a scenic treat with the sun setting over the snow-capped peaks of the 12,000-foot Alps surrounding us on all sides.

Once at the restaurant, we sat down at picnic tables and sampled *raclette engadina*. This was their signature dish—a Swiss form of fondue featuring melted cheese in a center pot surrounded by "dippable" food, including potatoes and bread. The funicular ride back down the mountainside in the darkness offered a stunning view of the lights of the valley, and Linda reminded us that many hikes could be started from funicular exit points. I made a mental note about that as a potential afternoon family activity.

Two weeks before the board meeting came the big "hiccup." Marcus called Friday morning out of the blue and sheepishly shared that the singing waiters at the resort were not going to be able to sing.

"But Marcus," I said in a panic. "You know that Dan HAS to have these singing waiters for our closing dinner. What are we going to do?" I knew I had to call Sandra and give her the bad news, but I decided to wait until the end of the day. When I called, her daughter asked me to hold while she tracked her down. Suddenly, a male voice came on the line.

"Kris?" It was Dan. I began to get nervous but decided I would keep my calm and act nonchalant. I certainly wouldn't mention the news.

"Yes, Dan?"

"We are in the middle of a fundraiser upstairs. I'll let you talk to her, but please remember in the future that she is not available to you 24/7—and especially not during Friday night cocktail hours."

"Of course, Dan. I just had something important I needed to share with her."

"Well, here she is. Have a good weekend and get the singing group to practice those two songs for our closing event." My heart began to race as he brought up the hot issue.

I waited for another moment, then heard her bubbling voice "Hi, Kris! What's up?"

"You may want to sit down because I have some not-so-great news," I started, hoping to prepare her for what was coming.

286

After I finished—and we volleyed a few questions back and forth—she asked if I would keep the news to myself to give her time to think, then she'd check back in on Monday.

Over dinner that night at my parents' house, I also shared what had happened. Dad immediately started thinking about what to do with the situation, but Mom changed the subject. "I've hired a masseuse for you, Kris. She'll be here tomorrow afternoon. Maybe that will de-stress you a bit."

I was touched by her thoughtfulness. The next day when the masseuse arrived and began working my body, I opened up about what was happening in my life (maybe for me, this verbal aspect of massages was more therapeutic than the body work?). When I got to what had just happened with the singing group, she burst out in enthusiasm, "I am part of a group that meets every Thursday morning at 5:30 am to pray. We will pray for a singing group for you, and I just *know* God will bring you one! In fact, let's end this massage with a prayer."

I felt great and relaxed—and even more than that, I felt encouraged. Little did Mom know what she had done when she hired this masseuse. That night at dinner, Mom revisited the singing group problem. "Remember how we used to enjoy the *Strolling Strings* in Washington, DC?"

My mind went back to high school and one of my favorite Sunday events at a military facility, Bolling Air Force Base, that had been founded in World War I as the closest military airfield to the National Capitol. Their Officers' Club was known for its excellent food, and Sunday brunch was one of our favorite times to go there. It was also the headquarters of a group of violin and viola players who walked around a room and use their instruments to provide a multi-dimensional concert-type experience without a conductor. If in town, they would play during the brunch—and listening to them was always a beautiful experience.

"I seem to remember that they perform in Europe too," my mom said. "Wouldn't they be the caliber you need for the event?"

I saw it in my mind now. It would be perfect…the musicians in formal uniforms, playing romantic music, walking around the dinner tables. She had a great idea! My only problem was that I needed acapella singers as well. But she reminded me that the group was part of the Air Force Band, and her friend's husband played for the European version of the band. "I got to know her while I was stationed in Germany. Do you want me to see what I can find out for you?"

I was so grateful to her, but the event was in two weeks—and I knew the slow pace at which the government works. But I also knew how crazily things often worked out for me. What would be the harm in asking?

When Monday morning rolled around, I called Sandra. We had no sooner started to talk when I saw our executive director, Sam, approach my desk briskly. Sam never came by my desk, so I knew something was up.

"Kris, I need to talk to you right away," he interrupted. He could see I was on the phone, and that didn't seem to dissuade him.

I told Sandra I would call her back, and heard her warn, "Watch out; Dan knows, and he called Sam."

Sam stood in front of me looking quite upset. "Dan just called me. Apparently, we no longer have an a cappella group for the closing dinner?" he asked, waiting for my reply.

"That is what the hotel just told me, Sam. But, I've—"

Sam interrupted again, "He's really upset. He told me that he didn't care what it costs, but we had better find a replacement."

I let him stand there and talk. I knew this issue wasn't about me or him. He had to be the one to hear Dan vent. "I've been racking my brain all weekend to come up with other ideas, but we only have

288

two weeks before the board meeting. I do have some feelers out for the Air Force Band in Europe at the moment."

"Good idea," he said, seeming a bit calmer. "Keep on top of it and let me know what you find out."

I called Sandra again, telling her my mom's idea about the Air Force Band. "You know how much I've been praying. Then, this weekend, I had a wonderful massage, and the lady who did it told me that she is having her whole prayer group make it one of their requests. Let's just watch and see what happens."

After we hung up, I thought about calling Nathaniel. I remembered from our initial dinner together and subsequent get togethers in New York City that he was strongly connected to the Orthodox Jewish church, and we had discussed our common experiences with prayer. I had been keeping him "in the loop" on the board meeting and wondered if he would pray with me about this. So, I dropped him an email explaining the situation—asking if he could talk.

A minute later, I heard my desk phone ringing. The number on the display read from Boston. It was Nathaniel!

"Hi, Kris. I just saw your message. What are you going to do?"

"I really need to resolve this singing group situation. My mother has an idea about a European group, but at this point something unusual has to happen to resolve this situation, so will you pray about this with me?"

"Of course, and it would be great if you keep me up to date."

We spent a moment in silence as we prayed separately. As I hung up, I thought about the first time after the University that I had returned to Manhattan. Nathaniel had shown me around New York City, taking me to the Museum of Modern Art, walking me rapidly through each room, stopping to glance only at the new pictures, then moved on. It had been all I could do to keep up with him.

Then, last month when Sandra, Susan, and I had been on our way home from Switzerland, we had stopped off in New York City to see *The Scarlet Pimpernel* on Broadway. I had loved the Jane Seymour movie version of the story—and Sandra was a big Broadway fan of musicals—so she offered to treat us to dinner and the show. She had heard me talk so much about Nathaniel that she asked if he would like to join us for dinner beforehand at La Grenouille.

"The flowers they have in the restaurant are gorgeous, and almost everyone famous has eaten there. Nathaniel will know it, and I'm sure he'll want to join us."

I emailed him, and he agreed, saying that he loved the restaurant but hadn't been there in a while.

After we checked into our hotel, I rang Nathaniel. No answer. A bit later, no answer. I began to get frustrated and embarrassed, as I had told Sandra and Susan that he would make a wonderful dinner companion. I also knew he and Sandra could discuss both Boston and New York given their familiarities with both cities.

When 5:30 pm came and there was still nothing from him, we moved on to dinner. I was so disappointed but tried to shift my hurt by focusing on the beautiful restaurant and wonderful French food. Sandra could sense that something was wrong and prompted me a few times for an explanation, but I kept my feelings to myself.

When we got to the show, the French Revolution-era adventure drew my mind off Nathaniel. Written by Barroness Orczy in 1905, the main character, whose secret ability to rescue those in danger from the guillotine, had inspired the characters of *Superman, Zorro, Batman*, and *The Shadow*. The intense songs, fabulous costumes, classic storyline, and good, clean fun (and "clean" didn't seem to happen much in "adult" Broadway shows!) kept me entertained for the rest of the evening.

That night, I suddenly awoke with a humorous idea of how to convey my disappointment to Nathaniel. I got out of bed, sat down at my computer, and rhyming words soon flowed freely:

There once was a great guy named Nathaniel

Who forgot to check in his etiquette manual

About how to dial and say with a smile

"I won't be able to join you."

Sandra, Susan, and Kris understand very much

How schedules get busy and things may come up

But it takes just five seconds to return a phone call

And it says to them that they weren't blown off after all.

Returning to bed, I fell asleep as I pondered when to send the communication. Returning to Dallas, I waited a day, and then another—finally realizing that if I waited much longer, he might not even remember the reason for my note. So, I looked at the email one last time—then pressed "send."

It didn't take long for Sandra to check in and say that she had received an apology from Nathaniel. He did the same thing to Susan, then followed by calling me to apologize as well. Mentioning his extremely busy schedule, he said he had forgotten about the whole thing but appreciated my humorous rhyme. Thinking about it all, I felt the incident had made it clear that we would—at most—be close friends and that was okay with me.

The next morning, Mom called with the phone number of Steve LeDeux, one of the members of the German Air Force Band. I left a message, saying I was making an "official" inquiry into an opportunity for the band—hoping it would generate a return call ASAP.

Steve promptly returned my call the next morning but said there were several problems with my request: First, any venue where they play must be an "official" event of some kind. Second, the band was always booked months in advance; in fact, they required ninety days to even *request* it. Third, they didn't have an a cappella group.

"I'm sorry, but there's just no way the Air Force Band can do the event."

I was deflated; there went that idea.

But he then offered, "I do have an idea for you. Laurie, one of the wives here just happens to have assembled an a cappella singing group, and I believe they travel to destinations. If you would like, I'll give her a call and tell her what you need."

I felt hope again, but it took several days for us to connect so I was sitting on pins and needles—especially since Dan now insisted on a daily update. Sandra also checked in because Dan was as much "on her case" as he was on mine. I loved her callings, always finding them a breath of fresh air. One day when she called in, she gushed about the *Anne of Green Gables* DVDs I had sent to her, and how much her girls were loving it. She made everything I did seem wonderful, and that made me want to work even harder for her.

When Laurie and I finally talked, it was an incredible conversation on many levels. It turned out her group was available the night we needed them—in exactly eight days! When I told her about the two songs from Rockapella and the re-do of their lyrics, to my amazement she told me she was friends with Rockapella and her group already sang those songs. The relief I felt was so great that I could feel my entire body relaxing from all the tension. The last thing to be discussed was the price, and that turned out to be well within budget (on the other hand, I didn't really have a budget after Dan's ultimatum, did I?). Then for some reason, I had a feeling that I should ask about her background.

"Sure," she responded, telling me that before marrying her husband in the Air Force, she had graduated from college in Boston in 1987.

"Were you at Harvard?" (I asked this thinking of Nathaniel, but knew I was taking a long shot).

"Yes, I was. Why do you ask? Did you go there as well?"

"No…I'm just good friends with someone who went there around the same time. His name is Nathaniel."

She gasped. "He was my best friend at Harvard! In fact, after we graduated, I worked for him in New York City."

Now *that* was just too big of a coincidence. "He belongs to this organization for whom you are going to sing—Young Presidents' Organization—though he won't be at this event," I continued. "The funny thing is that I just spoke with him about this situation, and he prayed with me about it!"

"He was always very philanthropic and spiritually-minded, so I'm not surprised," Laurie replied. "I haven't talked to him much since I moved over here. But, also, how funny—I helped him with YPO while I worked for him. He was really young when he joined."

I couldn't wait to get off the phone and email Nathaniel to update him. But my immediate goal was to track down Dan and Sandra and let them know. Sandra was aware how much I had been praying about this, and I was excited to give her the good news. I knew they had made plans to stop in Prague on the way to St. Moritz and wondered how to track them down. I started by calling his assistant, who was delighted with the news and gave me an international number where I could reach Dan.

When I dialed, it rang a few times then Dan's voice came on the phone. "What do you need? I am in the basement of a cathedral with the family, and this is an expensive call. Do you need Michele for something?" I heard some rustling noises, and him saying, "It's just Kris…"

When I emphasized that it was him I needed, he told me to make it quick.

"It looks like I found an a cappella group for you."

The phone was silent for a minute. "Really? How did you do that? Where are they from?" he asked, sounding as if he didn't believe me.

"It is a group headed up by a woman whose husband is stationed in Germany," I explained, my voice growing in confidence. "My parents had the idea and got me the contact. She personally knows Rockapella, and their group already sings the two songs that you want. I've emailed her your lyrics. And she was one of Nathaniel's best friends at Harvard—having worked for him in New York City and helped with YPO there. Small world!"

The tone of his voice suddenly grew warmer. "Kris, this is fabulous news. Great job! I can't believe it!" he said. "In fact, I am stunned."

At that moment, everything deep within me came to the surface about what *I* felt had made his wish come true. "Dan, this is not about me doing a great job! This is about the fact that I serve an amazing God who answers prayer. Do you know how many people are praying for your board meeting?"

His moment of silence indicated a loss for words. "Well… whatever it was…thanks for making it happen."

Sandra's voice jumped onto the phone, and I shared the news with her—also reminding her of all the praying that had been involved. Once again, it was "kudos" for God, and I had different motives in both of their lives for wanting to see this take place. The thrill in her voice was unmistakable, but I heard Dan in the background asking for the phone, so I rapidly ended the conversation.

From then on, it was all I could do to get ready for the global board meeting. My arrival into Zurich gave me just enough time to drop my suitcases at the Hauptbahnhof and get to Teuscher before my train headed out. The extra stop was due to a last-minute idea for a room gift—a box of champagne truffles for each of the families, an idea Sandra thought was perfect.

After arriving at the hotel, I wandered down to the area where the Encouragement Board was being set up. I was excited about this idea of Sandra's and hoped it would become one of the best memories of this meeting. One of my last projects was to print family names on the envelopes to hold notes from the special pads I had designed with our YPO Pontresina logo that were to be included in everyone's welcome packet.

The first night's ride up the funicular on Muottas Muragl to dinner at Panorama proved to be a success, and the descent after dark was particularly romantic and special. Riding the funicular had become my favorite thing to do during my planning trips over here, and as the stars appeared twinkling in the sky, I waited for the last open car and jumped on board.

Once I returned to the Kronenhof, I swung by the Encouragement Board area. Dan and Sandra had announced the concept during his welcome, and I had heard some buzz among the crowd—so I wanted to see if anyone had tried it yet. As I passed the bulletin board, I saw a few notes peeking out of the envelopes. Then, I noticed one sticking up out of mine! I had a feeling I knew who it would be from, but I decided to wait until later to look at it.

The first thing I did the next morning was pull out the note, and upon reviewing it my suspicions were confirmed that it was from Sandra. Her sweet words—followed by a big happy face—encouraged me a great deal. Later that morning, she asked me to join her at the wives' focus group later in the day. When I walked in, she announced, "I wanted everyone to know what a great job Kris did for this board meeting, and I brought a little surprise for her."

Sandra had seemed to notice everything I commented on, and during a recent event in Santa Fe I had seen Anastazia and her daughter wearing beautiful charm necklaces designed by a local artisan. Michele and I had discussed them, then I had forgotten all about it—but as she handed me a box from her bag, I saw the artisan's name on the box. Unwrapping the bow around the box, it revealed the beautiful necklace—with the exact charms I had mentioned. I tried to say something but was so emotional that I started to cry—so I bit my lip instead. I felt so special.

Another stop at the Encouragement Board, which was increasing in popularity, produced a few more notes in my envelope. One was from the New Zealand University chairman and another from Lynne. She and her husband James were the incoming YPO global chairmen and head of the next year's board meeting—as well as the reason for the special lyrics of the a cappella singing group. Her simple note complimented me on how I had handled this event and asked if she could tap my expertise during next year's planning period.

The next day flew by, and we spent the afternoon preparing for that evening's party featuring the a cappella singers. They had checked into their rooms, and I met Laurie ahead of time—who was even nicer in person than on the phone. We exchanged information about Nathaniel, then she had the group do a warm-up with the two re-written songs.

When the big moment came, Laurie's group performed wonderfully—and I felt all the stress had been worth it. The evening ended with Dan singing my praises in front of everyone, and I felt so good. The happy ending also reminded me about what I had said to Dan about the singing group being an amazing answer to prayer.

Tears came to my eyes as I realized this would be my last YPO international meeting, but I was elated knowing that I was leaving on a high note—literally and figuratively. Gazing around the room, I thought about all that had transpired since the seven years ago when my mother had first set up an interview with a strange organization for a job I didn't even know I wanted. My first project had been packing up 400 boxes of conference materials for an event in Vienna. Now I had managed an entire global board meeting and averted a last-minute disaster by finding an alternative singing group in the Swiss mountains!

Over these past seven years, I had worked for interesting CEOs, traveled to many places, and met world-changing people who had affected my life profoundly. And it had all started on a tiny, primitive island near Australia with my committing my life to impacting others on behalf of God.

Now it was time to move on. After talking to Nathaniel and applying at his suggestion to graduate school in New York City, something else had "divinely" opened with a YPO member offering me a job in Tulsa. So, it looked as if Nathaniel's idea had been put on hold with this unexpected side-step coming into play—though my new boss had agreed that I was welcome to leave the position if graduate school opened.

Years ago, I would have been thrown by this turn of events. But through everything I had learned by now—especially through my recent bungy jumping experience—I had gotten used to taking unknown steps and being confident in what came about. In my new role, I would be helping to coordinate YPO chapter and national events; who could predict what kind of doors that would open? I also realized I was beginning a new chapter in my life and could move forward with confidence by trusting in an amazing God. I had found my wings and was starting to fly.

Epilogue

The Titanic

I dissolved into tears as Jack drifted away from Rose into the icy sea. A friend had offered to take me to see the movie *Titanic*. As the closing credits rolled, I sat there unable to move, replaying the final heart-wrenching scene in my mind:

Out in the icy sea after the Titanic has sunk and the rescue boats pulled away, Rose and Jack are left floating, she on a large plank and him next to her in the ocean.

ROSE: *I love you, Jack.*

He takes her hand.

JACK: *No, don't say your good-byes, Rose. Don't you give up. Don't do it.*

ROSE: *I'm so cold.*

JACK: You're going to get out of this...you're going to go on...and die an old lady, warm in your bed. Not here. Not this night. Do you understand me?

ROSE: I can't feel my body.

JACK: Listen to me, Rose. Winning that ticket to get onto this ship was the best thing that ever happened to me...it brought me to you. And I'm thankful, Rose. I'm thankful.

Jack's voice trembles with cold, which is working its way to his heart. But his eyes are unwavering.

JACK: You must do me this honor...promise me you'll survive...you won't give up no matter what happens...no matter how hopeless. Promise me now and never let go of that promise, Rose. Never let go.

ROSE: I promise. I will never let go of that promise, Jack...I'll never let go.

She grips his hand, and they lie with their heads together. It is quiet now except for the lapping of the water around them.

Jack and Rose continue floating in the black water, hands locked together. Rose is in a semi-hallucinatory state but knows she is dying as she sings a song Jack taught her. Suddenly, a light from about fifty feet away shines toward them from a boat searching for survivors, and Rose hears voices sounding slow and distorted. But because the boat sees no motion, they move on. Rose lifts her head to turn to Jack.

ROSE: Jack...Jack...there's a boat, Jack.

There is no response, so she starts to shake him.

ROSE: There's a boat, Jack...a boat...Jack...Jack...there's a boat, Jack.

She can only stare at his still face as the realization of his stillness goes through her. Then, all hope, will, and spirit leave her. She looks at the boat, which is further away, and the voices fainter. She watches them go, then closes her eyes and lays back down, as there just seems to be no reason even to try

300

to get their attention. She wants to die with Jack. And then she seems to remember something. Her eyes snap open and she begins to whisper.

ROSE: *Come back…come back.*

BOAT CAPTAIN: *Helloooooooo…can anyone hear me? Is anyone alive?*

But the boat can't hear Rose due to the weakness of her voice and how far away she now is. She struggles to draw breath—calling again—then struggles to move. Her hand, she realizes, is actually frozen to Jack's. She breaks the ice between their hands and kisses his hand.

ROSE: *I won't let go, I promise.*

She lets him float away, then rolls off the plank and plunges into the ice water. She sees a whistle nearby, swims to it, then grabs and begins to blow with all her might. She keeps blowing as the boat comes to her and takes the whistle from her mouth as they haul her into the boat. She slips into unconsciousness as they scramble to cover her with blankets.

The movie showed Rose surviving and taking on the last name of Jack—the Jack who had changed her life on the Titanic and helped her choose to live through the icy water. Then, the movie flashed back to the present where she—now 101 years old—was standing at the back of an exploration ship as it searched for the famous "Heart of the Sea" diamond. Without anyone knowing that she still had that missing diamond, she stepped to the edge of the boat and dropped it into the deep. She then laid down on her bed—next to pictures of all she had done in her life—to think about these accomplishments she had achieved because Jack had encouraged her back in 1912.

After the credits finished rolling, my friend and I walked toward the theater exit, my mind spinning. He asked what I thought about the movie, but I couldn't answer—I almost couldn't breathe. I desperately needed some space because of the tremendous emotion rushing through my body. Asking if he could give me a minute, I darted into the bathroom, grateful for a means of escape. Why was

I having this overwhelming reaction? Why had this movie affected me so powerfully? I *loved* the story—although it was tragic—but my response seemed over the top.

Everything about the film had been awesome—the story, acting, costumes, cinematography, even the visual effects. But as I stood over the sink in the theater bathroom gazing in the mirror, I began to sob uncontrollably. The next thing I knew, I was transported to somewhere else, it was freezing cold, and I was shaking like a leaf. Next to me appeared Greg. When I saw him, I began crying even harder—feeling as if I were weighted down inside. Then I noticed his hand frozen to my body, keeping us attached. He didn't seem aware of his hand or of me, but I was totally aware of it all and didn't know what to do.

Suddenly, I heard a Divine voice telling me to break the icy bond between us. Continuing to cry while obeying, I began to feel a release—and the more I broke it, the lighter I felt. Finally, we were fully separated and he fell away from me (just as Jack had done in floating away from Rose). Had this maybe been God's signal all along and I was finally hearing it—eight years after our breakup? Whatever it was, I was feeling one hundred pounds lighter and incredibly free—then my need to cry gently ceased.

For some reason, I began comparing what had happened to me when I had separated from Greg eight years ago with had happened to Rose. While engaged to her fiancé, she had worried about not being in love with him, whether he was the right person to marry, and how controlling he seemed. I remembered those same fears running through my mind as I pondered marrying Greg back in 1990—whether it was because of him or my fear of commitment.

Then I thought about the parallels between Jack and God. Jack had been the person to save and encourage Rose and even die on her behalf. The more I looked back over my life, I saw the amazing things that had happened because of my surrender to and trust in Him—and intense love and warmth filled my heart.

302

Suddenly it dawned on me that my friend was still waiting outside to go to dinner. Attempting to regain my composure, I turned to exit but my heart was still pounding between my ears. Taking a few breaths allowed me to walk out—albeit unsteadily.

"Are you okay?" he asked, studying my face.

I nodded. Once outside the theater and settled into his car, we headed towards our dinner restaurant. Sensing something going on in my mind, he let there be silence and I was grateful.

As he drove, I compared Rose and my lives after losing our fiancés: traveling the world, maturing in amazing ways, meeting incredible people, and experiencing things most other people never had. If I had married Greg, I never would have danced a waltz in the Hofburg Palace…or met Prince Edward in St. James Palace…or safaried in South Africa and met Nelson Mandela… or worked in India for Mother Teresa…or bungy jumped from 1200 feet on a beautiful South Pacific Island…or impacted other people's lives by praying for and encouraging them.

Looking back on all those memories, relief and encouragement flooded me. With my new job in Tulsa—and finally letting go of Greg—the possibilities in my life were endless. And based on all the amazing things that had taken place the last eight years with God in control, who knew what might happen next? One thing was for sure—I was open for more divine adventures!

Lightning Source UK Ltd.
Milton Keynes UK
UKHW020746220222
399066UK00011B/637